**St. Louis Community
College**

**Library**

5801 Wilson Avenue
St. Louis, Missouri 63110

# FICTIONS IN AUTOBIOGRAPHY

*Studies in the Art of
Self-Invention*

# FICTIONS IN AUTOBIOGRAPHY

## Studies in the Art of Self-Invention

PAUL JOHN EAKIN

PRINCETON UNIVERSITY PRESS

PRINCETON, NEW JERSEY

Published by Princeton University Press, 41 William Street,
Princeton, New Jersey 08540

In the United Kingdom: Princeton University Press, Guildford, Surrey

Library of Congress Cataloging in Publication Data will be
found on the last printed page of this book

ISBN 0-691-06640-X

This book has been composed in Linotron Janson

Clothbound editions of Princeton University Press books are printed on
acid-free paper, and binding materials are chosen for strength and
durability. Paperbacks, although satisfactory for personal collections, are
not usually suitable for library rebinding

Printed in the United States of America by Princeton University Press
Princeton, New Jersey

*For Jean and Sybil*

# CONTENTS

# ACKNOWLEDGMENTS

FORMERLY NEGLECTED by critics, autobiography is now receiving the lively attention it deserves, and it becomes increasingly difficult for me to identify all those whose work on this subject has contributed to the development of my own ideas. The principal ones, however, Philippe Lejeune, the late Elizabeth Bruss, and others, are named in the pages that follow. In addition, I want to thank Gilbert Chaitin, who advised me about translations from the French, and Karen Hanson, who helped me to trace the history of the concepts of self and person in Western philosophy.

I am grateful to Indiana University for a Grant-in-Aid of Research that enabled me to consult manuscripts of Henry James in New York and Boston. Gordon N. Ray kindly allowed me to examine the typescript of James's *Notes of a Son and Brother* in his possession. Unpublished manuscript letters in the James family collection at the Houghton Library are quoted by permission of the Houghton Library, Harvard University and Mr. Alexander R. James. Chapter Two, "Henry James and the Autobiographical Act," appeared in a slightly different form in *Prospects: An Annual of American Cultural Studies*, 8 (1984), and is reprinted here with the kind permission of the Cambridge University Press. Excerpts from Henry James's *A Small Boy and Others* and *Notes of a Son and Brother* are reprinted by permission of Charles Scribner's Sons.

To two friends I owe a special debt. David Bleich stimulated my thinking about language, and the example of his engagement with theory was an unfailing source of encouragement. James Olney's generous response to my first published essay on autobiography persuaded me to persevere in what was then for me a new field of study, and his wise and searching criticism provoked me to a deeper understanding of the perennial problems of referentiality and the self in autobiographical discourse.

Finally, I would like to express my appreciation to two editors at the Princeton University Press, Miriam Brokaw, who believed in this project at an early stage, and Marjorie Sherwood, who knew how to say the right things at the right time.

My admiration for a survivor and my gratitude for a sustainer are recorded in the dedication.

# FICTIONS IN AUTOBIOGRAPHY

*Studies in the Art of
Self-Invention*

# CHAPTER ONE

## Fiction in Autobiography:
## Ask Mary McCarthy No Questions

### I. "IN TALKING ABOUT THE PAST WE LIE
### WITH EVERY BREATH WE DRAW"

MOST READERS naturally assume that all autobiographies are based on the verifiable facts of a life history, and it is this referential dimension, imperfectly understood, that has checked the development of a poetics of autobiography. Historians and social scientists attempt to isolate the factual content of autobiography from its narrative matrix, while literary critics, seeking to promote the appreciation of autobiography as an imaginative art, have been willing to treat such texts as though they were indistinguishable from novels. Autobiographers themselves, of course, are responsible for the problematical reception of their work, for they perform willy-nilly both as artists and historians, negotiating a narrative passage between the freedoms of imaginative,creation on the one hand and the constraints of biographical fact on the other. Accordingly, in order to deal with the vexing issue of factuality that readers of these texts confront, it is essential to reach some understanding of the state of mind that motivates autobiographical discourse in the first place. On the basis of my research into the autobiographical act as performed by the twentieth-century writers discussed in the chapters that follow, I shall argue that autobiographical truth is not a fixed but an evolving content in an intricate process of self-discovery and self-creation, and, further, that the self that is the center of all autobiographical narrative is necessarily a fictive structure. In these pages I seek to identify the fictions involved in autobiography and the sources—psychological and cultural—from which they are derived.

It is not my intention, however, to expel truth from the house of autobiography and to install fiction in its stead. One could conflate autobiography with other forms of fiction only by willfully ignoring the autobiographer's explicit posture *as autobiographer* in the text. It is, nevertheless, hardly surprising that the traditional version of the problematic of autobiography has focused on the apparently antithetical claims of truth and fiction that are necessarily involved in any attempt to render the materials of a life history in a narrative form. Jean-Jacques Rousseau is often recognized as the father of modern autobiography, and perhaps he deserves credit, too, for inaugurating the conception of autobiographical truth that has stunted until very recently the growth of a criticism devoted to autobiography. Rousseau's stance in the opening lines of *The Confessions* (1781), hand over heart, grandly invoking "the last trump" of Judgment and his "Sovereign Judge" to bear witness to the truth of his account of his life, has probably been more memorable for most of his readers than anything else in the book, including even the pleasurable spankings and the notorious theft of the ribbon: "I have resolved on an enterprise which has no precedent, and which, once complete, will have no imitator. My purpose is to display to my kind a portrait in every way true to nature, and the man I shall portray will be myself." When Rousseau goes on to state, "I have displayed myself as I was,"[1] he affirms the possibility of a total revelation of human personality, and his readers have been arguing ever since whether to accept his claim for *The Confessions* as truth told with complete and unshrinking candor, or to dismiss it as the shameless magniloquence of a monstrous self-deception.

Edgar Allan Poe, for one, grasped the revolutionary import of a project like Rousseau's when he addressed the art of confession in a passage of his "Marginalia" in *Graham's American Monthly Magazine of Literature and Art* for January, 1848:

---

[1] *The Confessions of Jean-Jacques Rousseau*, trans. J. M. Cohen (Harmondsworth, England: Penguin, 1953), p. 17.

4

If any ambitious man have a fancy to revolutionize, at one effort, the universal world of human thought, human opinion, and human sentiment, the opportunity is his own—the road to immortal renown lies straight, open, and unencumbered before him. All that he has to do is write and publish a very little book. Its title should be simple—a few plain words—"My Heart Laid Bare." But—this little book must be *true to its title.*

Poe correctly surmised that the lure of this model of autobiography, its appeal for the opportunist with an itch for notoriety ("STAR TELLS ALL"), is irresistible, and constantly exploited. Poe himself, however, would have none of it, because he believed that the psychological resistance to such a revelation was insurmountable: "No man dare write it."[2] Radically opposed though they are about the possibility of enacting the confessional model of autobiography, Poe and Rousseau are united in their view that the challenge posed by autobiographical truth is in essence a matter of volition, of having the courage to utter it, leaving unexamined the problematical nature of the truth to be told, the epistemological difficulty of ascertaining what it is.

Adventurous twentieth-century autobiographers have shifted the ground of our thinking about autobiographical truth because they readily accept the proposition that fictions and the fiction-making process are a central constituent of the truth of any life as it is lived and of any art devoted to the presentation of that life. Thus memory ceases to be for them merely a convenient repository in which the past is preserved inviolate, ready for the inspection of retrospect at any future date. They no longer believe that autobiography can offer a faithful and unmediated reconstruction of a historically verifiable past; instead, it expresses the play of the autobiographical act itself, in which the materials of the past are shaped by memory and imagination to serve the needs of present consciousness. Autobiography in our time is increasingly understood as both an

[2] *Marginalia* (Charlottesville: Univ. of Virginia Press, 1981), p. 150.

art of memory and an art of the imagination; indeed, memory and imagination become so intimately complementary in the autobiographical act that it is usually impossible for autobiographers and their readers to distinguish between them in practice. It is in this spirit, for example, that two hundred years after the publication of Rousseau's *Confessions* we find the writer William Maxwell meditating on the nature of autobiographical truth in *So Long, See You Tomorrow* (1980), a narrative with equal claims to being a memoir and a novel (it is both):

> I seem to remember that I went to the new house one winter day and saw snow descending through the attic to the upstairs bedrooms. It could also be that I never did any such thing, for I am fairly certain that in a snapshot album I have lost track of there was a picture of the house taken in the circumstances I have just described, and it is possible that I am remembering that rather than an actual experience. What we, or at any rate what I, refer to confidently as memory—meaning a moment, a scene, a fact that has been subjected to a fixative and thereby rescued from oblivion—is really a form of storytelling that goes on continually in the mind and often changes with the telling. Too many conflicting emotional interests are involved for life ever to be wholly acceptable, and possibly it is the work of the storyteller to rearrange things so that they conform to this end. In any case, in talking about the past we lie with every breath we draw.[3]

It is this process of storytelling that I want to investigate, this drive toward narration of the self, and the autobiographers I have chosen to work on share my interest in the fictions of autobiography. Characteristically, they have little use for the narrow, no-nonsense, "nothing but the facts, Ma'am" approach to the realities of biographical experience. Jean-Paul Sartre's stance is representative. When an interviewer asks him

---

[3] *So Long, See You Tomorrow* (New York: Knopf, 1980), p. 27.

whether he has "come closer to [his] own truth through Roquentin or Mathieu than in writing *The Words*," Sartre's reply demonstrates the limitations of hard and fast taxonomical distinctions between autobiography and novel: "Probably. Or rather, I think that *The Words* is no truer than *Nausea* or *The Roads of Freedom*. Not that the facts I report are not true, but *The Words* is a kind of novel also—a novel that I believe in, but a novel nevertheless."[4] Most of the autobiographers I shall be discussing—not only Sartre but Mary McCarthy, Henry James, and Maxine Hong Kingston as well—freely avow the presence of fiction in their art. Rejecting the traditional view of fiction as a potential threat to the success of the autobiographical process, antithetical to the truth they propose to tell, they regard fiction instead as a central feature of that truth, an ineluctable fact of the life of consciousness.

My inquiry into the fictions of autobiography begins with a consideration of the referential dimension of autobiographical discourse in the case of Mary McCarthy, who teaches us that fiction can have for an autobiographer the status of remembered fact. In the chapters that follow, I study the dialectical interplay between an autobiographer's impulse to self-invention and the received models of selfhood in the surrounding culture. My investigation of Henry James's autobiography (Chapter Two) explores the dynamics of the autobiographical act, in this case devoted to the invention of an existential fiction. The fiction is double here, for James's tale is not only the story of young Henry's creation of a self designed to surmount the crisis of identity and vocation posed by his non-participation in the Civil War, but also, in its telling, a strategy of self-invention designed to aid the ailing novelist to achieve a recovery of his imaginative powers. In the case of Jean-Paul Sartre (Chapter Three), the model of selfhood is specifically literary, for young Sartre, pre-empting the autobiographer he would later become, proposes to transform

[4] *Life/Situations: Essays Written and Spoken*, trans. Paul Auster and Lydia Davis (New York: Pantheon, 1977), p. 15.

himself into a text. This curious circumstance of a text about a self who would be a text offers a privileged occasion to inquire into the origins of the autobiographical impulse, that drive toward narration which Maxwell posits as the central act of memory: is this storytelling limited to the art of retrospect, something imposed on life history as a consequence of the autobiographical act, or can narrative itself be said to constitute an experiential category?

The examples of McCarthy, James, and Sartre demonstrate that self-invention refers not only to the creation of self in autobiography but also to the idea that the self or selves they seek to reconstruct in art are not given but made in the course of human development. Thus, in the final chapter I place self-invention in the context of the history of the self as a concept in Western culture and in the context of current ontogenetic and phylogenetic speculations in linguistics, psychology, and philosophy about the nature of the self in the developmental history of the human individual. Investigation of the ontology of the self, both as entity and as idea, suggests the wisdom of abandoning the familiar formulation of the relation between the self and the language that is its means of expression in autobiography. Instead of debating the old either/or proposition—whether the self is a transcendental category preceding language in the order of being, or else a construct of language brought into being by it—it is preferable to conceptualize the relation between the self and language as a mutually constituting interdependency, for study of early human development reveals an intimate and necessary linkage between the acquisition of language and the emergence of self-awareness. In the ontogenetic schema of self-realization I present in Chapter Four, the autobiographical act (when it occurs) figures as a third and culminating phase in a history of self-consciousness that begins with the moment of language in early childhood and subsequently deepens in a second-level order of experience in childhood and adolescence in which the individual achieves a distinct and explicit consciousness of himself or herself as a self. In this developmental perspective, the autobiographical act is revealed as a mode of self-invention that is always practiced first in living and only eventually—sometimes—formalized in writing. I view the rhythms of the autobiographical act as recapitulating the fundamental rhythms of identity formation: in this sense the writing of autobiography emerges as a second acquisition of language, a second coming into being of self, a self-conscious self-consciousness.

My study of the fictions that structure autobiography, then, is finally intended as an exploration of the relation between narrative and the fundamental structures of consciousness, for I believe that the impulse to write autobiography is but a special, heightened form of that reflexive consciousness which is the distinctive feature of our human nature. I have chosen to conclude the last chapter with commentary on the recently published autobiographies of Saul Friedländer and Maxine Hong Kingston because these texts help to answer why the autobiographical imperative, a seeming anachronism derived from the old belief in self and presence, continues to exercise its creative force with undiminished urgency, vitality, and originality in what our newest critics would have us accept as an age of absence and privation.

## II. "MEA CULPA"

We readily accept the presence of autobiographical elements in fiction, and any reader with an interest in the life of an author takes pleasure in identifying them. Thoreau wisely reminds us of the inevitable presence of autobiography in fiction when he observes that "it is, after all, always the first person that is speaking." The presence of fiction in autobiography, on the other hand, tends to make us uneasy, for we instinctively feel that autobiography is—or ought to be—precisely not-fiction. We want autobiography to be true, we expect it to be true more or less, and most of us are content to leave untested the validity of its claim to a basis in verifiable fact; most of the time we are not in a position to make such a test anyway. In those cases when we are forced to recognize that an autobiography is only fiction, we may feel cheated of the promised encounter with biographical reality.

To abandon expectations of the sort I have just described would be to abandon autobiography itself. Why would we bother to read it in the first place if we did not believe in autobiography as a primary expression of biographical truth? Realizing this, most autobiographers refrain from any behavior that would disturb the delicate entente between writer and reader that Philippe Lejeune has described as the autobiographical pact;[5] indeed they are apt to encourage our trust in the historicity of their accounts lest we leave them in the lurch with their lives on their hands.

Mary McCarthy, however, risks violating the convention of the autobiographical pact at the very opening of her "*memoirs*" when she argues that any autobiographer, acting in the best of faith, is going to produce a narrative that will have fiction in it, like it or not. The presence of fiction in autobiography is not something to wish away, to rationalize, to apologize for, as so many writers and readers of autobiography persist in suggesting, for it is as reasonable to assume that all autobiography has some fiction in it as it is to recognize that all fiction is in some sense necessarily autobiographical. The practice of Mary McCarthy provides an ideal opportunity to launch an investigation of this presence, not only because she explicitly addresses herself to this issue but because her performance offers such a distinctly problematical illustration of it. In her case the autobiographer is an established writer of fiction recalling in a series of sketches that look very much like short stories the truth about a self she portrays as a liar.

McCarthy herself dramatizes the ambiguity of the fiction writer turned autobiographer when she observes of one of the chapters of her "*memoirs*," "*This is an example of 'storytelling'; I arranged actual events so as to make 'a good story' out of them. It is hard to overcome this temptation if you are in the habit of writing*

[5] Lejeune, *Le pacte autobiographique* (Paris: Seuil, 1975), pp. 13-46.

*fiction; one does it almost automatically.*"[6] McCarthy was, in fact,
a well-known writer of short stories when she began in 1944
to publish a series of sketches about a character with the same
name as her own. There were to be eight of these pieces, and
thirteen years later she presented them in a single volume,
which she called *Memories of a Catholic Girlhood* (1957). At that
time she arranged the sketches in a chronological sequence,
adding a commentary or afterword for each one, and providing a long preface ("To the Reader") in which she described
the problems and motivation for her autobiographical project.
To be sure, autobiographies are frequently many years in the
writing, and there are numerous instances where manuscript
drafts exist of different versions and revisions; what is unusual
in the case of McCarthy's *Memories* is that the form of the text
itself, with its alternation of chapters and interchapters, displays the evolution of the autobiographical act as an essential
feature of the autobiography, an evolution which is usually
masked by the publication of only a final draft.

McCarthy's commitment to autobiography is manifested not
only in the structure of the text but in the tenor of her opening remarks in the preface as well. Even though some readers,
finding her *"memories"* in a magazine, took them for *"stories,"*
even though the author herself often states that she wished
she were writing *"fiction"* (3), she asserts at the outset that *"this
record lays a claim to being historical—that is, much of it can be
checked,"* and she invites anyone detecting *"more fiction in it
than I know"* (4-5) to come forward with corrections. More
fiction in it than she knows, for she is the first to point out
the presence of fiction in her enterprise. Conversations, for
example, *"are mostly fictional"*; she can only vouch that *"a conversation to this general effect took place"* (4). Again, after the first
sketch, the added commentary begins, *"There are several dubious points in this memoir"* (47), and of one of the scenes she

[6] *Memories of a Catholic Girlhood* (New York: Harcourt, 1957), pp. 164-65.
Subsequent references are to this edition and will appear in the text. Note:
McCarthy's interchapter commentaries are printed in italics in her text and
in mine.

writes, "*I believe this is pure fiction*" (48). Of another sketch she observes, "*this account is highly fictionalized*"; "*the story is true in substance, but the details have been invented or guessed at*" (97). Of the penultimate sketch, however, she states firmly, "*Except for the name of the town and the names of the people, this story is completely true*" (192). And sometimes she is hard put to distinguish fact from fiction, as when she comments on yet another sketch, "*This story is so true . . . that I find it almost impossible to sort out the guessed-at and the half-remembered from the undeniably real*" (124). That a story may be "*so true*" without being "*undeniably real*" offers some measure of the difficulty we face in dealing with the presence of fiction in autobiographical narrative.

Do McCarthy's commentaries on the extent to which she has manipulated her materials—sometimes consciously, sometimes not—discredit the autobiographical nature of her project, or do they confirm it? McCarthy's own position on this score is unmistakable. In collecting the eight "*stories*" she had written about herself since 1944, she clearly believed that she was assembling the material of her autobiography, and all of the framing commentary she added to bind the pieces together as a group stresses the dynamics of the autobiographical process in which she thought she was engaged. What, then, are we to make of her candid discussion of the ubiquitous presence of fiction in her "*memories*"? Nowhere is this issue posed more strikingly than in the chapter and interchapter on "A Tin Butterfly," which, taken together, dramatize the complexity of McCarthy's relation to autobiographical truth.

In McCarthy's recreation of the remembered world of "A Tin Butterfly," the boundaries between autobiographical fact and narrative fiction seem to dissolve. Orphaned at six by the sudden death of her parents in the flu epidemic of 1918, Mary, along with her three younger brothers, began to live out an unhappy childhood along the lines of classic Victorian fiction—the Murdstone chapters of *David Copperfield*, or Kipling's "Baa Baa, Black Sheep." In the first two chapters of *Memories*, "Yonder Peasant, Who Is He?" and "A Tin Butterfly," she gives an account of the years she spent in the home of her McCarthy guardians, Uncle Myers and Aunt Margaret, and it is an existence filmed in black and dark black. The health regimen imposed by Aunt Margaret—repulsive meals to be endured by day, followed by grim nights spent with lips taped shut to prevent mouth breathing—was repressive, and the capricious beatings meted out by the tyrannical Uncle Myers were endless. Not surprisingly, the child responds to this "totalitarian" (70) world of harsh rules and arbitrary punishments by adopting "a policy of lying and concealment": "for several years after we were finally liberated, I was a problem liar" (65). McCarthy herself suggests that one appropriate model for the bleak reality of this period of her life is literary: "It was as though these ignorant people [her guardians], at sea with four frightened children, had taken a Dickens novel—*Oliver Twist*, perhaps, or *Nicholas Nickleby*—for a navigation chart" (64). However much these early memories may resemble the stuff of Victorian fiction, McCarthy also observes that the concentration camp and the prison are equally valid models, and she is careful to point out in the concluding section of her commentary on "A Tin Butterfly" that she has received letters from readers testifying to the verisimilitude of her portraits of her guardians. Her materials may remind us of familiar fictions, but she argues that they are nevertheless squarely rooted in biographical fact.

An evocation of an environment in which the extremity of living conditions resembles the melodramatic exaggeration we associate with sentimental fiction, and a characterization of the self as a deliberate liar—these are the salient features of the context that McCarthy provides for the most elaborately presented memory in her entire autobiography, the episode of the tin butterfly, which brings her story of her life with the cruel guardians to a climax. One day, in an uncharacteristically expansive mood, the usually stingy Uncle Myers buys a whole box of Crackerjack for six-year-old Sheridan McCarthy, the youngest of Mary's brothers, and the favor at the bottom of the box turns out to be a painted tin butterfly with a little pin on it. The butterfly immediately becomes the boy's most cherished possession, coveted openly by his two older brothers, but scorned by ten-year-old Mary, who was too proud to show her feelings. When the butterfly disappears a week later, however, suspicion settles on Mary, and Aunt Margaret and her sister force Mary, despite her protestations of her innocence, to ransack the house looking for it. "Uncle Myers thinks you took it" (75), Aunt Margaret confides, but the search is fruitless. After dinner, however, when the tablecloth is lifted, the butterfly is found pinned to the pad underneath at Mary's place, whereupon the adults conclude that Mary is guilty, and proceed to whip her in the lavatory. Aunt Margaret begs Mary to confess to Uncle Myers ("Say you did it, Mary Therese, say you did it" [77]), but Mary stubbornly refuses to sacrifice her innocence to satisfy her uncle, so she is whipped again. The proud, defiant girl emerges from this confrontation "with a crazy sense of inner victory, like a saint's," for she had not "recanted" (78). Six or seven years later, on her way east to college, Mary stops in Minneapolis to see her brothers at the home of their new guardian, Uncle Louis, and as they sit one night on the screened porch, they fall to talking about Uncle Myers and the past. She now learns from her brother Preston "that on the famous night of the butterfly, he had seen Uncle Myers steal into the dining room from the den and lift the tablecloth, with the tin butterfly in his hand" (80). This vindication of Mary's innocence ends the chapter; the "problem liar" turned "saint" had been punished for telling the truth.

This is the version of the episode that McCarthy published in *The New Yorker* in 1951. But did the autobiographer tell the truth about the aftermath of the episode, the conversation with Preston that ends the story? In the commentary on it that she wrote for *Memories*, the author confesses her misgivings about the truth of the dramatic ending. As she begins to describe her doubts here as "*a struggle with my conscience*," she observes parenthetically, "*the first Communion again*" (83). The "*again*" alludes both to a pattern of behavior in a series of recollected experiences and to her treatment of its prototype in the preface to the autobiography, "To the Reader." In the first Communion episode the child chooses to lie about a fatal sip of water, accepting the Host without first confessing that she has broken her fast. Generalizing on the child's transgression, McCarthy suggests that her performance as an autobiographer—especially, we should note, her ostensible failures to tell the truth about herself—is of a piece with the most characteristic pattern of behavior that her autobiography relates. "A Tin Butterfly" is a case in point. Rereading the story, she suddenly remembers that she had started to write a play on this very subject in college, and she wonders whether the idea that Uncle Myers put the butterfly at her place was suggested to her by her drama teacher at Vassar. "*I can almost hear her voice saying to me, excitedly: 'Your uncle must have done it!'*" (82). Consulting two of her brothers about her doubts, she learns that neither Kevin nor Preston recalls the statement she attributed to Preston about the butterfly, although Kevin remembers the scene on Uncle Louis' screened porch. McCarthy speculates that she herself may have put forward the drama teacher's idea during this family reunion in Minneapolis. But then she admits that she cannot remember whether she took the course in play-writing "*before or after the night on Uncle Louis' porch.*" "*The most likely thing,*" she concludes, "*is that I fused two memories.* Mea culpa" (83).

Of what exactly is McCarthy guilty here? Of an involuntary lapse from fidelity to autobiographical truth into the irresponsible manipulations of fiction? When she states, as she does in this commentary, "*About the tin butterfly episode, I must make a more serious correction*" (82), she seems to be measuring the account in the story against the record of unvarnished fact and to be judging its truth value accordingly. It would be easy enough to assume that the distinction she is getting at is the one between fiction and fact, that what we have here is a short-story writer confessing her autobiographical sources. Certainly McCarthy herself sought to emphasize the distinction between the stories or chapters proper and the commentaries or interchapters: the former are printed in roman type, the latter in italic. The upshot of McCarthy's commentary on "A Tin Butterfly" is *not*, however, to disconfirm her original version of the episode: *"But who did put the butterfly by my place? It may have been Uncle Myers after all. Even if no one saw him, he remains a suspect: he had motive and opportunity. 'I'll bet your uncle did it!'—was that what she* [the college drama teacher] *said?"* (83). We can only conclude that the fundamental distinction that the use of the two typefaces represents is not between art and criticism, between fiction and fact, but rather between different phases of a single, autobiographical mode of discourse. One phase reflects the autobiographical act as it was expressed at a series of discrete moments from 1944 until 1957 in each of the individual, separately published chapters, while the other reflects the most recent content of the autobiographical act that immediately preceded the publication of the earlier material in book form in 1957.

McCarthy concludes that she must have *"fused"* two memories in the first version of the episode, the memory of the reunion with her brothers on the porch in Minneapolis and the memory of her work with a playwriting teacher in college. Moreover, each of these memories has to do with writing about the episode. That is to say that what is presented in the commentary is not an alternative version of the original, disputed incident itself but rather a series of earlier recallings of it, a series of prototypes for the autobiographical act. Following her reconstruction of the writing of the story about Uncle Myers, McCarthy even attempts to reconstruct the motivation of her commentary: what was it that triggered her memory of the college course in playwriting as she reread "A Tin Butterfly"? The play, she recalls, *"was set in my grandmother's sun parlor and showed our first meeting with our guardians. It was thinking about that meeting, obviously, that nagged me into remembering Mrs. Flanagan and the play"* (83). *"Obviously?"* The play was about the guardians; thinking about the guardians recalled the play— we simply do not know why McCarthy recalled her first meeting with Myers and Margaret at this point, and we may well be less than sure that McCarthy knows either. In any case, she drops the issue, leaving us to contemplate the mystery of autobiographical motivation.

The "mea culpa" in the commentary on "A Tin Butterfly," then, can scarcely be advanced as evidence of McCarthy's failure as an autobiographer in the story unless we are prepared to forget that her memory is equally the source of both versions of the episode. Instead, the double presentation of the ending of "A Tin Butterfly" should teach us that autobiographical truth is not a fixed but an evolving content, what we call fact and fiction being rather slippery variables in an intricate process of self-discovery. In view of the complex interrelationship between the remembered incident and its expression in art, we must discard any notion of the juxtaposition of story and commentary as representing a simple opposition between fiction and fact, since fiction can have for the author, as it does here, the status of remembered fact (remembering something that is not true—a frequent refrain in *Memories*). The making of fictions, moreover, is central to McCarthy's identity, in her character early on as a problem liar, and eventually as a writer, and it forms a critical part of the mass of autobiographical fact that she is dealing with. What the commentary on "A Tin Butterfly" makes clear is that McCarthy accepts the presence of fiction in autobiography and seeks to understand it as a natural function of the autobiographical process. Following McCarthy's example, are we then prepared to accept fiction as an inevitable and even essential ingredient of autobiography, generated as much by the unconscious workings of memory as it is by the conscious agency of the imagination? Yet in so far as we do accept the presence of fiction in autobiography, are we not blurring by just so much the fundamental working distinction between autobiography and other forms of writing?

### III. BEYOND THE TEXT

In a recent study entitled "Unsettling the Colonel's Hash: 'Fact' in Autobiography," Darrel Mansell reminds us that Mc-

Carthy herself asserts that autobiography can be distinguished from fiction. She had written a narrative called "Artists in Uniform," to which the editors of *Harper's* added the subtitle, "A Story," when they published it in 1953. Put off by the misreadings generated by the subtitle, McCarthy tried to set the record straight a year later in an essay called "Settling the Colonel's Hash." She rejected the identification of her piece as "a story," claiming instead that it was more properly regarded as "a fragment of autobiography" because of its basis in events that had happened to her "in real life." Consequently, readers were misguided in wondering if details such as the colonel's having hash for lunch were symbolic; "the colonel had hash because he had hash" in the real-life experience on which the narrative was based. Mansell sums up McCarthy's view by stressing that it is the basis in fact that separates autobiography from narrative fiction. We have seen that McCarthy's performance in *Memories* is a good deal more complex than her simplistic remarks about the colonel's hash might lead us to expect. Nevertheless, Mansell argues that McCarthy's assertion of a fundamental distinction between autobiography and fiction is "the assumption we all make except in our stern philosophical moments."[7]

When Mansell puts McCarthy's distinction to the test, however, it collapses, since we "almost never know the actual relation of literary events to what 'happened, in real life' "; "the large-scale probability, the verisimilitude, of what an author says in his book therefore has to be considered merely a rhetorical strategy." It is at this point in his argument that Mansell shifts to a consideration of the author's intention as the decisive criterion in the identification of a given text as an autobiography, since "we *do* know, or think we know, what the author *intends* the relation [between literary events and real life] to be." It is precisely in the area of intention that present research has developed a new sophistication in dealing with this most refractory of literary genres. If to steer toward the

[7] *Modern Language Quarterly*, 37 (1976), 115-16.

open water of the extra-textual is doubtless problematic, it is also true that to do so is to move with the prevailing current of the autobiographical text, which signals to us that it is to be considered as autobiography by referring to a biographical reality lying beyond itself and upon which it claims to be founded. It is not surprising, however, given the formalist hegemony of the previous generation, that autobiographical criticism has been so late in blooming, and even Mansell, for one, despite his admirable willingness to grapple with the referential dimension of the autobiographer's art, settles for a disappointingly formalist conclusion: the critic "reads autobiography as fiction." The referential dimension of autobiographical texts, hitherto decisive, is now to be exorcised as irrelevant: "the critic tries to assume that over every autobiography is hung a sign that says, 'The opinions expressed here are not necessarily those of the management.' "[8]

Mansell's dilemma is hardly unique, as Louis Renza suggests in "The Veto of the Imagination." Renza performs a balanced and careful scrutiny of the implications of the view of autobiography that identifies it as an imaginative kind and that stresses the primacy of the act of creation rather than the nagging issue of verisimilitude. "Desiring to colonize autobiography in the name of literary art," he concludes, "the apologist for autobiography is apt to fictionalize the object about which he theorizes," attenuating "autobiography's explicit, formal claim to be a legitimate personal-historical document."[9] Despite this apparent impasse, recent critics have launched a promising double-pronged inquiry into the issue posed by the vexingly unverifiable referentiality of autobiographical texts. On the one hand, phenomenological, linguistic, and psychohistorical methodologies open up the possibil-

---

[8] *Ibid.*, 121, 131.

[9] *New Literary History*, 9 (1977), 4-5; rpt. in *Autobiography: Essays Theoretical and Critical*, ed. James Olney (Princeton: Princeton Univ. Press, 1980), p. 273. Hereafter this volume will be referred to as *Autobiography*. See, e.g., Burton Pike, "Time in Autobiography," *Comparative Literature*, 28 (1976): "The past does not exist" (337).

ity of investigating the author's motivation for adopting an autobiographical stance in the first place. On the other, the consequences of the reader's identification of the author's stance as such have been explored through case studies of individual reader responses and through literary historical analysis of the institutional existence of genres.

Intention becomes the decisive consideration in dealing with both the generation and the reception of autobiographical texts. This consideration, according to Philippe Lejeune, is characteristically expressed within such texts—explicitly or implicitly—in the form of an autobiographical pact between author and reader.[10] It is this contract that determines our manner of reading the text, creating the effects that, attributed to the text, seem to us to define it as autobiography. Lejeune's view has been confirmed in part by the work of Norman Holland, whose experiments have led him to conclude that reader responses vary "according to the expectation or 'set' the reader brings [to a given text], . . . one kind of 'set' for non-fiction, another for fiction."[11] Moving from the individual case to the historical group, Elizabeth Bruss has attempted to formulate the "set" that defines the context in which autobiography is written and read within "a particular community of writers and readers." Calling for an end to the countless misguided efforts to prescribe what autobiography is, Bruss sensibly states that even the most superficial acquaintance with the diversity of works customarily received as autobiographies should lead us to recognize that "there is no intrinsically autobiographical form." It is nevertheless possible, she argues, to offer limited generalizations about "our notion of the functions an autobiographical text must perform." She proceeds accordingly to formulate such generalizations in terms of a list of interrelated

[10] Lejeune, p. 44.

[11] "Prose and Minds: A Psychoanalytic Approach to Non-Fiction," in *The Art of Victorian Prose*, eds. George Levine and William Madden (New York: Oxford Univ. Press, 1968), p. 321. See also Francis R. Hart, "Notes for an Anatomy of Modern Autobiography," *New Literary History*, 1 (1969-1970), 488.

"rules" that must "be satisfied by the text and the surrounding context of any work which is to 'count as' autobiography."[12] All these rules, moreover, address the issue of the ostensible referentiality of such texts.

Research into the genesis of autobiographical texts would seem, then, to be the most promising approach to the problem of referentiality that these texts by definition propose. The source of all the difficulties that bedevil autobiographical criticism is, after all, the decision of an author to adopt an autobiographical stance in the first place, a stance which, signalled in the text, generates the kind of expectations in readers that Lejeune, Bruss, Holland, and others have been at pains to document. But what can we know of intention? Are we in any better position as readers to get at the truth of the autobiographical act than we were to verify the truth of the author's past as narrated in the text? Much of the recent criticism devoted to autobiography would seem to promote just such an inquiry, largely as a consequence of the rejection of the traditional view of the referentiality of autobiographical texts and the concomitant conception of the autobiographical act.

Lionel Abel's review of Jean-Paul Sartre's *The Words* in 1965 typifies the older, commonsense belief in the absolute existence of the past events in a life history and hence in the possibility of their recovery in autobiographical narrative. Thus he defines autobiography as "a recounting of the events of the author's life as they happened, together with what the author may have felt or thought at the time of these happenings, insofar as he can remember them exactly." Abel rejects Sartre's volume as an autobiography because he feels that the narrative offered nothing of the child Sartre but only the adult's opinion of him. Abel would have the autobiographer "separate out of his response to any fact or meaning present before his mind the impact of that fact or meaning before he reflected on it

---

[12] Bruss, *Autobiographical Acts: The Changing Situation of a Literary Genre* (Baltimore: Johns Hopkins Univ. Press, 1976), pp. 15, 10.

and its impact after reflection began."[13] In this view the autobiographer's present consciousness threatens to disrupt the proper functioning of the autobiographical act conceived as a disciplined recovery of past consciousness. In practice, Abel's distinction has proved to be untenable because the autobiographer's access to the past is necessarily a function of his present consciousness of it. That is to say that the past that any autobiographical narrative records is first and foremost the period of the autobiographical act itself. As Burton Pike puts it, writing on "Time in Autobiography" in 1976, "what is real to the autobiographer is the present moment, the time of writing, and not the past as it may have 'happened,' either empirically or as the nexus of a set of feelings."[14] In the words of James Olney, who is largely responsible for this shift in our conception of the autobiographical enterprise, an autobiography is, "intentionally or not, a monument of the self as it is becoming, a metaphor of the self at the summary moment of composition."[15] Thus, if autobiographical texts do not tell us as much about the autobiographer's past history as earlier students of the genre wished to believe, they may nevertheless have a good deal to tell us about the autobiographer in the moment of his engagement in the act of composition.

As Jean Starobinski suggests in "The Style of Autobiography," "No matter how doubtful the facts related, the text will at least present an 'authentic' image of the man who 'held the pen.' " Rejecting the definition of style as "form" superadded to a "content," to be viewed with suspicion for its potential interference with the record of autobiographical truth, Starobinski argues for the special importance of the individual mark of style in autobiography, "since to the explicit self-reference

[13] "The Retroactive I," *Partisan Review*, 32 (1965), 257, 258. Commenting on Sartre's repudiation of the commonsense belief in the existence of the past, Lejeune suggests nevertheless that some form of this belief is necessary to the pursuit of any autobiographical project (p. 235).

[14] Pike, 334.

[15] *Metaphors of Self: The Meaning of Autobiography* (Princeton: Princeton Univ. Press, 1972), p. 35.

of the narration itself the style adds the implicit self-referen-
tial value of a particular mode of speaking."[16] This sensible
notion of style as an organic constituent of autobiographical
content has been given a more ambitious theoretical elaboration by Elizabeth Bruss. Drawing on speech act theory as
developed by J. L. Austin, P. F. Strawson, and John R. Searle,
she presents the thesis that however private an autobiographer's world may be, "it is a world to which, in writing, he
cannot help but give us a key." Adopting this model, in which
the autobiographical act is conceived as a form of speech act
of which the text constitutes the primary expression, it then
becomes a question of reconstructing the original context by
following "certain clues embedded in the language of the text."
Bruss begins her study by providing an inventory of the available clues or "linguistic markers sensitive to context" (person,
space, time, modality, etc.),[17] but it would be hard to say that
her subsequent analyses of individual autobiographies exemplify the procedures her model proposes. However sharp and
packed with insight her commentaries may be, they look very
much like the kind of close readings practiced by the New
Critics, who would have rejected her determination to use the
text to explore the author's private world as a familiar form
of the intentional fallacy, albeit in a new guise.

Whether a speech act model of this kind can offer valid
insights into the autobiographical act has yet to be demonstrated; it does offer a valuable perspective on the nature of
the referentiality in which the autobiographical text is implicated. Moving away from the traditional view of testing autobiographical narrative against some extra-textual order of fact,
which is, inevitably, largely based in its turn on other texts
(dignified as documents), we begin to see the text itself as
constituting the primary biographical fact with which we have
to deal: if the text is derived from the self, then its factuality

---

[16] In *Literary Style: A Symposium*, ed. Seymour Chatman (London: Oxford
Univ. Press, 1971), pp. 287, 286; rpt. in *Autobiography*, pp. 75, 74.
[17] Bruss, pp. 31, 19, 31.

would be self-made. Should we not, then, be able to approach knowledge of the self through scrutiny of its acts of self-expression? Such a proposition is hardly novel, moreover; it is, in fact, a commonplace of the so-called psychological approach to art. When it comes to autobiography, however, the application of psychoanalytic theory has been limited mostly to brief passages or isolated parts of a text. Freud's analysis of the function of screen memories in a childhood episode of Goethe's autobiography, A. W. Levi's identification of John Stuart Mill's repressed wish for his father's death as the cause of his "mental crisis," Saul Rosenzweig's anatomy of the complex of guilt and impotence involved in Henry James's traumatic experience of an "obscure hurt" in the early days of the Civil War, Richard L. Bushman's account of the role of infantile conflict in Benjamin Franklin's choice of a vegetarian diet—these are characteristic examples of the psychological criticism of autobiography.[18] On the whole, psychobiographers devote relatively little attention to their subjects' performance as autobiographers. Perhaps this is because they instinctively regard the autobiographical act as a precursor of their own inquiries and hence, like these latter, somehow extrinsic to the life history it purportedly documents, rather than as a biographical manifestation in its own right requiring the same explications as the life events it records.[19]

To be sure, a good many biographers have affirmed the therapeutic value of the autobiographical act, yet this notion has not been systematically demonstrated in particular cases. The most promising contributions here have tended to be

[18] Freud, "A Childhood Recollection from *Dichtung und Wahrheit*," 1917; rpt. in *Collected Papers*, ed. Joan Riviere, 5 vols. (New York: Basic Books, 1959), IV, 357-67; Levi, "The 'Mental Crisis' of John Stuart Mill," *Psychoanalytic Review*, 32 (1945), 86-101; Rosenzweig, "The Ghost of Henry James: A Study in Thematic Apperception," *Character and Personality*, 12 (1943-1944), 79-100; Bushman, "On the Uses of Psychology: Conflict and Conciliation in Benjamin Franklin," *History and Theory*, 5 (1966), 225-40.

[19] E.g., Bruce Mazlish, in a book on Mill of more than 400 pages, devotes only four pages to Mill's engagement in the autobiographical act. *James and John Stuart Mill: Father and Son in the Nineteenth Century* (New York: Basic Books, 1975), pp. 162-65.

largely theoretical. Erikson's essays on his work on Gandhi are exemplary in their self-conscious account of the sensitive methodological problems that face any inquiry into autobiographical motivation, and I suspect that any major research into the psychological dynamics of the autobiographical act is going to be heavily indebted to Erikson's proposed model for such analysis. In his biographical study of James and John Stuart Mill, Bruce Mazlish acknowledges Erikson's contribution in this regard as follows: "with great subtlety he has shown how the writing and reading of an autobiography is not a timeless process, but embedded in ongoing history and the search for identity of both the individual writer and reader, and the communities in which they live."[20]

It is just here, however, when the insights of linguistic, stylistic, and psychohistorical methodologies promise to penetrate the private world of the self and its autobiographical motivation, that we meet the grinning face of fiction at the door. "Abandon all hope, ye who enter here," the French structuralists seem to say, the late Roland Barthes foremost among them when he reminds us, "The one *who speaks* (in the narrative) is not the one *who writes* (in real life) and the one *who writes* is not the one *who is*."[21] To Barthes' wise sense of the need to discriminate among the plurality of identities concealed in the "person" of the first-person singular we could

[20] Mazlish, p. 163. In comparison with the authoritative voice of Erikson's practice as a clinician, other theorists of the autobiographical act are apt to sound excessively abstract. Louis Renza's fascinating phenomenological speculations on the mystery of autobiographical motivation would be a case in point. He is obliged to conclude as follows: "Needless to say, the typologies of autobiographical writing which I have tried to elucidate in this essay refer to autobiography's 'idea,' to how we can think of its verbal identity from the imagined perspective of the writer immediately situated in the act of writing" (19). The imagined perspective here is, of course, Renza's own.

[21] "Introduction à l'analyse structurale des récits," *Communications*, 8 (1966), 20; rpt. "An Introduction to the Structural Analysis of Narrative," *New Literary History*, 6 (1974-1975), 261. Barthes is speaking here not specifically of autobiography but of narratives in general. In a note of his own he cites Jacques Lacan's parallel query: "Is the subject to which I refer when I speak the same as the one who speaks?"

add the challenge of Jacques Lacan, who argues that the self is not a presence but an absence. In these views, the very concept of autobiographical referentiality thus becomes altogether a matter of fiction, whereas it should by definition be a matter of fact. From the perspective of the age of absence, the autobiographer's familiar injunction—"this is no book/Who touches this touches a man"—shows as nothing more than a piece of Romantic bravado.

Interestingly, the existence of such theorizing has done nothing to inhibit the autobiographical pursuit; if anything, quite the reverse. The impulse to take the fiction of the self and its acts as fact persists, a more than willing suspension of disbelief in which the behavior of writer and reader refuses to coincide with theory. Barthes himself has written his autobiography. Even so extreme example as the Welshman Goronwy Rees, who prefaces his autobiography with the assertion that "at no time in my life have I had that enviable sensation of constituting a continuous personality," defining autobiography as "the art of creating a self which does not exist," concludes his foreword with this revealing speculation about his intention: "But perhaps, in putting these episodes together, I have not been entirely free from a certain curiosity whether someone else may not be able to find in this bundle of sensations a greater degree of continuity than I have been able to do." Autobiography offers the individual an opportunity to reify, to constitute, to create an identity precisely because referentiality is the *sine qua non* of such texts. However, if the autobiographical process engaged in by the writer is not truly reversible in the case of the reader or critic—that is, if the premise of autobiographical referentiality that we can move from knowledge of the text to knowledge of the self proves to be a fiction—the text becomes paradoxically not less precious but more: in making the text the autobiographer constructs a self that would not otherwise exist. As Rees would have it, "all we expect of [an autobiographer] is to invent *himself*."[22]

[22] *A Bundle of Sensations: Sketches in Autobiography* (New York: Macmillan, 1961), pp. 9, 15, 17, 15. John N. Morris first drew my attention to Rees.

Let us grant the very concept of the self as a fiction, let us speak in the French way of the textuality of the self. After such knowledge, why do authors still indulge in, and readers still consent to, a fiction of this kind? It may well be that our quest for the self is rooted in the same human need that Frank Kermode identifies as the motive for our invention of endings; such fictions become "necessary to life," mediating as they do the limitations of human consciousness in an intractable universe.[23] What we would want to understand is the motivation for writing autobiographical narrative, which is doubtless parallel to the motivation for reading it. How does making something up—a self, a text—answer to the search for self-knowledge? In such an inquiry we do well to begin with the author's own account of the autobiographical act, accepting the text as the author's model for the self and for its interpretation. Bearing in mind Barthes' caveat that the "I" of the text is identical to neither the author of the text nor to the biographical individual who is its subject, let us return to Mary McCarthy and examine the author's autobiographical stance as it is dramatized in her narrative.

## IV. "C.Y.E."

On a certain day in February of 1943, on her way to the subway station in Union Square, Mary McCarthy passes a store called Cye Bernard. To her surprise, the name on the storefront elicits violent and uncontrollable feelings of embarrassment and shame, a queer and extravagant sense of indecent exposure mixed with martyrdom:

> I averted my eyes from the sign and hurried into the subway, my head bent so that no observer should discover my secret identity, which until that moment I had forgotten myself. Now I pass this sign every day, and it

See *Versions of the Self: Studies in English Autobiography from John Bunyan to John Stuart Mill* (New York: Basic Books, 1966), p. 11.

[23] *The Sense of an Ending: Studies in the Theory of Fiction* (New York: Oxford Univ. Press, 1968), p. 155.

is always a question whether I shall look at it or not. Usually I do, but hastily, surreptitiously, with an ineffective air of casualness, lest anybody suspect that I am crucified there on that building, hanging exposed in black script lettering to advertise bargains in men's haberdashery.

The strangest part about it is that this unknown clothier on Fourteenth Street should not only incorporate in his name the mysterious, queerly spelled nickname I was given as a child in the convent but that he should add to this the name of my patron saint, St. Bernard of Clairvaux, whom I chose for my special protector at a time when I was suffering from the nickname.[24]

In this curious fashion begins "C.Y.E.," the first of McCarthy's autobiographical sketches, published in *Mademoiselle* in April of 1944.

As far as the published record is concerned, any attempt to trace the motivation for McCarthy's autobiography to its origins must come to rest in the involuntary recall of the past triggered by the fortuitous circumstance of this episode of 1943. Surely "the strangest part" of the passage is that McCarthy herself should choose to advertise in her story and in its title—and in the very "black script lettering" she abhors—a painful experience which she claims to wish to conceal. McCarthy's stated concern, however, is not to explain the contradictory intentions implied by her decision to publish such a confession but rather to understand the unpredictable behavior of her memory. To account for the ease with which she had forgotten the past for twenty years, McCarthy invokes the mechanism of repression. Developing a political metaphor for personality, she likens the tyranny of consciousness over the exercise of memory to a Soviet-style dictatorship which decrees that "discarded selves languish in the Lubianka of the unconscious"; "the past is manipulated to serve the in-

[24] *Cast a Cold Eye* (1950; rpt. New York: New American Library, 1972), p. 121. Subsequent references will appear in the text.

terests of the present." "But a moment comes at last," she writes, "after the regime has fallen, . . . when the archives are opened . . . and history must be rewritten in the light of fresh discoveries" (122). This is McCarthy's model for the complex interplay between conscious and unconscious motivation for the control of memory that determines the autobiographical act in "C.Y.E." What she does not tell us is the nature of the fallen regime, nor does she suggest why it should have been overthrown at a given moment in 1943.

Liberated from the prison of the unconscious, a discarded self from childhood is once more in possession of the author's consciousness and of the movement of her narrative as well: "I was back in the convent, a pale new girl sitting in the front of the study hall" (122). Eager to be accepted by the most popular girls in the school, the eleven-year-old Mary of twenty years ago naively trusts in the unaided power of her own identity to achieve the social success she desires. She soon learns to her cost, however, that power in her world rests with others. It is the two school clowns, an unprepossessing pair named Elinor Henehan and Mary Heinrichs, who confer on girls of their choice the prestige and notoriety of the nicknames they invent. Accordingly, and as sure as fate, recognition comes to Mary one night when these self-appointed arbiters of identity bestow on her the name "Cye," "C-Y-E"; "the next day it was all over the school" (125). Convinced that the name represents some profound—and unpleasant—truth about herself, some "wrongness," some "taint," some "miserable effluvium of the spirit" (126) that has made her the laughingstock of the convent, the girl is consumed with a desire for the very knowledge that all the others conspire to withhold. "The hateful name" (127) dooms her to isolation and painful self-examination, inverting her dreams of success into a nightmare of failure. The special mark of Mary's vulnerable condition is that her deepest private anxieties, given a name, crystallize into a secret identity that is condemned to constant involuntary exhibition. Mary is forced to become an autobiographer in spite of herself. It is no wonder, then, that when the time comes to leave the school, the girl should resolve to forget the convent altogether, and this she did for twenty years.

According to McCarthy, it is a force from her unconscious that sets her autobiographical narrative in motion, and it is again a force from her unconscious that brings it to a close. "Yesterday," in the vicinity of the shop with its embarrassing sign, the words "Clever Young Egg" rise unbidden to her lips. She experiences that "sharp, cool sense of relief and triumph that one has on awakening from a nightmare" at the thought that her anguish over the nickname had been groundless, that her enemies "really divined nothing" about her. Armed with a solution to the riddle that bedeviled the child, the adult Mary prepares for a reconciliation with the past and with her earlier self:

> "Now I can go back," I thought happily, without reflection, just as though I were an absconding bank teller who had been living for years with his spiritual bags packed, waiting for the charges against him to be dropped that he might return to his native town. A vision of the study hall rose before me, with my favorite nun on the platform and the beautiful girls in their places. My heart rushed forward to embrace it.

As the passage continues, however, the story concludes with a shocking reversal of this gesture of self-acceptance:

> But, also, it is too late. Elinor Henehan is dead, my favorite nun has removed to another convent, the beautiful girls are married—I have seen them from time to time and no longer aspire to their friendship. And as for the pale, plain girl in the front of the study hall, her, too, I can no longer reach. I see her creeping down the corridor with a little knot of her classmates. "Hello, Cye," I say with a touch of disdain for her rawness, her guileless ambition. I should like to make her a pie-bed, or drop a snake down her back, but unfortunately the convent discipline forbids such open brutality. I hate her,

for she is my natural victim, and it is I who have given
her the name, the shameful inscrutable name that she
will never, sleepless in her bed at night, be able to puzzle
out. (128)

What takes place is nothing less than another re-enactment of
the painful event of the name, this time as deliberate as the
earlier re-enactment had been involuntary. Now the Mary of
1943 adopts the role of the hateful pair of clowns, so much so
that she can speak of her earlier self as "my natural victim."
Her motivation in doing so is complex, to say the least, as the
puzzling image of the "absconding bank teller" implies, with
its suggestion of a guilty act (but the charges have been dropped
and were groundless anyway?) that condemns her to exile (but
the banishment was not only self-imposed but unnecessary?).
The distinction between "I" and "her," moreover, that the
psychological confrontation between these warring selves requires, is unstable, for just as swiftly as the gesture of love
transmutes to hate, so the identity of the "I" shifts without
warning from a post-convent present ("I have seen them from
time to time") back to the convent past ("the convent discipline forbids such open brutality").

There is much that is problematical in the behavior of this
personality in conflict as it is portrayed in "C.Y.E.," and the
tension between the Marys of 1923 and 1943 derives as much
from their similarities as from their obvious differences. To
begin with, we can be fairly sure that the original childhood
experience of injury retains a peculiar power to compel, despite any attempts of an older self turned autobiographer to
exercise control. It is re-enacted twice within the narrative, as
we have seen, and the writing and publication of the sketch
constitute an additional mimesis of the original episode. To
be sure, to the extent that she becomes the author of "C.Y.E.,"
the older McCarthy can be said to make good the failed am-
bitions of the proto-autobiographer schoolgirl, whose initial
resolve to make a name for herself in the convent was supplanted by an equally firm, anti-autobiographical determina-

31

tion that she would "never, never, never again let anybody see what I was like" (127). Thus she can write at the last, "it is I who have given her the name," but the tough, aggressive stance and the tone of superiority that accompany this show of power seem rather hollow, a wishful display not of the knowledge but only of the knowing air of the original authors of the nickname. The "happy solution" to the mystery of Mary's "secret identity" is never demonstrated, the promised reconciliation is never effected. The import of the dramatic ending and its striking self-betrayal is undermined by the rest of the narrative, which betrays the autobiographer's unresolved ambivalence toward the past (to be remembered or repressed) and toward her earlier self (to be embraced or repudiated). The very existence of the text testifies against the truth of the conclusion that the earlier self and its history are inaccessible to the autobiographer. How can we believe in the impossibility of the return to the past ("her, too, I can no longer reach") when the opening of the sketch and indeed all of its subsequent content dramatize the ease and spontaneity of the movement backward in time ("I was back in the convent . . . I see myself perfectly . . . I am ambitious")? It would be more accurate to say of "C.Y.E." that both its Marys, then and now, are simultaneously attracted to and repelled by the consequences of the quest for identity.

The ambivalence that characterizes McCarthy's behavior in "C.Y.E." is confirmed by the subsequent history of her autobiographical writing. The apparently abortive encounter with the past proved in the event to be the beginning of an autobiographical project that would occupy her, on and off, for the next thirteen years. Eventually, however, a new repression, this time conscious and deliberate, was exercised over the involuntary recall of her convent shame. Collecting several short narratives in a volume called *Cast a Cold Eye* in 1950, McCarthy included "C.Y.E." without change, for at this point, as she recalled in an interview with Elisabeth Niebuhr in 1962, she did not realize how much she "disliked" it. But seven years later she could not "stand" the sketch: "When I was reading the book [*Memories*] in proof, I decided to tear it out, to reduce it to a tiny tiny incident. As it stood, it was just impossible, much too rhetorical."[25] And so the McCarthy of 1956-1957 suppressed the McCarthy of 1943 as completely as the McCarthy of 1923 had repressed the original episode of the nickname for twenty years. "Names," as the new version is titled in *Memories of a Catholic Girlhood*, is quite different in feeling from "C.Y.E." No mention is made of the drama of memory unleashed by the sight of the storefront of Cye Bernard; the painful experience itself, reduced to a page, is supplied with an altogether new context; and the last names of the two school clowns are changed.

In "Names," the event of the nickname becomes the climax of a pattern of lying that surrounds McCarthy's quest for identity in her convent years. Her desire for prominence in the school leads her to pretend to have lost her faith and to regain it showily in a simulated confession during a retreat. This is the subject of the sketch that precedes "Names" in *Memories*, "C'est Le Premier Pas Qui Coûte." When she really does lose her faith in the process—an unforeseen complication—she is obliged to go through with her conversion or risk exposure as a liar. This public imposture is presently succeeded by a private one: when blood from a cut stains her bedsheet, McCarthy finds herself involved in an impossible situation with an all-too-understanding dormitory nun who is convinced that the girl has "become a woman." It is her fate, it seems, to become entrapped in false identities which she must maintain through a deliberate program of lying:

> There I was, a walking mass of lies, pretending to be a Catholic and going to confession while really I had lost my faith, and pretending to have monthly periods by cutting myself with nail scissors; yet all this had come about without my volition and even contrary to it. But the basest pretense I was driven to was the acceptance of

[25] "The Art of Fiction XXVII: Mary McCarthy," *Paris Review*, No. 27 (1962), 64.

the nickname. Yet what else could I do? In the convent,
I could not live it down. To all those girls, I had become
"Cye McCarthy." That was who I was . . . the kind of
girl I hated. (136)

Mary's wish for recognition in the school is fulfilled but never
on her own terms; this girl, unlike her counterpart in "C.Y.E.,"
receives the autobiographer's sympathy for her unnerving experience of the loss of control over her own life and identity.

Taken together, the writing of "C.Y.E." and its subsequent
transformation into "Names" dramatize two quite different
concepts of autobiographical motivation. In "C.Y.E." the narrative is structured by the rhythms of memory, and the author is led to investigate both why she suddenly remembers
and why she had earlier resolved to forget. Even though
memory necessarily plays a central role in the autobiographical act, so much so in fact that many self-historians like to
think of it as the autobiographical faculty *par excellence*, the
agency of memory is not, after all, equivalent to the sum of
autobiographical motivation. McCarthy's practice of revisionist life history in "Names" reminds us that what is recalled is
subject to the conscious shaping of the autobiographer. In both
versions of the past autobiographical motivation remains elusive. For all the apparent deliberateness of McCarthy's behavior in 1956-1957, we do not finally know why she does not
like "C.Y.E." and (by implication) the McCarthy of 1943 any
more than we know why the McCarthy of 1943 "hates" the
McCarthy of 1923. "C.Y.E." and "Names" together suggest
that conflicting impulses of repression and confession govern
McCarthy's autobiographical narrative. Confession itself,
moreover, as we have seen in the episode of the first Communion, offers an equivocal model for the expression of autobiographical truth, involving as it does in McCarthy's case
the partly involuntary, partly voluntary, public performance
of a lie about one's self. As far as we know, the history of the
autobiography begins with the involuntary recall of the C.Y.E.
episode; it is equally true, again, as far as we know, that this

beginning is the only part of the history that McCarthy later cancelled. The cancellation is all the more remarkable given the author's decision to structure the completed narrative in terms of a counterpoint between chapters and interchapters that explicitly dramatizes shifts in autobiographical perspective. What, then, is the source of her hostility to "C.Y.E.," and why did she choose not to speak of it in the interchapter commentaries whose leading feature is their pretense to candor? It seems safe to infer from the fact of the initial confession and its subsequent cancellation that some special kernel of truth about the self is latent in the episode of the nickname, a truth that governs the behavior of McCarthy as a girl in 1923, as a young woman in 1943, and as an older woman in 1956-1957. In each case, in both the event and its two retellings, the impulse to reveal is accompanied by an equal and opposite impulse to conceal. The episode, with its emphasis on public exposure of some secret truth about the self, expresses both the desire for autobiographical confession and its ultimate defeat, for what "C.Y.E."—hidden or displayed—signifies for all these Marys is the unknowable mystery of one's inmost identity. What the troubled psychological and literary history of the nickname suggests is a deeply ambivalent view of the autobiographical act; whether the revelation of the self to the self and to others is either desirable or even possible remains unclear.

## V. "The word for mirror"

"A Tin Butterfly" (1951) and its commentary (1957) supply two alternative versions of a decisive event in Mary McCarthy's past; so do "C.Y.E." (1944) and "Names" (1957). In the one case the difference is apparently the result of an unconscious fusion of two memories; in the other it is the result of a deliberate revision for reasons undisclosed. Such evidence suggests the difficulty of locating any fixed points of reference in a life history; it underscores the limitations of any definitions of autobiography that are based on presumably stable concepts of times and identities past and present. Instead, autobiography is better understood as a ceaseless process of identity formation in which new versions of the past evolve to meet the constantly changing requirements of the self in each successive present. Accordingly, any necessity to choose between competing versions of the past—between the two accounts of the theft of the butterfly, between "C.Y.E." and "Names"—simply evaporates. It would, moreover, be equally foolish to reject both versions of an event as though acceptance of the truth of the one necessarily required rejection of the truth of the other. Truth and identity in autobiography are plural, and, therefore, so is the autobiographical text, as McCarthy's counterpoint of chapter and commentary makes clear. Nevertheless, the various Marys—the autobiographer and her earlier, discarded selves (including selves who performed as autobiographer)—share a single name, and the composite text we read, the *Memories* of 1957, for all its multiple parts, is one, beginning once and ending once. Is this formal unity of the narrative nothing but formal, an aesthetic construct, or is it the manifestation of an underlying psychological unity to which it ostensibly refers? Such a narrative, with its double view—singular and plural—of the self and its history, poses the question whether the very idea of autobiography is not in its deepest sense a fiction, some wish or dream of a possible unity of personality underlying the apparent accidents of an individual life. Do the vicissitudes of the autobiographical act in McCarthy's case, for example, predicate the existence of a continuous identity of the self, or do they represent nothing more than a set of discrete, randomly shifting gestures? Investigation of her performance as an autobiographer suggests both the possibilities and the limitations of the creation of a text as an instrument to negotiate—and renegotiate—the terms of an individual's psychological reality. Autobiography becomes a privileged bridge of discourse of the self with itself across lapsing time.

If we consider the history of the composition of McCarthy's

*Memories* as a sequence, it dramatizes a series of deepening returns to the past. Risking the schematic in order to highlight the presence of a coherent pattern of behavior, we can identify three distinct phases or waves of autobiographical recollection, each reaching further back into the past than its predecessor. In the first of these McCarthy returns to the period of her life in the convent, which is the subject of "C.Y.E." (1944) and "The Blackguard" (1946); in these pieces she is a girl of eleven and twelve. In the second phase, she returns to her life with the guardians, beginning after the death of her parents when she is six and continuing more or less chronologically through her years in the convent and still later in a public high school; this is the order of the next five sketches as originally published: "Yonder Peasant, Who Is He?" (1948), "A Tin Butterfly" (1951), "C'est Le Premier Pas Qui Coûte" (1952), "The Figures in the Clock" (1953), and "Yellowstone Park" (1955). In a last phase, McCarthy returns to her own earliest memories of the first six years of her life before her parents died, and beyond these to the history of her parents and her mother's mother before she was born; these are the subject of "To the Reader" (1957) and "Ask Me No Questions" (1957) which, respectively, begin and end the narrative of McCarthy's *Memories* published in 1957. Something was drawing the autobiographer steadily backward into the past; somehow, as she came to believe, the central issues of her life history were connected with her loss of her parents in the influenza epidemic of 1918. From "C.Y.E." to "Ask Me No Questions"—the history of the autobiographical act begins with the middle of her story and it comes to an end with the beginning.

Philippe Lejeune argues that the most general order in which autobiographical narrative can unfold is that of the inquiry, which alone arises naturally from the very circumstances in which autobiography is produced. The final object of every autobiographical quest, he believes, is the impossible search for one's birth; one returns to the past in an attempt to pen-

etrate the mystery of one's origins.[26] McCarthy's pursuit during her thirties and forties of the story of her early years,
especially her recurrent sense of an inscrutable darkness lurking at the heart of self-knowledge, would seem to corroborate
this thesis quite specifically, but in a more general way all
autobiographers might be said to do so. Erik Erikson theorizes
that man's creation of myths, of " 'ideal' realities in which we
become and remain the central reality," mediates against his
ego-chilling awareness that his "nonexistence . . . is entirely
possible." He proceeds to give an account of the process of
identity formation that offers a major insight into the invention of autobiography:

> The sense of identity, which is not wanting in most
> adults, prevents such feelings of panic. To be adult means
> among other things to see one's own life in continuous
> perspective, both in retrospect and in prospect. By ac-
> cepting some definition as to who he is, usually on the
> basis of a function in an economy, a place in the sequence
> of generations, and a status in the structure of society,
> the adult is able to selectively reconstruct his past in such
> a way that, step for step, it seems to have planned him,
> or better, he seems to have planned *it*. In this sense, psy-
> chologically we *do* choose our parents, our family his-
> tory, and the history of our kings, heroes, and gods. By
> making them our own, we maneuver ourselves into the
> inner position of proprietors, of creators.[27]

[26] Lejeune, p. 201. Martha R. Lifson takes McCarthy as her primary example to illustrate her thesis that the quest for the secret self is a central
motive in the creation of autobiography. Lifson shares my view that Mary's
grandmother Preston functions as a surrogate for Mary in the final section of
*Memories*, although she leaves the role of Tess, Mary's mother (for me the
crucial, mediating term in the dynamic of the relationship), largely out of
account. "Allegory of the Secret: Mary McCarthy," *Biography*, 4 (1981), 249-
67.

[27] *Young Man Luther: A Study in Psychoanalysis and History* (1958; rpt. New
York: Norton, 1962), pp. 111-12.

Thanks to this reversible teleology ("it seems to have planned him, or better, he seems to have planned *it*"), autobiographical narrative offers a unique opportunity to affirm the godlike existence of the self—the self as a *causa causans*, Erikson suggests—against the threat of nonidentity. Thus the autobiographical act would be merely a special instance of the psychological imperative motivating any individual to the work of self-creation.

In "To the Reader" McCarthy presents the loss of her parents as the central fact with which she had to reckon in the creation of her autobiography. In its essence autobiography is for her an art of memory, and memory is not only fallible but in her case beyond correction:

> *One great handicap to this task of recalling has been the fact of being an orphan. The chain of recollection—the collective memory of a family—has been broken. It is our parents, normally, who not only teach us our family history but who set us straight on our own childhood recollections, telling us that* this *cannot have happened the way we think it did and that* that, *on the other hand, did occur, just as we remember it, in such and such a summer when So-and-So was our nurse.*

In this perspective the death of her parents illuminates the problematical relationship to truth that links all of the various Marys past and present in the narrative: lying becomes a sign of her orphan condition, the making of fictions a function of her loss. In addition, this statement contains a latent wish that provides a major clue to the motivation for the autobiography: if "*this task of recalling*" is completed, if the broken link in "*the chain of recollection*" is repaired, then, at least in narrative, the orphan will repossess her missing parents.[28] Such a view helps

[28] In his suggestive study of the parallels between the situation of the writer and that of the patient undergoing a psychoanalysis, Bernard Pingaud describes the fantasy of wish-fulfillment that can inform the creation of narrative as follows: "Tandis que le patient utilise un allocutaire réel, présent matériellement comme support de ses fantasmes, l'écrivain s'invente à mesure

to account for the urgency with which McCarthy can speak of her project, as when she says of it, *"It has been a kind of quest"* (5). Thus, when she writes of the *"burning interest in our past,"* which she and her brother Kevin try *"to reconstruct together, like two amateur archaeologists"* (6), the autobiographical act emerges as her opportunity to acquire a past she would otherwise have lacked. Paradoxically, her status as an orphan simultaneously inhibits and stimulates the functioning of the autobiographical impulse: the loss of her parents becomes the pivotal, identity-conferring event in her life, the breaking and the making of her narrative. This McCarthy herself seems in part to see when, reflecting on the fact that she and her brother *"are the only members of the present generation of our family who have done anything out of the ordinary,"* she asks: *"Was it a good thing, then, that our parents were 'taken away,' as if by some higher design?"* (16-17). She professes not to know the answer, but leaves little doubt about her own view of the matter when she conjures up a vision of the banal, conventionally middle-class self she might otherwise have become, a *"rather stout,"* unreflecting Catholic *"married to an Irish lawyer and playing golf and bridge"* (16).

Interestingly, the loss of her parents, which McCarthy presents in "To the Reader" as the focal event in her history, at once obstacle and incentive to its recovery in narrative, seems to be lurking in the background of the very first of her autobiographical writings that we know of. According to the commentary on "A Tin Butterfly," the only completed part of the play she had planned to write in college on this episode dealt with *"our first meeting with our guardians"* (83). In *Memories*, this meeting occurs in the first of the sketches, "Yonder Peasant, Who Is He?" (1948), where it is associated with the period

---

un destinataire, le fantasme de l'écriture étant précisément la conviction que l'oeuvre obligera, en fin de compte, cet interlocutaire désiré et impossible à se présenter en chair et en os. Ainsi Kafka écrit sa *Lettre au père* non pas pour s'expliquer, ni pour se disculper, mais pour que l'image paternelle que l'écriture appelle naisse de l'écriture elle-même, pour que ce soit *ce père-là* qui lise la lettre." "L'écriture et la cure," *Nouvelle Revue Française* (Oct. 1970), 154.

immediately following the death of her parents, at a point when the child refuses to acknowledge the reality of her loss: "Those weeks in my grandmother's house come back to me very obscurely, surrounded by blackness, like a mourning card: the dark well of the staircase, where I seem to have been endlessly loitering, waiting to see Mama when she would come home from the hospital. . . ." In the context of this delicate phase in the formation of her identity, when she hovers between regression and development, "a dangling, transitional creature, a frog becoming a tadpole" (38), the maid's announcement one afternoon that "there is someone here to see you" necessarily comes as a shock: "My heart bounded; I felt almost sick (who else, after all, could it be?), and she had to push me forward. But the man and woman surveying me in the sun parlor with my grandmother were strangers . . ." (39). Who else indeed if not "Mama"? In the commentary she wrote in 1957 for "Yonder Peasant," however, McCarthy singles out this passage for special criticism, dismissing it as *"pure fiction,"* for *"in reality, I had already seen the people who were going to be my guardians sometime before this"* (48). She says that she no longer remembers what made her *"change this story to something decidedly inferior, even from a literary point of view—far too sentimental"* (49). This harsh judgment is misleading, for the power of the scene as it is presented in "Yonder Peasant" derives from the fact that the meeting with the guardians functions as a screen for the fantasy of a reunion with the lost parent. The real *"fiction"* in the account is the narrative re-enactment of the child's need to believe that the mother is not dead.

Taken together, the episode in "Yonder Peasant" and McCarthy's subsequent criticism of it in the commentary represent the two most characteristic postures of her performance as an autobiographer in *Memories*. On the one hand, she constantly criticizes herself—as a child telling lies, as an autobiographer making fictions—for infidelities to the truth; on the other, she willingly conspires with her earlier selves in the invention of wish-fulfilling fictions. In this case neither memory nor imagination succeeds in dispelling the darkness that

shrouds the primal event of death and loss. In the narrative a
break occurs at just this point, coinciding and symbolizing the
psychological blackout involved, and the author's subsequent
researches, reported in the commentary, fail to close the gap.
The newspaper accounts contradict each other on the date of
death, and discussions with brother Kevin yield no certainty
on the date of burial. As to this last, McCarthy is obliged to
settle for "*the feeling of 'remembering'* " (48). In "Ask Me No
Questions," the final sketch in the series, she makes one last
effort to repair the break in her lifeline, and nearly succeeds,
by means of a subtle and daring fiction, in placing herself in
the presence of the determining event in her story. It is an
instructive failure.

INITIALLY, the terminal position of "Ask Me No Questions" in
*Memories* comes as a surprise, a strategic error in the literary
design, for it violates the rhythm generated by the more or
less chronological progress from childhood to high school in
the first seven sketches. As the sketches succeed one another,
the autobiographer gradually moves away from the family
portraits that cluster in the early portion of the narrative to a
more focused concern with her own development, which she
dramatizes in terms of her relationships with various school
friends and teachers. She could so easily have capitalized on
the momentum generated by the sixth and seventh sketches,
"The Figures in the Clock" and "Yellowstone Park," which
portray a distinctly adolescent Mary finishing high school and
learning the ways of the world, to pursue her development at
Vassar in the final chapter. Instead, seeming to exchange autobiography for biography, McCarthy devotes the last and
longest of the chapters to a portrait of her mother's mother,
Augusta Morganstern Preston.

The commentary immediately preceding "Ask Me No
Questions" addresses the issue of the curious final position of
the story in the narrative, latest in the sequence of composition, earliest in terms of the personal history with which it
deals. As in the genesis of her very first autobiographical sketch,

McCarthy's stance is again distinctly ambivalent. She had waited to write partly because her grandmother was still living *"while most of these memoirs were being written."* However, McCarthy continues, *"even when she was dead, I felt a certain reluctance . . . as toward touching a sensitive nerve,"* for *"it meant probing . . . into the past, into my earliest, dimmest memories, and into the family past behind that."* Again, as in the case of "C.Y.E.," the motive for repression of the past is balanced by a compulsion to explore and solve some underlying enigma in her story: *"I knew I was going to have to touch on her, or the story would not be complete. . . . [T]he sense of a mystery back of the story I had already told traced itself more and more to the figure of my grandmother"* (193). *"Touch on her," "touch on a sensitive nerve"*— the autobiographer is intimately linked to her biographical subject; the identification between the two women is crucial, as we shall see, for McCarthy intuitively understands that the anatomy she intends to perform on her subject involves a laying bare of the nervous system of her own personality. And so "Ask Me No Questions" begins with this statement: "There was something strange, abnormal, about my bringing-up; only now that my grandmother is dead am I prepared to face this fact" (195).

"Ask Me No Questions" clearly demonstrates that McCarthy did experience her grandmother's death as a kind of release, opening up previously forbidden territory in her own past. The movement backward in time steadily accelerates in the first few pages; three, six, almost twenty, more than forty years ago. Only in "To the Reader," also written at this time, is the prose so richly autobiographical in texture, not only in the comprehensiveness with which all phases of her life are recalled but also in the explicitness with which the process of recollection itself is dramatized. Nevertheless, the first act of this newly liberated autobiographical consciousness is the evocation of a memory of Grandmother Preston that restores the very prohibition so freshly lifted by her death. "Six years ago," three years before she died, the old woman and Mary go over a collection of family photographs, and the grandmother in the confusion of senility charges Mary with having written "bad things" about her in her autobiographical sketches, whereas in fact McCarthy has hitherto avoided treatment of this most important of her relatives. In this revealing moment life history and the autobiographical narrative devoted to it intersect, for the set of photographs becomes a metaphor for the portraits McCarthy assembled in *Memories*, a symbolism carried over into the published text, moreover, which includes an album of family pictures.

Here McCarthy is again on the defensive, rehearsing once more her desire to write and not to write about her grand-mother and, ultimately, herself. She explains that she had not written because she knew that her grandmother hated to have her likeness taken, and so the portrait in "Ask Me No Questions" is to be understood as the equivalent of the presence conspicuously missing in so many of the photographs ("a shadow on the lawn . . . may indicate where she was standing"). Thus she embarks on her telling of this story with "a distinct uneasiness," imagining her grandmother's shade interposing to forbid her projected revelation:

> Limbo is where I can best imagine her, waiting for me at some stairhead with folded arms and cold cream on her face, as she used to wait in her pink quilted Japanese bathrobe or the green one with the dragons when I turned my key softly in the front door at two or three in the morning, with a lie, which I hoped not to need, trembling on my lips. She would never forgive me for what I am about to do, and if there is an afterlife, it is God who will have to listen to my explanations. (198)

This striking image captures the moral ambiguity of McCarthy's autobiographical situation: the identity of the object of her search is concealed behind a threatening mask, and the truth she seeks to unlock and utter shows here as a lie; the passage suggests that to practice such revelation is to commit a sin, a violation of the privacy of the self. Moreover, in the context of her own reluctance toward the inquiry she is about to pursue, the scene on the stairhead dramatizes an internal confrontation between two opposed motives in her own personality: the opposition to the aggressive quest for knowledge, suggested here by the daughter's return home from a mature world of late-night experience, takes the form of a forbidding and hostile parent.

In this evocation, McCarthy's autobiographical stance in the concluding phase of her project in 1957 is every bit as contradictory and conflicting as it was at its inception in 1943. A clue to the latent tension lies in the roles assumed in the primal confrontation on the stairs—the disobedient daughter and the unforgiving mother—and the mystery of unreciprocated love that keeps them apart. It is a no-win situation, for any attempt to justify to her grandmother the story she is going to write would be as "hopeless" as the attempt to justify what she had already written:

> You could never explain anything to her or make her see you loved her. She rebuffed explanations, as she rebuffed shows of affection; they intruded on her privacy, that closely guarded preserve—as sacrosanct as her bureau drawers or the safe with a combination lock in her closet— in which she clung to her own opinion. "Look, Grandma," I began, but then I gave it up. (197)

I would argue that this curious linkage of the issue of her autobiographical motivation to her desire to love and be loved is governed by the logic of McCarthy's great loss, the vulnerability of her orphan state, a logic which we might reconstruct as follows. The pre-eminently missing figure among the family photographs is Mary's grandmother; in its counterpart, *Memories*, it is Mary's mother. To write the grandmother's story is to recapture the mother and give her love; the apparent aggression of the intrusion on privacy is to be understood, paradoxically, as a "show of affection." But why is the fantasy of such a reunion colored by the need for reconciliation that the encounter on the stairs seems to imply? Why indeed, unless the absence of the loving mother, early taken from the child in the influenza epidemic of 1918, was somehow experienced by McCarthy as a rejection? Her position here, in this autobiographical present (imagined, significantly, in terms of a memory from the past), as so often in her story—in "A Tin Butterfly," in "Names"—is defined by her sense of guilt for something she has not done, as though the mother had died because the child had inadequately loved her. Such a sense of guilt would doubtless be encouraged by the sudden shift in the children's domestic circumstances from a life of happiness and indulgence by adoring parents (this is the picture in "To the Reader") to one of discipline and punishment under the loveless regime of the guardians ("Yonder Peasant, Who Is He?" and "A Tin Butterfly"). The climax of McCarthy's autobiographical quest would be to come to terms at last with the event that had made her an orphan, shaping her life and her story. Viewed in this light, the stairway setting of the imaginary encounter with the dead grandmother seems more than accidental, for it links this scene with McCarthy's fantasy of a reunion with her dead mother in "Yonder Peasant, Who Is He?" In a suggestive reversal of roles, Mary assumes here the part played in the earlier scene by her mother, whose death had abandoned the child to a shadowy limbo of loitering by the stairs.

Although I am convinced that something very like the pattern of the "logic" I have described structures the working out of the autobiographical impulse in McCarthy's case, I would be the first to point out that such speculations are necessarily unverifiable. They are offered as a possible background for the central issue that I would like to study in McCarthy's performance in "Ask Me No Questions": her transformation of the grandmother and her story into a special kind of fiction to meet the requirements of her autobiographical quest into her own identity and its mysterious origins. If the grandmother is perceived as a barrier to the pursuit of the past, in what sense, we may ask, is the telling of her story an appropriate ending to McCarthy's own story, as she urges that it is and had to be? The subsequent narrative, in thirteen sections of varying length, unfolds as a series of four attempts to pass beyond the unforgiving figure at the head of the stairs into the knowledge the autobiographer seeks to possess.

In the second section, in which McCarthy delves into her earliest childhood memories, the recurring image of the grandmother that links them all is that of a woman wearing a veil or mask, culminating in the recollection of a "strange lady . . . with a different kind of veil on, a black one, which hung all the way down over her face" (201), who visited the six-year-old Mary during her convalescence from the flu in Minneapolis in 1918. Only months later did the child surmise that her own parents "were not coming back," and that "the strange lady had come and cried on my bed because her daughter was dead" (202). This initial clarification, however, fails to dissipate the darkness that McCarthy associates early and late with the elusive figure of Augusta Preston. In the third section, as the author studies various photographs of her grandmother, she is struck by the shift in her appearance from a young woman of "gentle, open, serious mien" to an older woman with a "sharp" and "jaunty" air (203), and finds herself at a loss to account for so "profound a change": " 'What happened?' " (204).

McCarthy proceeds in this and the following sections to assemble the facts of Mrs. Preston's story despite her subject's avowed lack of any autobiographical curiosity—" 'Why do you keep asking me all those old things?' " (204). A brief review of her grandmother's childhood—Mrs. Preston, like Mary, is an orphan—leads into a more extended but finally inconclusive examination of her Jewish background. The author is obliged to settle for her own nagging sense of a biographical significance that refuses to be captured, a "*something*—a shying away from the subject, an aversion to naming it in words" (211). Mrs. Preston's accounts of her own motivation are reluctant and unenlightening, and McCarthy can find little resemblance between her grandmother's characterization of herself as a perennial "loser" in the anecdotes she liked to tell and her own memory of her as a "disconcerting," "impassive,"

"forbidding" woman ("most people . . . were afraid of her")
(217).

The seventh section rounds off this sequence of retrospect
by returning once more to the "oddity" of Augusta Preston's
appearance; this, McCarthy asserts, was "the first thing that
would have struck an outsider about her in her later years"
(217). Studying the image of her grandmother arrayed for her
unvarying daily routine of afternoon shopping, she highlights
the "consummate artifice" involved, especially the cosmetic
disguise of the face, "the rouge and the powder and the van-
ishing cream underneath" (218). Despite this "blazonry of make-
up," "she did look remarkably young," so much so that flat-
tering salespeople urge her to make Mary "pass for your
daughter"; the granddaughter adds, significantly, "she *could*
have passed for my mother" (220). McCarthy reads a "garish"
loneliness in her grandmother's appearance, but she confesses
her inability to account for it, for "she had nothing to com-
plain of in life" (221):

> . . . until she reached her second childhood, she seemed,
> on the surface, a contented woman, well situated in life,
> self-contained, unemotional. The only blights she had
> suffered, so far as I knew, were the unseasonable death
> of my mother and a mastoid operation that had left her
> with some scars, just under her ears, in her neck and
> lower cheeks. (222)

This second attempt at clarification of the mystery of this life
is avowedly unsatisfactory. As Faulkner's Mr. Compson puts
it, after his elaborate reconstruction of the motivation of the
dead Sutpens in *Absalom, Absalom!* ends in failure, "It just
does not explain."

In the first seven sections of "Ask Me No Questions,"
McCarthy ranges freely backward and forward from the earliest to the latest phases of her grandmother's story and her
own points of contact with it. In the second half of the narrative, beginning with section eight, she presents a sustained
evocation of the years she spent living in the Preston house,

while she attended first a Catholic convent and later a public high school. This is the period in which Mary's orphan circumstances structure her relationship with her grandmother as that of mother and daughter. After five years of deprivation with the hateful guardians in Minneapolis, the eleven-year-old girl is overwhelmed by the luxury of the affluent Preston household. Repeating the pattern of the earlier portions of the narrative, the focus narrows swiftly to the grandmother's body and Mary's chilling intuition of the "mature sensuality" with which her grandmother satisfied its hunger:

> I conceived an aversion to apricots—a tasteless fruit, anyway, I considered—from having watched her with them, just as though I had witnessed what Freud calls the primal scene. Now I, too, am fond of them, and whenever I choose one from a plate, I think of my grandmother's body, full-fleshed, bland, smooth, and plump, cushioning in itself, close held—a secret, like the flat brown seed of the apricot. (225)

The girl gradually perceives the grandmother's body as a kind of "cult object," the *omphalos* of the family world, and the bathroom as "the temple" of its worship. Here Mrs. Preston secludes herself for hours each day in preparation for her public display of herself in the ritual afternoon shopping, and here, inevitably, Mary, now twelve, is tempted one day to enter the inner sanctum and appropriate its "relics" (225-26).

Significantly, McCarthy prefaces this episode of the bathroom with an allusion to another scene of revelation much later on, in Mrs. Preston's seventies, when Mary caught "a disturbing glimpse of her thighs": "Disturbing, because I knew she would not want to be looked at, even in admiration" (226). This allusion parallels—and closely follows in the text—the author's analysis of the child's watching the grandmother eat as the equivalent of witnessing "what Freud calls the primal scene" (225), and suggests an undercurrent of sexuality as a latent content in the forbidden knowledge that McCarthy, then as a child, now as an autobiographer, pursues. McCarthy shows herself as imitating her grandmother, early and late, in the application of cosmetics, in the eating of fruit, as though through symbolic gestures of impersonation she could become and hence possess what she seeks to know.

Her transgression betrayed by the forbidden cosmetic disguise of rouge and powder she has applied, the guilty granddaughter adopts the familiar recourse of lying in the "terrible scene" with her grandmother that follows. The pair of women in opposition, the mask (here worn by Mary), the lying that accompanies the revelation of the truth—all these suggest the scene as a prototype for the stairhead encounter that introduces the final phase of McCarthy's autobiographical quest. The bathroom, she writes, "figured to me as the center of everything in the Preston family life from which I was excluded" (228). From here on the narrative presents the autobiographer facing the fact that she presents as the occasion for writing "Ask Me No Questions": "There was something strange, abnormal, about my bringing-up" (195).

The picture of family life as McCarthy reconstructs it is one of "shut doors and silence," which symbolizes the painful lack of communication between Mary and her relatives. Repeated attempts at conversation with her grandmother invariably end in failure: "We could never be 'like mother and daughter' to each other, in spite of what people said" (231). Gradually McCarthy comes to see her family as "remarkably inhospitable." The Prestons rarely entertain and make no effort to supply a social life for their adopted granddaughter. As with the hated nickname, the girl is led to blame her lack of social life on herself, as though "there was something wrong with me, like a petticoat showing, that other people could see and I couldn't" (235). It is at this point that the autobiographer takes up for the first time the relationship between her grandmother and her mother, for "in my mother's day, so I was told, things had been very different" (237). In the thirteenth section of the narrative McCarthy presents the third in the series of attempts to read aright the enigmatic figure guarding the stairhead against the autobiographer's determined ascent to knowledge. "My mother," she begins, "had been my grandmother's darling" (237).

The "official explanation" for the "oddities" of the Preston household was that Mary's grandmother "had never recovered from the shock of my mother's death" (238), and McCarthy speculates that her own failed relationship with Mrs. Preston may have been the result of her painful resemblance to her mother. In this view the paired lives of grandmother and granddaughter, the paired narratives of "Ask Me No Questions" and *Memories of a Catholic Girlhood*, would be similarly determined by the same central shaping event of loss. McCarthy, however, rejects the "official" version of the grandmother's story in favor of her own instinctive insight as a child that Mrs. Preston's mourning was "willful and obdurate": "My grandmother's grief had taken a form peculiar to herself, stamped, as it were, with her monogram—the severe 'AMP,' in scroll lettering, that figured on her silver, her brushes and combs, her automobile." For "my mother's darling," read "AMP"; the identity of the beloved other is stamped—and stamped out—with the sign of the voracious ego. Her analysis traces the experience of grief to her grandmother's "coquetry," to her preoccupation with her "beauty"; it becomes merely an adjunct, a prized possession serving the conspicuous consumption of self: "life itself was obliged to court her" (239). Pursuing this thesis, McCarthy proposes that her grandmother's story was structured by a series of three "mortal" affronts to her ego: a conjectured injury to her Jewish pride (occurring, perhaps, early in her marriage), a tragic face lifting (in 1916 or 1917, when she was in her forties), and, finally, the death of her daughter Tess (in 1918). All the puzzling aspects of the biographical materials that McCarthy has assembled in the narrative so far seem to fall into place in this penultimate moment of clarification, a clarification, however, which fails to make good the autobiographer's sense that the grandmother's character held "the key" to the "mystery back of the story" she had already told about herself. Significantly, the death of Tess is displaced here by the face lifting as the central event of "Ask Me No Questions." To the aftermath of the botched surgery belong the daily cult of the bathroom and the ritual of the afternoon shopping, the withdrawal from society into silence; the legacy of "pouchy disfiguring scars" (240) explains all the makeup, the veils, the refusal to be photographed.

In the concluding section of the narrative McCarthy returns once more to the last years of her grandmother's life; here, with her account of Mrs. Preston's response to the death of her sister Rosie, McCarthy's search for knowledge of her grandmother comes to an end. In this climactic scene, heralded by "a terrible" and "unearthly" scream, she seems for once to witness the always veiled and impassive woman in the throes of undisguised and violent emotion:

> Flinging open her bedroom door (even then with a sense of trepidation, of being an unwarranted intruder), I saw her, on her bed, the covers pushed back; her legs were sprawled out, and her yellow batiste nightgown, trimmed with white lace, was pulled up, revealing her thighs. She was writhing on the bed; the cook and I could barely get hold of her. My uncle appeared in the doorway, and my first thought (and I think the cook's also) was to get that nightgown down. The spectacle was indecent, and yet of a strange boudoir beauty that contrasted in an eerie way with that awful noise she was making, more like a howl than a scream and bearing no resemblance to sorrow. (242)

This, like its predecessors, is one more version of the experience of revelation that the narrative is designed to supply. The allusion to the indecent exposure of the thighs links this scene with the episode of Mary's trespass in the bathroom as a girl of twelve, where it is also mentioned; this earlier scene is in its turn a version of the stairhead encounter that frames the entire narrative. In this nocturnal display of naked emotion the autobiographer seems at last to behold the inmost truth about the woman whose story, so she had believed, could illuminate the darkness at the center of her own life history: "It seemed clear to me that night, as I sat stroking her hair, that she had never really cared for anyone but her sister; that was her secret." However, undercutting her sense "that some sort of revelation had taken place," echoed by her belief that the family "too, felt that she [Mrs. Preston] had revealed something" (243), is her inability to determine for sure what actually has been revealed. And so this last of the series of clarifications of the grandmother's story, like all the others, gives way once more to a sense of the unsolvable mystery at the heart of personality.

Displaced first by the face lifting and then by the death of Rosie, the death of Mary's mother, the missing event of McCarthy's own story, recedes from the autobiographer's grasp. "She had never really cared for anyone but her sister"; recognition of this truth forecloses definitively the possibility that McCarthy could re-enact and symbolically recover the exchange of love interrupted by her mother's early death. Biographically speaking, there is nothing surprising in McCarthy's involvement in a behavior pattern of this sort, first during her adolescence in Seattle, and then, many years later, during the autobiographical act. To the contrary, such behavior seems altogether natural, given the circumstances. In an obvious way the grandmother functioned as a substitute for Mary's mother, and, reciprocally, Mary functioned as a substitute for her as well; this aspect of the mother-daughter tie is ever-present in their relationship—even the casual comments of admiring salespeople kept it in view. What "Ask Me No Questions" proposes, however, with its juxtaposition of the grandmother's story on Mary's own history, is a more daring perspective on the mother-daughter axis in which the grandmother would function as a surrogate for Mary herself. She would be a Mary who consciously experienced the loss of Tess, a Mary who loved the mother and who was genuinely bereaved by her death, as opposed to the six-year-old girl for whom the event of loss was wrapped in a blackout of sickness and repression. Thus it is, as we have seen, that McCarthy is capable of playing the role of either the unmasker or the masked in the various scenes of revelation. The dual role suggests the identity of subject and object, of self and other, that makes possible the fulfillment of the wish: McCarthy wants to witness what "she" has experienced. To this extent the biographical facts about the grandmother would operate as an autobiographical fiction designed to recover the missing event of McCarthy's own life story.

The very premise of this fiction, however, the bereavement that they shared, is disconfirmed by the ultimate scene of revelation at the time of Rosie's death. In an ironic reversal of roles, the orphan autobiographer offers maternal consolation and love to the "mother" in her loss ("I sat stroking her hair"), while the grandmother, swiftly slipping into senility, becomes precisely such a "child" as Mary describes herself to have been in "To the Reader" and "Yonder Peasant, Who Is He?", believing that the dead sister had " 'gone away,' . . . just as children believe that this is what happens to their dead relations" (243-44). And so the end of "Ask Me No Questions," and with it, *Memories of a Catholic Girlhood*, circles back to its beginning and the unfathomable mystery of origins.

At the last the powers of language—and, by extension, narrative—atrophy. One afternoon, the old lady, in a state of agitation, asks Mary to get her something—the " 'wachama-callit' "—from her bureau, and Mary is at a loss to discover what she wants until the nurse supplies the answer: "She's forgotten the word for mirror" (245). The autobiographical act, we might say, is the attempt to find the word for mirror. McCarthy speaks of her project in the preface as "a kind of quest," and the story in *Memories* of its pursuit over a period of thirteen years reveals that the presence of fiction in autobiography is properly regarded not as an interference with the search for the truth about the self but rather as an inevitable and invaluable resource for its recovery. McCarthy's position at the end of *Memories* repeats her position in the very first of her autobiographical sketches. As in "C.Y.E.," she is dealing in "Ask Me No Questions" with the presence of something about herself, some deep truth, which she cannot get at but which she believes to be central to her identity and its story.

The autobiographer has pursued her symbolic manipulations of fact to the limit, attempting to fashion in her grandmother's story and in her own an instrument of vision in which she can witness the reflection of her inmost self; her narrative can do no more.

Did McCarthy recognize that to write a life is in effect to embrace a strategy for translating the incommunicable self into a communicable substance, incommunicable because not finally knowable? Had she engaged in the making of fictions about what is, perhaps, itself only a fiction? In any case, some five years after the publication of *Memories*, in an interview in 1962, McCarthy announces her definitive abandonment of the view of autobiography that governs the creation of *Memories*:

> I think I'm really not interested in the quest for the self any more. Oh, I suppose everyone continues to be interested in the quest for the self, but what you feel when you're older, I think, is that—how to express this—that you really must *make* the self. It's absolutely useless to look for it, you won't find it, but it's possible in some sense to make it.[29]

After such knowledge, an autobiographer can only say of the truth of her story, "ask me no questions," for the telling of lies is inextricably implicated in the writing of her memories. The lesson of McCarthy's experience of the autobiographical act is that the process of self-discovery is finally inseparable from the art of self-invention.

[29] "The Art of Fiction," 93-94.

# CHAPTER TWO

# Henry James and
# the Autobiographical Act

ROY PASCAL has observed that autobiography involves an interplay or collusion between the past and the present, that indeed its significance is more truly understood as the revelation of the present situation of the autobiographer than as the uncovering of his past.[1] As readers of autobiography we ordinarily do need to be reminded of this obvious truth, even though Freud and his followers have shaken our faith in the ability of memory to provide reliable access to the contents of the past. When we settle into the theater of autobiography, what we are ready to believe—and what most autobiographers encourage us to expect—is that the play we witness is a historical one, a largely faithful and unmediated reconstruction of events that took place long ago, whereas in reality the play is that of the autobiographical act itself, in which the materials of the past are shaped by memory and imagination to serve the needs of present consciousness. This mediation of the past by the present governs the autobiographical enterprise, as we have seen in the explicitly revisionist performance of Mary McCarthy in Chapter One, and it frequently supplies a frame for narrative in modern autobiography. In Henry James's autobiography this mediation is prominently displayed in the foreground of the text, and it is for this reason that James's narrative has seemed to me especially suited to an inquiry into the nature of the autobiographical act.[2]

[1] *Design and Truth in Autobiography* (Cambridge: Harvard Univ. Press, 1960), p. 11.

[2] "Like all autobiographies," William Hoffa has commented, "James's is about the early life of its author, but it is just as much about the autobiog-

It is impossible to remain indifferent to James's insistent and obtrusive dramatization of the process of composition. Some readers have found it involving, others have been repelled by it. Either way, there is no question that it gives the prose its distinctive self-conscious coloration. It accounts, moreover, for much of the length of this massive narrative, which eventually ran to two volumes, *A Small Boy and Others* (1913) and *Notes of a Son and Brother* (1914), and a posthumous fragment, *The Middle Years* (1917). Is James's emphasis on the performative values of his undertaking merely one more illustration of his inveterate fondness for dramatizing the creative process, acted out in countless monologues in the notebooks and lovingly memorialized in the New York prefaces? Considering the circumstances of the composition of the autobiography, the pacing up and down in the Chelsea flat as he dictated his story to Theodora Bosanquet, we could conclude that this procedure only heightened the tendency to display the workings of the creative process in his art, and let it go at that. On the other hand, if we make as much of James's preoccupation with the autobiographical act as he made of it himself, we can only infer that the writing of the autobiography, ostensibly a rehearsal of the completed history of the past, is better understood as a manifestation of some imperative drama of consciousness going forward in the present.

Robert Sayre has argued that James's recollection of his early youth was motivated by a need to regain his creative powers.[3] James himself wrote to his nephew Harry on January 19, 1913, that in pursuing the project he was "working off" "the heritage of woe of the last three years,"[4] and Leon Edel has spelled out the nature of the woe in the final volume of his biography

---

rapher's reaction to the process of telling his story, about the present re-experiencing of his early life." "The Final Preface: Henry James's Autobiography," *Sewanee Review*, 77 (1969), 284.

[3] *The Examined Self: Benjamin Franklin, Henry Adams, Henry James* (Princeton: Princeton Univ. Press, 1964), pp. 144-45.

[4] *The Letters of Henry James*, ed. Percy Lubbock, 2 vols. (New York: Scribner's, 1920), II, 289.

of James. Devastated by the financial failure of the New York Edition of his work, which was to have been the culmination of his extremely long and productive career, James became increasingly depressed during 1909 and suffered a nervous breakdown at the beginning of 1910. By midsummer he had recovered, only to succumb to a second blow, the death of his beloved brother William in August. A period of renewed depression and illness followed, accompanying the early phases of the autobiographical project begun in the late fall of 1911 and continuing to trouble James during the writing of *A Small Boy and Others* in 1912. Edel believes that the act of composition ministered not only to James's physical recovery but to his psychological health as well, allowing him to resolve the old "family" drama of tensions and sibling rivalries that is the theme of Edel's five-volume biography. Edel links the crisis of these years, both its cause and its resolution, to the better-known earlier one that followed the failure of *Guy Domville* and the collapse of James's career as a dramatist in 1895. The effect of the failure of the New York Edition, he writes, "was as if [James] had faced a booing audience again [as in 1895], and were being told that his life work was no good, and that he was unwanted."[5] Similarly, the recall of childhood in the autobiographical act "held in it the same form of release from discouragement and depression he had experienced a decade earlier [in the later 1890s] when he had written out of his fantasies a series of novels and tales about children."[6] Edel clarifies the theoretical implications of these observations in the preface to the fourth volume of his biography, where, speaking of the *Guy Domville* crisis, he states that James "performed on himself what Freud was busily demonstrating—he showed man's capacity to heal himself by a retreat to earlier experience."[7]

[5] Edel, *Henry James: The Master, 1901-1916* (Philadelphia: Lippincott, 1972), p. 434.

[6] *Ibid.*, pp. 455-56.

[7] Edel, *Henry James: The Treacherous Years, 1895-1901* (Philadelphia: Lippincott, 1969), p. 16.

The autobiographical act would, on the face of it, seem to offer a natural, even a privileged, instance of this notion of art as therapy. Students of psychoanalytic procedure, however, insist on the radical differences between autobiography and autoanalysis, emphasizing the extent to which writing characteristically functions as a defense mechanism. Still more important, they stress the absence from both of these of the crucial relationship between patient and analyst that is the source of the therapeutic value of psychoanalysis.[8] In any case, although both Sayre and Edel assert that the writing of the autobiography was instrumental in James's recovery, they do not demonstrate how the literary project accomplished this therapeutic task. We can test this view and enlarge our understanding of the autobiographical act by examining James's own testimony, both in the text itself and in his many letters to others about it.

## I. "I at any rate watch the small boy dawdle and gape again"

James frequently addresses himself to the nature of the autobiographical process in which he is engaged, but his numerous pronouncements in the text do not add up to any coherent view. Two characteristic passages, one from the opening of *A Small Boy* and the other from the final chapters of *Notes*, will suggest both the insights and the limitations of James's account of the autobiographical process. In his introductory statement, James makes the autobiographical act practically synonymous with the act of recollection. He asserts that the motive for the project is his desire "to place together some particulars of the early life of William James." As he continues, however, it becomes clear that the undertaking is dominated by the agency of his own memory, which first creates formal problems for the autobiographer and then proceeds to

---

[8] See, e.g., Bernard Pingaud, "L'écriture et la cure," in Philippe Lejeune, *L'autobiographie en France* (Paris: Armand Colin, 1971), pp. 257-62 passim.

solve them: "To knock at the door of the past was in a word to see it open to me quite wide—to see the world within begin to 'compose' with a grace of its own round the primary figure, see it people itself vividly and insistently. Such then is the circle of my commemoration and so much these free and copious notes a labour of love and loyalty."[9] The act of recollection emerges here as an autonomous, structuring process, supplying the materials for James's commemorative intention and conferring a form on them as well. By this account, James is hardly to be held responsible for any ambiguity we may detect about the true identity of "the primary figure," who proves in the end to be not William but Henry himself.

By the end of the second volume, however, James offers a distinctly different formulation of the autobiographical act, of "the principle governing, by my measure, these recoveries and reflections." This time he casts himself as the artist, the "teller of tales," who has found in the story of his own life the "long-sought occasion" for the working out of a peculiarly challenging aesthetic "task," the presentation of the "personal history . . . of an imagination." "Haunted" as he was by "the man of imagination" as "the hero of a hundred possible fields," James emphasizes that he was slow to recognize that he himself could serve as his model:

> . . . he [the man of imagination] was to turn up then in a shape almost too familiar at first for recognition . . . He had been with me all the while, and only too obscurely and intimately—I had not found him in the market as an exhibited or *offered* value. I had in a word to draw him forth from within rather than meet him in the world before me, the more convenient sphere of the objective, and to make him objective, in short, had to turn nothing less than myself inside out. What was *I* thus, within and essentially, what had I ever been, and could

[9] *Henry James: Autobiography*, ed. Frederick W. Dupee (1956; rpt. Princeton: Princeton Univ. Press, 1983), pp. 3-4. Subsequent references are to this edition and will appear in the text.

I ever be but a man of imagination at the active pitch?—
so that if it was a question of treating *some* happy case,
any that would give me what, artistically speaking, I
wanted, here on the very spot was one at hand in default
of a better. (454-55)

The entire passage, considerably longer than the part I have
quoted, is an impressive and sustained utterance, and the authoritative tone of the New York prefaces is unmistakable. If
we take our cues from it, we should have to conclude that it
is the strenuous and deliberate agency of the creative process
that shapes the narrative. In this view, the autobiographical
act becomes merely a special instance of the novelist's enterprise, and James himself only a representative case, a convenient resource for the maker of fiction.

Measuring the second passage against the first, we find that
the two positions cancel each other out. If we are to believe
that the autonomous functioning of memory conveniently
performed according to the dictates of some innate principle
of aesthetic form, there really was no heroic task for the teller
of tales to perform. Obviously these formulations are fashioned on the spot to serve the purpose at hand. Thus the
initial tribute to the power and art of memory at the beginning of A *Small Boy* seems to deal with the personal and artistic consequences of a shift in the focus of the project from a
memoir of "the early life of William James" to an emphatically
autobiographical account of James's own childhood. In the
second passage a counter-strategy is at work, in which James
seeks to persuade us that the narrative is really much less
personal than the immediately preceding chapters dealing with
his "obscure hurt" and its aftermath lead us to believe, as we
shall see.

If we turn from these apparently contradictory formulations and examine instead James's dramatization of the autobiographical act in the text, we find that it is consistently
structured by a dialectical relationship between the autobiographical narrator in the present and the character of his ear-

lier self in the past. The distinction implied by such a pair of terms, however, between James as small boy and James as autobiographer, proves to be deceptive. As we examine James's first full-scale presentation of the relationship between past and present in the text, a lengthy reminiscence in the second chapter of *A Small Boy* about walking home from school, we observe that the opposition between younger and older selves, which characteristically structures James's—or anyone's—autobiographical discourse, dissolves before our eyes.

In this passage the autobiographer defines his earliest self in terms of a pattern of behavior that was destined to be a calling: the small boy was a gaper and a dawdler, an observer who feasted on vision. When, in 1851, the eight-year-old Henry had finished his day at Mrs. Lavinia D. Wright's school, there were two routes across Manhattan that could take him home. One way involved a "test" of his courage: the child and his schoolmates passed as close as they dared to a railroad construction project where blasting was going on, for "it was our theory that our passage there . . . was beset with danger." It was the other way home, however, that James was destined to prefer, "a sphere of a different order of fascination and bristling . . . with more vivid aspects, greater curiosities and wonderments." The chief of these was a large house on the northeast corner of Eighteenth Street and Broadway, and the boy liked to lean against the iron palings of the fence and peer through at the animals that "peopled" the grounds: "a romantic view of browsing and pecking and parading creatures, not numerous, but all of distinguished appearance: two or three elegant little cows of refined form and colour, two or three nibbling fawns and a larger company, above all, of peacocks and guineafowl, with, doubtless—though as to this I am vague—some of the commoner ornaments of the barnyard" (15-16).

We may be sure that this reminiscence contained some special significance for James, since he prefaces his account by announcing that he is determined to explore it even at the risk of seeming to make "too much of these tiny particles of history." What he makes so much of is the intense identification of the autobiographical "I" with his earlier self: three times he adopts the stance of the dawdling gaper at the fence. In the first instance the identification of the two selves seems to signify the autobiographer's successful recapture of an earlier state of consciousness; as such we recognize in it a familiar rhetorical strategy of so much autobiographical narrative: "I have but to close my eyes in order to open them inwardly again, while I lean against the tall brown iron rails and peer through. . . ." To stand at the fence was, and is, it seems, to stand at the gateway to romance. The autobiographer embraces the child's point of view enthusiastically, affirming the "note of greatness" experienced by the boy, and he reads in the child's solitude "in these and like New York *flâneries* and contemplations" (16) a sense of confident mastery.

Reflecting, however, on "the liberty of range and opportunity of adventure allowed to my tender age" leads James to conjecture that his parents must have believed "that the only form of riot or revel ever known to me would be that of the visiting mind." Then he proceeds to attribute this conjectured sense of limitations to the small boy of long ago: "Wasn't I myself for that matter even at that time all acutely and yet resignedly, even quite fatalistically, aware of what to think of this?" Thus, when he adopts the child's stance a second time, it is no longer to participate in the small boy's mode of vision. Instead, distancing himself from it, the autobiographer reinterprets the child's station at the fence as an emblem of privation: "I at any rate watch the small boy dawdle and gape again, I smell the cold dusty paint and iron as the rails of the Eighteenth Street corner rub his contemplative nose, and, feeling him foredoomed, withhold from him no grain of my sympathy." Continuing in a vein of parental solicitude for the small figure at the bars, the autobiographer gives himself up to an extended meditation on the boy whose condition was destined to become his own. I quote at length here in order to display the intricate shifting of identity and attitude, the interpenetration of past and present, that makes up the texture of James's autobiographical prose:

> He is a convenient little image or warning of all that was to be for him, and he might well have been even happier than he was. For there was the very pattern and measure of all he was to demand: just to *be* somewhere—almost anywhere would do—and somehow receive an impression or an accession, feel a relation or a vibration. He was to go without many things, ever so many—as all persons do in whom contemplation takes so much the place of action; but everywhere, in the years that came soon after, and that in fact continued long, in the streets of great towns, in New York still for some time, and then for a while in London, in Paris, in Geneva, wherever it might be, he was to enjoy more than anything the so far from showy practice of wondering and dawdling and gaping: he was really, I think, much to profit by it. What it at all appreciably gave him—that is gave him in producible form—would be difficult to state; but it seems to him, as he even now thus indulges himself, an education like another: feeling, as he has come to do more and more, that no education avails for the intelligence that doesn't stir in it some subjective passion, and that on the other hand almost anything that does so act is largely educative, however small a figure the process might make in a scheme of training. (16-17)

If we all too readily assume that it is the business of the autobiographical act to resurrect the departed earlier self and make it live again before our eyes, James gives us fair warning here that the autobiographer's art necessarily involves a talented impersonation. It is, of course, the autobiographer speaking in the guise of the small boy, who observes "but it seems to him, as he even now thus indulges himself. . . ."

The distinction between identities and characteristic states of consciousness past and present is not easy to sort out in the passage, because James discusses both simultaneously. The terms of the one become interchangeable with those of the other, so that when we encounter the final instance of identification between the two selves, which terminates the passage and introduces a new chapter, we are entitled to wonder which of the two he is really talking about: "But I positively dawdle and gape here—I catch myself in the act" (17). Such a statement seems to assert the power of the past over the present ("I" am "he" once more, and so my narrative presents the contours of his walk); yet we have been told in this same passage that the past is made or made over by the present (the small boy is "a convenient little image" fashioned by the autobiographer for purposes of his own). We stand in a hall of mirrors in which the autobiographer can claim to be under the spell that he has himself cast. So this mimesis of past experience by the autobiographical act is not just the obvious demonstration of the autobiographer's sense of continuous identity with his earlier self but something more. Whatever the small boy's state of mind may have been (and James reminds us repeatedly that what he has to say of it is largely inferential), it is obviously the autobiographer's present consciousness that pre-empts the scene as he lingers with the boy at the fence. In the elaborate commentary triggered by the initial evocation, the pleasure of gaping stands for the activity of the imagination, and the boy's preference for the second way home prefigures the artist's choice of vocation. It is James's present sense of the consequences of this commitment that seems to generate the contradictory assessments that cloud the passage as it moves from celebration to apology. Thus the boy's happiness is somehow a "warning"; the younger James, blessed with the freedom to do what he liked best, becomes presently a James "foredoomed" to privation.

What we get from the passage as a whole amounts to a curious double exposure in which James superimposes on an apparently authentic and charming memory of untroubled childhood pleasure (what the child saw as he looked through the fence) a more complicated projection of problems he was to experience only later on (what the autobiographer sees as he looks at the gaping child). In the mirror formed by the record of the past, we begin to make out the reflection of present consciousness engaged in the autobiographical act, especially on occasions like this one when James attempts to probe "the so far from showy practice of . . . gaping" that forms the core of his earlier identity.

James's candor about the creative process in such passages as this one obliges us to modify our conception of the autobiographical narrator and the earlier self in view of the necessarily loose correspondence between these fictions and the biographical realities to which they refer. The point, however, is not to abandon all hope of any valid encounter with biographical truth in an autobiographical text, especially since the making of such fictive selves is likely to be in itself a central biographical event. Any practicing autobiographer is perforce sustained by such a hope; only by belief in the possibility of its realization does the autobiographical enterprise as distinct from an avowedly fictional project have any meaning. Accepting James's version of the past as his truth at the time of composition, what interests us is why he chooses now to recall this particular version of the past, what is in it for him. Pursuing our inquiry into the relationship between autobiographical narrator and small boy as the key to the biographical significance of the autobiographical act, we may be in a better position to make out what the small boy and the telling of his story could do for the autobiographer if we first establish what the autobiographer could do for the small boy.

## II. "Taking in"

Even though James's statements in the text about the nature and purpose of the autobiography cannot be easily reconciled with each other, they add up to a consistent characterization of the autobiographical narrator as a good deal of an exhibitionist. If the elaborate, expansive prose records James's pulse as he performs each moment of the autobiographical act, we cannot help noticing that the showiness of the autobiographer's self-display is occasioned by the story of an apparently featureless earlier self who had nothing to show. James states the thesis of his narrative in the very first of his characterizations of himself as a small boy, which strikes the note for all that follow:

> I lose myself in wonder at the loose ways, the strange process of waste, through which nature and fortune may deal on occasion with those whose faculty for application is all and only in their imagination and their sensibility. There may be during those bewildered and brooding years so little for them to "show" that I liken the individual dunce—as he so often must appear—to some commercial traveler who has lost the key to his packed case of samples and can but pass for a fool while other exhibitions go forward. (8)

Even after the small boy had shed the servitude of his duncelike appearance, discovering in his vocation the key to the locked case of the imagination, this sense of the self as negligible in the eyes of the world persisted. Midway through *The Middle Years* we find James as a young man of twenty-six, already the author of a considerable number of reviews and a few stories, bewildered by the thought that he "could be of interest" to others, in this case a group of Englishmen breakfasting at Albert Rutson's table in London. "My identity for myself," he writes, "was *all* in my sensibility to their own exhibition, with not a scrap left over for a personal show." James describes his state of mind as "the proved humiliation of my impotence"; like the small boy, the young man had to settle for "an abject acceptance of the air of imbecility" (559). If we are to credit James's account, there were precious few to guess what lay hidden within the unprepossessing boy. Louis De Coppet, a childhood friend, is honored as one of the exceptions, although James confesses that he is "quite unable to conceive my companion's ground for suspecting a gift of which I must at that time quite have failed to exhibit a single in the least 'phenomenal' symptom" (22). (Interestingly, for all his praise of his parents in the course of the autobiography, James does not attribute to them a comparable degree of insight in these early years.)

Following the logic of this self-conception, it becomes the function of the autobiographer to unlock the treasure house of past consciousness in order to display the unguessed wealth of the boy's imaginative life. Thus, if the elderly autobiographer is drawn to imagining the sense that others must have had of him—it is almost invariably a diminishing perspective—he cannot resist reminding us that the child's perceptions and the rendering of them in the text itself are anything but small. When James pauses to wonder, for example, why he had been taken while only "a mere mite of observation" to his cousin Kitty Emmet's " 'grown-up' " evening party, he writes: "Was it that my mother really felt that to the scrap that I was other scraps would perhaps strangely adhere, to the extent thus of something to distinguish me by, nothing else probably having as yet declared itself—such a scrap for instance as the fine germ of this actual ferment of memory and play of fancy, a retroactive vision almost intense of the faded hour and a fond surrender to the questions with which it bristles?" (25-26). In this passage, only one of many of this sort in the narrative, James explicitly suggests that some causal, sequential relation connects the condition of small boyhood in the past and the autobiographical act in the present. Somehow, belatedly, the "actual ferment of memory and play of fancy" preserved in the autobiography retroactively complete the child's identity. We behold James giving to James what he once had lacked, "something to distinguish me by."

James recognized that there was some compensatory mechanism at work in the commerce between the present and the past in which he was engaged. We need only reflect, however, that in becoming "the Master" of the assembled *oeuvres* of the New York Edition, the "mite" had surely exhibited his powers to the full, and that anything that the autobiography might add to the sum of vindication would seem to be superfluous. We must suppose, then, that a good deal more was at stake in the autobiographical transaction than anything I have suggested so far. To be sure, James's brimming account of his numerous and colorful relatives, of the theaters and schools and city sights at home and abroad, suggests that a small boy who only demanded "just to *be* somewhere . . . and somehow receive an impression" was certainly well provided for. Indeed, in the several striking passages that seem to take us furthest inside the sensibility of this unusually sensitive child, he seems to have been most happily and fully occupied when he wasn't doing anything at all, not even gaping, but just listening to life, listening to himself listen. The finest of these passages recalls a summer of convalescence in Geneva in 1855, when the slow pace of the boy's recovery confined him largely to his room:

> I had never before lived so long in anything so old and, as I somehow felt, so deep; depth, depth upon depth, was what came out for me at certain times of my waiting above, in my immense room of thick embrasures and rather prompt obscurity, while the summer afternoon waned and my companions, often below at dinner, lingered and left me just perhaps a bit overwhelmed. That was the sense of it—the *character*, in the whole place, pressed upon me with a force I hadn't met and that was beyond my analysis—which is but another way of saying how directly notified I felt that such material conditions as I *had* known could have had no depth at all. My depth was a vague measure, no doubt, but it made space, in the twilight, for an occasional small sound of voice or step from the garden or the rooms of which the great homely, the opaque green shutters opened there softly to echo in—mixed with reverberations finer and more momentous, personal, experimental, if they might be called so. . . . (163-64)

The "haunted interior" inhabited by the child seems to be that of his own mind. Vagueness, obscurity, "depth upon depth"—James finds a notation to record the pulse of consciousness itself, permitting us a shadowy glimpse of the life of the self.

Such prose contrives to show that the inwardness of the small boy with nothing to show was overwhelmingly rich, his apparent nullity the house of plenitude, so much so that it is all the more remarkable that the retrospective James cannot content himself with evocation alone. In any account of the condition of small boyhood the autobiographer pushes on with predictable regularity, as he does here, to measure his own early identity against other available models. Thus he proceeds in this instance to contrast his "comparatively so indirect faculty for what is called taking life" with the "directness" (163) of his younger brother Wilky, and he suggests that he was even then "already aware . . . that one way of taking life was to go in for everything and everyone, which kept you abundantly occupied, and the other way was to be as occupied, quite as occupied, just with the sense and the image of it all, and on only a fifth of the actual immersion: a circumstance extremely strange." James concludes: "Life was taken almost equally both ways—that, I mean, seemed the strangeness; mere brute quantity and number being so much less in one case than the other. These latter were what I should have *liked* to go in for, had I but had the intrinsic faculties . . ." (164). Again and again in the autobiography we see James engaged in the mathematics of experience, trying to balance his account with life, trying to prove that his own sum was equivalent to that of others.

The autobiographer performs the saving addition time after time, construing the potentially negative circumstances of the child's condition as the occasion for affirmation. The full measure of what he could do for the small boy becomes clear when James gives a name to the child's mode of being and explores it as a process in a series of contiguous and interrelated episodes that occur shortly after the child's removal to Europe with his family in 1855. In these experiences, "taking in" gave the boy a sense of possibilities and power, especially when the impression received was "proportioned to [his] capacity" (161), when the scale of life was reduced to a "far off hum." On these terms sickness, solitude, and confinement become enabling conditions, providing a secure environment where the activity of the imagination, frequently associated with eating, can operate freely without interruption. In the first of these scenes, Henry is sick in bed in London:

> . . . I lay, much at my ease—for I recall in particular certain short sweet times when I could be left alone—with the thick and heavy suggestions of the London room about me, the very smell of which was ancient, strange and impressive, a new revelation altogether, and the window open to the English June and the far off hum of a thousand possibilities. I consciously took them in, these last, and must then, I think, have first tasted the very greatest pleasure perhaps I was ever to know—that of almost holding my breath in presence of certain aspects to the end of so taking in. It was as if in those hours that precious fine art had been disclosed to me—scantly as the poor place and the small occasion might have seemed of an order to promote it. We seize our property by an avid instinct wherever we find it, and I must have kept seizing mine at the absurdest little rate, and all by this deeply dissimulative process of taking in, through the whole succession of those summer days. (158)

The autobiographer confers on the apparent passivity of the process of "taking in" the force of violent action: the seizing of his own property becomes a metaphor for the formation of identity going forward here. Further, by suggesting that the child masked the pleasure involved by a deliberate policy of dissimulation, he makes inwardness show as an act of choice. The dignity of "taking in" as chosen action is sealed when James makes it shine with the purpose of his life to come, revealing it as an initiation into the life of art.

In the last of these experiences of 1855, "an hour that has never ceased to recur to me all my life as crucial, as supremely determinant" (159), all the features of "taking in" are reiter-

ated in a culminating, "ecstatic vision" of all that " 'Europe' "
was to mean to James, "a bridge over to more things than I
then knew." As before, James beholds the nourishing of his
imagination ("by a long slow swig . . . of the wine of perception") going forward in the midst of seemingly impoverished
opportunities ("small," "poor," "scant"). But, despite—or because of?—the diminishing perspective and the self-deprecat-
ing remarks ("my absurdly cushioned state"), which invariably accompany any major assertion of the value of his identity,
James commemorates his practice of "taking in" in this climactic instance of the series as an irrevocable dedication of
his imaginative powers: "supremely . . . was 'Europe' . . . expressed and guaranteed to me—as if by a mystic gage, which
spread all through the summer air, that I should now, only
now, never lose it, hold the whole consistency of it" (160-61).

James presents "taking in" as the most important feature of
the small boy's inward life, the very core of his identity, and
it is the only aspect of the child's consciousness that he inves-
tigates in any detail. The autobiographer's appraisal of this
private exercise, however, is distinctly ambivalent: was its latent aggression to be admired or condemned? There are occasions in *A Small Boy*, complementary to those we have looked
at, when James expresses serious reservations about the morality of his grasping imagination and its acts of appropriation,
occasions when the child recoils in fear from the predatory
aspect of "taking in," which he brands as "a sort of spiritual
snatching" (101) of the supposedly richer consciousness of
others. Given James's thesis, that when the small boy adopted
the observer's stance—as gaper, as taker-in of impressions—
he was most like the artist he was to become, it seems especially revealing that the autobiographer should contrive to keep
constantly in view a negative assessment of the education so
constituted. Although he confidently announces early on that
"the history of my fostered imagination" (65) is his theme in
*A Small Boy*, James's view of the matter seems to have been
unsettled, for he goes over the ground again and again with
the reader, with his brother William, with himself, always

seeking the reply that will silence the nagging critic he imagines observing of the boy and his story, " 'That won't do for a decent account of a young consciousness' " (124). James frequently anticipates the reader's response to his narrative—is it moving too slowly? is it too detailed? is it too private?—but only once does he engage in an extended colloquy with him, an imaginary exchange concerning the systematically unsystematic nature of the formal schooling that Henry and his brothers received as a consequence of their father's special views. The reader, cast as the representative of methodical training, is portrayed as horrified by the "waste" involved in the Jamesian scheme, and his sentiments are echoed by William James in the running debate with Henry about their formative years that shapes the final third of *A Small Boy*.

Although William is rarely in the foreground of James's narrative, disappearing from it altogether for long stretches, numerous allusions along the way demonstrate the extent to which he functioned for Henry as an alternative model of identity, a foil in his manifold capacities and successes for Henry's deep-seated sense of inadequacy and failure. William figures most prominently and consecutively in that portion of *A Small Boy* where he becomes for a brief time the companion of Henry's walks in London and Paris. It is as though for once, with a basis in shared experience, William were in the position of trying on Henry's habitual identity—the gaper at the fence—for size. This put him in a position to judge it, and judge it he did—or so it must have seemed to Henry when, in the course of a conversation between the two brothers in "after days," William assumed the autobiographer's retrospective stance. James's account of their discussion is especially interesting, for in it we see William acting out both phases of Henry's double role as boy and man in the autobiography. Only this once, moreover, does James refer in *A Small Boy* to an act of retrospection preceding the autobiographical act, and given the subject involved we may regard it as an anticipation of the motives behind James's ambitious autobiographical project later on:

It is a very odd and yet to myself very rich and full reminiscence, though I remember how, looking back at it from after days, W.J. denounced it to me, and with it the following year and more spent in Paris, as a poor and arid and lamentable time, in which, missing such larger chances and connections as we might have reached out to, we had done nothing, he and I, but walk about together, in a state of the direst propriety, little "high" black hats and inveterate gloves, the childish costume of the place and period, to stare at grey street-scenery (that of early Victorian London had tones of a neutrality!) dawdle at shop-windows and buy watercolours and brushes with which to bedaub eternal drawing-blocks. We might, I dare say, have felt higher impulses and carried out larger plans—though indeed present to me for this, on my brother's so expressing himself, is my then quick recognition of the deeper stirrings and braver needs he at least must have known, and my perfect if rueful sense of having myself had no such quarrel with our conditions: embalmed for me did they even to that shorter retrospect appear in a sort of fatalism of patience, spiritless in a manner, no doubt, yet with an inwardly active, productive and ingenious side. (170)

The experience may have been substantial ("rich and full") and the boy as well ("inwardly active, productive and ingenious"), but the concessive mood of fraternal piety, momentarily in the ascendant, leads James to entertain an alternative vision of his past, utterly reversing the tenor of his own assessment of the small boy at the fence: "we had done nothing."

As though instinctively recognizing that William's devastating case rejects the very assumptions about the small boy's identity and experience that constitute the argument of Henry's autobiography, James cannot let the matter rest. Exploiting the survivor's advantage of the last word, he proceeds to rehearse the conversation all over again by way of rebuttal.

In this version William's charges are presented as irrelevant, based as they were on a failure to make out just what kind of a person Henry really was:

> . . . what could one have asked more than to be steeped in a medium so dense that whole elements of it, forms of amusements, interest and wonder, soaked through to some appreciative faculty and made one fail at the most of nothing but one's lessons? My brother was right in so far as that my question—the one I have just reproduced— could have been asked only by a person incorrigible in throwing himself back upon substitutes for lost causes, substitutes that might *temporarily* have appeared queer and small; a person so haunted, even from an early age, with visions of life, that aridities, for him, were half a terror and half an impossibility, and that the said substitutes, the economies and ingenuities that protested, in their dumb vague way, against weakness of situation or of direct and applied faculty, were in themselves really a revel of spirit and thought. (170-71)

By italicizing *"temporarily"* James directs our attention to the article of faith that sustains the autobiographical act. In theory, vindication of the existence of the small boy was to come in the fullness of time, when the fruits of dawdling would become visible in James's art and especially—now—in the art of his autobiography. "Taking in" was indeed so private an affair that even William had remained uncomprehending early and late; only the autobiographical "I" could serve as the ideal "other," the right audience, the sympathetic witness of the small boy and his works. The rhetorical energy expended here, however, the elaborate effort to read "revel" in "aridity," suggests that James, in answering William's objections, was answering himself as well. In fact, William's reservations are only a variation of those James elsewhere makes his own: his doubts, namely, that his narrative of the inward life, necessarily "a tale of assimilations small and fine," might seem to be merely "refuse," an accumulation of "absurdities," "directly interesting to the subject-victim only" (105). Did the autobiographical act and the process of "taking in" enjoy a complementary relationship, each justified by, and justifying, the other? Or was the autobiographical act, given over to what had been originally negligible, merely a self-indulgent re-en-actment of a child's trivial existence?

### III. "A DREAM-ADVENTURE"

In the twenty-fifth chapter of *A Small Boy*, which opens and closes with allusions to the debate with William, James attempts to lay these doubts definitively to rest. The chapter brings the story of his early years to a climax, and in so doing it offers one of the most fascinating demonstrations of the complex interrelationship that can exist between the past and the present in this or any autobiographical narrative. To William's obstinate refusal to find anything of value in their European experience, James, speaking always for himself, begins by spelling out the most obvious of the uses of the past, doubtless assumed by the reader early on as the underlying point of the autobiography although never named until now: the seemingly pointless dawdling had been in truth the education of an artist. If Henry and William—and sometimes Henry alone—were drawn to repeat a favorite walk in Paris that took them across the Seine to the Left Bank and up the Rue de Seine and the Rue de Tournon to "the great Paris museum of contemporary art" (192), it was because "it somehow held the secret of our future." The autobiographer presents the walk as a metaphor for an interior journey, the various stages of the itinerary symbolizing the progressive development of the child's inveterate practice of "taking in." It begins to dawn on the small boy that his inward life has a purpose, and the purpose finds a voice in the very houses they pass along the way: " 'Art, art, art, don't you see? Learn, little gaping pilgrims, what *that* is!' " (191).

The final destination of this aesthetic pilgrimage is not the Luxembourg Palace, however, but the Louvre, and " 'the small

staring jeune homme' " (191) arrives there not by retracing his
steps to the Right Bank, as Edel would have it, but more
swiftly by way of the autobiographer's own imperative train
of remembered association.[10] Thus when James sums up the
small boy's entrance into the world of art, as we expect him
to, the bridge spanning the distance that he must cross is no
longer the bridge over the Seine that led to the Luxembourg
but the bridgelike Galerie d'Apollon in the Louvre: "This comes
to saying that in those beginnings I felt myself most happily
cross that bridge over to Style constituted by the wondrous
Galerie d'Apollon, drawn out for me as a long but assured
initiation and seeming to form with its supreme coved ceiling
and inordinately shining parquet a prodigious tube or tunnel
through which I inhaled little by little, that is again and again,
a general sense of *glory*." This shift from the Luxembourg to
the Louvre seems to testify to a more fundamental shift taking
place in the course of this decisive reminiscence. Up to this
point the autobiographer has been speaking up for the small
boy, but now, as the narrative continues, we witness the small
boy and the memory of his experience intervene on behalf of
an older James many years later on in "the most appalling yet
most admirable nightmare" (196) of his life. The autobiographer has arrived at the moment when he must demonstrate
that the value of the past lies in its preparation for the boy's
future as an artist; instead reversing the prevailing temporal
movement in the narrative, he takes us from a point in that
future to its origin in the past in order to exhibit a value that
is first and foremost psychological rather than artistic.

Although James's account of his magnificent nightmare in
the long passage that follows has been frequently quoted, I
give it in full in order to make clear how it functions for James
in two distinct contexts: as a memorable psychological event
in the inner life of an older James who dreamed a dream "many
years later" and, for an autobiographer older still, as definitive

---

[10] Edel, *Henry James: The Untried Years, 1843-1870* (Philadelphia: Lippincott, 1953), p. 69.

textual evidence proving the truth of his thesis about his early years:

The climax of this extraordinary experience—which stands alone for me as a dream-adventure founded in the deepest, quickest, clearest act of cogitation and comparison, act indeed of life-saving energy, as well as in unutterable fear—was the sudden pursuit, through an open door, along a huge high saloon, of a just dimly-descried figure that retreated in terror before my rush and dash (a glare of inspired reaction from irresistible but shameful dread,) out of the room I had a moment before been desperately, and all the more abjectly, defending by the push of my shoulder against hard pressure on lock and bar from the other side. The lucidity, not to say the sublimity, of the crisis had consisted of the great thought that I, in my appalled state, was probably still more appalling than the awful agent, creature or presence, whatever he was, whom I had guessed, in the suddenest wild start from sleep, the sleep within my sleep, to be making for my place of rest. The triumph of my impulse, perceived in a flash as I acted on it by myself at a bound, forcing the door outward, was the grand thing, but the great point of the whole was the wonder of my final recognition. Routed, dismayed, the tables turned upon him by my so surpassing him for straight aggression and dire intention, my visitant was already but a diminished spot in the long perspective, the tremendous, glorious hall, as I say, over the far-gleaming floor of which, cleared for the occasion of its great line of priceless vitrines down the middle, he sped for *his* life, while a great storm of thunder and lightning played through the deep embrasures of high windows at the right. The lightning that revealed the retreat revealed also the wondrous place and, by the same amazing play, my young imaginative life in it of long before, the sense of which, deep within me, had kept it whole, preserved it to this thrilling use; for what in the world were the deep embrasures and the so polished floor but those of the Galerie d'Apollon of my childhood? (196-97)

We have no more information about the immediate psychological context of this nightmare than what James provides in this passage; not even Edel can tell us for sure when the dream was dreamed. But, on the basis of some cryptic notations in James's datebook (red and black crosses inscribed on different dates in varying number and frequency), Edel speculates that James may have had his dream of the Louvre on July 21, 1910, a date James explicitly recognized as marking the end of the weeks of illness and depression that had brought his creative life virtually to a standstill. Pursuing this hypothesis, Edel summarizes the function of the nightmare in these circumstances as follows: "Since the dream contained a vigorous moment of self-assertion and putting to flight of a frightening other-self (or brother) it may have helped restore to James that confidence and faith in himself which had crumbled in his life when he received the news of the failure of the Edition."[11] If the nightmare is indeed linked to James's crisis of 1910, and that crisis in its turn is connected in its circumstances to the earlier crisis of his failure as a dramatist in 1895, then the dream would seem to be involved in a complex and recurring pattern of illness and recovery: twice the mature artist had shown something to the world and had been rejected; the nightmare would seem to triumph over such self-doubts in a dazzling moment of self-display. In any case, the dream itself seems to be about recovery in the sense that the self is portrayed as successfully meeting a threat. Moreover, since this success results from an appropriation of the palace of art, the dream logic seems to predicate the view that art—and the praise, the recognition of self that it generates—is therapeutic.

[11] Edel, *The Master*, p. 445. Edel has taken various positions on the date of the nightmare. See also Edel, *The Untried Years*, pp. 68, 75. For a judicious examination of the relation between the dream and James's art, see Cushing Strout, "Henry James's Dream of the Louvre, 'The Jolly Corner,' and Psychological Interpretation," *Psychohistory Review*, 8 (1979), 47-52.

If Edel's speculation about the biographical circumstances of the nightmare is correct, it may help us to see why the autobiographer should have chosen to formulate the story of the small boy in precisely the terms he does (the condition of someone who seemed to have nothing to show for himself), for what the autobiographical act shares with the dream is an appropriation of the past to meet the needs of present consciousness. Something was drawing the small boy across the Seine from the Luxembourg to the Louvre; something is drawing the autobiographer across time forward from the past: James's inclusion of the dream material is the only major instance in *A Small Boy* in which he advances his retrospect to dramatize an event that occurred later than the period of his youth.[12] Did this more recent memory seem to hold the key to the earlier memories whose significance he sought to uncover in this chapter? If we approach the text from this perspective, it seems as though James is using the symbolism of the dream consciously in his analysis of his earlier identity in a way that parallels its unconscious function in his illness and recovery of 1910. For the small boy, inward existence posed a double problem despite its pleasures and consolations: the child experienced certain anxieties about the act of appropriation on which the very life of his imagination depended, and then this process of "taking in," because it took place unseen, had the further disadvantage of leaving the boy *"temporarily"* with nothing to show, at least until the day when it would find expression in his art. The experience of the dreamer, by contrast, seems to offer a solution to the difficulties of small boyhood, portraying as it does a James not only able to give himself over decisively to the appropriation necessary to the inward life but privileged as well to behold the glory of his own imagination, incarnate in the "endless golden riot and relief" of the magnificent hall.[13] The creative process was risky,

---

[12] Except, of course, the debate with William about the value of their wandering education abroad.

[13] Our curiosity naturally focuses on the identity of the mysterious "visitant"-intruder (was it William? was it some frightening aspect of Henry's own

even perilous, but the artist arrived home safely; better still, the acts of the imagination had themselves already the beauty and the glory of art. Like the dream, the autobiography could exhibit the invisible wonders of the inward life.

Although James introduces his account of the dream with the observation that the Galerie d'Apollon was destined to become for him "the scene of things, even the quite irrelevant or, as might be, almost unworthy," I feel that the ornate structure is, in fact, the perfect emblem of James's autobiographical text, which, similarly elaborate, houses the workings of the boy's imagination in the splendor of a work of art. James's instinct to include the nightmare in his story of the past is absolutely appropriate because it performs the autobiographer's task with the breathtaking economy of symbolism, offering a paradigm of the inward drama of the entire autobiography: the dream culminates in an act of self-display that reveals precisely the aspect of the small boy's consciousness that the mature artist sought to dramatize in his autobiographical narrative, "my young imaginative life . . . of long before." The reassuring message of the dreamer for both the small boy and the autobiographer was that James had it in him to come into his own, to emerge in glory. James's autobiography would tell this story, and in the telling of it the artist would prepare himself to enact it yet again. In this sense the nightmare can be read as a double prophecy of a future now past and a future yet to come, anticipating the confident stance of the earlier James at the end of the entire narrative, successfully launched on his long career as a novelist, and projecting perhaps as well the aging Master's longed-for re-

---

identity?), so much so that we tend to neglect the rest of James's revelation, that he was in a position (as is the case anyway with dreams) of actually seeing the creative process in action. In this respect there is perhaps an analogy to be drawn between James's nightmare and Wordsworth's apocalyptic vision of the power of imagination in the passage about "Crossing the Alps" in *The Prelude* (1850 ed.). Here the poet wrote: ". . . to my conscious soul I now can say— / 'I recognise thy glory' " (VI, 598-99).

turn to the house of fiction, which he had left almost without knowing it several years before.

Indeed, the autobiographical act seems to have supplied James with a medium quite as wonderful and restorative as the dream consciousness that he describes in the nightmare, a medium in which the various Jamesian identities—the dreamer, the small boy, the autobiographer—could enjoy a mutually supportive and sustaining relationship. In a letter of January 19, 1913, James wrote to his nephew Harry that he regarded the completion of *A Small Boy*, despite continuing ill-health, as "the proof of my powers," terms that could be applied with equal justice to the nightmare. He places his work on the autobiography in a pattern of illness and recovery that clearly parallels the one reconstructed by Edel for the "dream-adventure" of the Galerie d'Apollon. Work on "the Book" would, he hoped, bring a long and painful passage of personal history to an end. He traced his troubles to his "fatally interrupted production of fiction . . . six years or more ago," when he had devoted himself to "fatal-to-everything-else" preparation of the New York Edition of his work. "The disaster of my long illness of Jan. 1910" prolonged the interruption, laying "a paralysis" on everything. As James saw it, only by taking up the writing of fiction once more could the destructive cycle be broken: "it becomes *vital* for me to aim at returning to the production of the Novel, . . . only when this relation is renewed shall I be again on a normal basis." The autobiographical project emerges in this context as a sign of returning health, demonstrating "my vitality, my still sufficient cluster of vital 'assets,' to say nothing of my will to live and to write," and James could conclude by commending himself to Harry as his "all unconquered and devoted old Uncle."[14]

James's project, however, was still far from completion; the nightmare's prophecy of the climactic moment when the small

[14] *Letters*, II, 289, 291-92. In the letter James begins by referring specifically to financial troubles, but consideration of these difficulties leads him into a larger complex of problems revolving around his health and his art.

boy would come into his own was not to be fulfilled until several hundred pages later, at the end of *Notes of a Son and Brother*. Immediately following his account of the dream, James reverts to his very first memories of the Louvre, which present in contrast an almost regressive picture of a "small scared consciousness" clinging to the courier Nadali's arm as it beheld the splendors of Géricault and David with a mixture of "bliss" and "alarm." "Taking in" was clearly a problematic exercise, a mixture of pleasure and threat; if it forecast "all the fun . . . that one was going to have, and the kind of life, always of the queer so-called inward sort . . . that one was going to lead," it warned as well of the annihilation that might follow from "a freedom of contact and appreciation really too big for one" (198). The various accounts of the small boy's imaginative activity—gaping through a fence, listening while sick in bed—provide a revealing index of James's ambivalent attitude toward his creativity. Although these passages characteristically situate the receiving consciousness in the presence of the objects of its desire, they rarely fail to evoke the intervening distance, sometimes as protective, sometimes as privative. When some degree of separation between the self and "life" is maintained—vision filtered through the palings of a fence, sound coming through an open window—aesthetic experience is distinctly pleasurable. When, however, it is a question of exchanging the security of assured passivity for the risks of a more active engagement, imaged as the crossing of a bridge or more often as the opening of a door, the potential for aggression becomes a source of anxiety.

To employ such phrases as "the objects of its desire" and "aesthetic experience," however, is to fail to do justice to the richness and complexity of what James is attempting to describe in these passages. Because the small boy is so frequently portrayed as looking *at* or listening *to* something, and because the things observed are just as frequently valued as sources of knowledge later employed in his art, it is all too easy to adopt a false sense that an opposition between self and not-self is the governing dynamic of these episodes, a misleading view that the nature of the experiences in question is exclusively aesthetic. To behold the paintings of Géricault, to listen to the far off hum of London—these, James understood, were metaphors for wholly inward experience, mirrors of selfhood, memorable occasions when consciousness seemed to achieve a new awareness of its own nature.

It is this deepest level of experience that James manages to capture in his autobiography, nowhere more so than in the moving final chapter of *A Small Boy*, in which he recounts his memories of Boulogne and a dangerous bout with typhus that he came to regard as "the marked limit of my state of being a small boy" (224). He opens, to be sure, by sounding the familiar refrain that his illness reduced him "to operations of that mere inward and superficially idle order at which we have already so freely assisted," reduced him, that is, to living "almost only by seeing what I could, after my incorrigible ambulant fashion—a practice that may well have made me pass for bringing home nothing in the least exhibitional" (223). What James has to say of the illness itself, however, strikes a new note in the autobiography, more in the key of *Notes of a Son and Brother* than anything we have encountered in *A Small Boy*: "I took on, when I had decently, and all the more because I had so retardedly, recovered, the sense of being a boy of other dimensions somehow altogether, and even with a new dimension introduced and acquired; a dimension that I was eventually to think of as a stretch in the direction of essential change or of living straight into a part of myself previously quite unvisited and now made accessible as by the sharp forcing of a closed door" (224). The meaning of this statement is partially obscure, probably unavoidably so, for James attempts not merely to record the fact of a basic shift in his earlier identity but also to evoke as a felt experience his original recognition of this turning point in his inward development. Making his way through the shadowy underworld of his own personality toward the hidden core of his earlier self, he resorts instinctively to a symbolic language, one which repeats—not surprisingly—a motif from the "dream-adventure"

84

of the Galerie d'Apollon. This echo provides, perhaps, a clue to the unnamed "new dimension" the small boy had "acquired" at Boulogne, the undesignated "part" of himself that he was now in a position to explore, for the dreamer had first defended a door, and then, "forcing" it outward, had taken possession of the world of his own imagination.

Whatever likeness obtains between the two situations is presently overturned when James, having presented the period of his protracted convalescence, moves backward at the end of the chapter to describe the onset of his illness:

> Present to me still is the fact of my sharper sense, after an hour or two, of my being there [in bed] in distress and, as happened for the moment, alone; present to me are the sounds of the soft afternoon, the mild animation of the Boulogne street through the half-open windows; present to me above all the strange sense that something had begun that would make more difference to me, directly and indirectly, than anything had ever yet made. I might verily, on the spot, have seen, as in a fading of day and a change to something suddenly queer, the whole large extent of it. I must thus, much impressed but half scared, have wanted to appeal; to which end I tumbled, all too weakly, out of bed and wavered toward the bell just across the room. The question of whether I really reached and rang it was to remain lost afterwards in the strong sick whirl of everything about me, under which I fell into a lapse of consciousness that I shall conveniently here treat as a considerable gap. (236)

Here the gesture toward self-preservation leads not, as it had in the Galerie d'Apollon, to an explosive revelation of the self and its creative powers but to collapse and extinction of consciousness. The familiar stance of the small boy—alone, in bed, with the sound of experience coming through the window—identifies this episode as yet another version of the process of "taking in." The "something" appropriated here, however, seems not to have been a knowledge of "life," of

"Europe," but a pre-vision of the cost and consequences of the small boy's own development. It is as though the child, momentarily endowed with the hindsight available only to the autobiographer, drew back from the unfolding of his own story in this waking nightmare. Overwhelmed by "the whole large extent of it," by the profound changes taking place within him, boy and text end rather ominously in a blackout.

## IV. "*My* truth, to do what I would with"

In the opening pages of *Notes of a Son and Brother* James presents the story of his education in the same terms he used in *A Small Boy and Others*, so much so, in fact, that the first two chapters, which concern his residence in Geneva and then in Bonn in 1859 and 1860, read like a summation of the themes of the earlier volume, a continued rebuttal of William's case against their formative years abroad. Once more we find young Henry James adopting his customary strategy for coping with his nagging sense of inferiority—this time in mathematics at the Institution Rochette—as he consoles himself by thinking of the compensatory richness of his consciousness, "little as any item of it might have passed at the time for the sort of thing one exhibits as a trophy of learning" (241). To indulge himself with "taking in" was to be happy, as before, but the boy was now aware of a new voice calling into question the charmed equilibrium of his inward life: "They had begun, the impressions—that was what was the matter with them—to scratch quite audibly at the door of liberation, of extension, of projection; what they were *of* one more or less knew, but what they were *for* was the question that began to stir, though one was still to be a long time at a loss directly to answer it." Continuing, James writes that he contemplated this "dark difficulty" "secretly" because he was "somehow ashamed of its being there" (253), and did not want to be caught in the act of watching it. His analysis of his embarrassed reticence about the life of impressions, its pleasures and problems, focuses on his sense that he was not yet prepared to acknowledge his creativity openly:

> . . . one would have gone to the stake rather than in the first place confessed to some of them [impressions], or in the second announced that one really lived by them and built on them. This failure then to take one's stand in the connection could but come from the troubled view that they were naught without a backing, a stout stiff hard-grained underside that would hold them together. . . . (254)

The inward life, which James chronicled as the given condition of his small boyhood, emerges now for the youth of seventeen as a problem of vocation, an act of choice requiring masculine self-assertion. In *Notes* James tells how he came to terms with his "dark difficulty."

Just at this point when the autobiographer projects a new and problematic phase of his own story, he seems to devote himself increasingly to the lives of others, almost as though he were throwing out so many decoys—to the reader, to himself—to interrupt the tracking of his earlier identity. The autobiography begins to look rather like the sort of "Family Book" James had originally discussed with William's widow[15] and which he had outlined to his secretary, as she recalled it, as "a set of notes to his brother William's early letters, prefaced by a brief account of the family into which they were both born."[16] Chapter 3 sounds this new note most clearly, opening with James voicing an editor's point of view in a vein that is reminiscent of his biographical memoir, *William Wetmore Story and His Friends* (1903). Each of the first three chapters includes excerpts from William's letters, and they are displayed prominently in Chapters 5 and 12. In addition, letters

[15] Henry James to Henry James II, November 15-18, 1913, *Letters*, II, 345-46.

[16] Theodora Bosanquet, "Henry James at Work," *The Hogarth Essays*, eds. Leonard S. Woolf and Viginia S. Woolf (1928; rpt. Freeport, N.Y.: Books for Libraries Press, 1970), p. 252.

by James's father fill Chapters 6 through 8, while Chapters 11 and 13 (the last) are devoted, respectively, to letters by Wilky and by James's cousin Mary (Minny) Temple. Given the sheer bulk of this documentary material, it is not surprising that the form of *Notes* has been described as "a series of notes, of associations, surrounding the quoted letters of, chiefly, his brother William, his father, and Minnie."[17] And in the only comprehensive commentary that *Notes* has ever received, Jane P. Tompkins states that the narrator "rarely focuses the narrative directly upon himself," that "the important roles are all assigned to others."[18] In her account, *Notes* becomes a gallery of shining portraits of others, while the image of the son and brother remains in the shadows. In the autobiographical act, she concludes, James became the adversary of time and dissolution, performing a saving ritual of commemoration.

The initial impulse behind the autobiography does seem to have been largely commemorative, and Edel records that an early working title for *Notes* was "Early Letters of William James with Notes by Henry James."[19] Moreover, when letters of other members of the family came into his hands during the composition of *Notes*, James expanded the text to make room for them. It would be a mistake, however, to assert, as Tompkins does, that the autobiographical narrator "was interested in his own history only as it related to 'other matters and other lives.' "[20] It was really quite the other way around, as William's son Harry must have suspected when he wrote to his uncle about revisions that James had freely made in the texts of William's letters. In his reply of November 15-18, 1913, after he had finished *Notes*, James asserted tactfully but firmly the prerogatives of the autobiographer. Reconstructing the genesis of the project, he claimed that from the very mo-

[17] S. P. Rosenbaum, "Letters to the Pell-Clarkes from Their 'Old Cousin and Friend' Henry James," *American Literature*, 31 (1959), 56.

[18] Tompkins, "The Redemption of Time in *Notes of a Son and Brother*," *Texas Studies in Literature and Language*, 14 (1972-1973), 681.

[19] Edel, *The Master*, p. 457.

[20] Tompkins, 682.

ment of its inception he had been guided by "a spirit and a vision as far removed as possible from my mere isolated documentation of your Father's record." James had a different relation of picture and frame in mind: it was a question rather of working "these Cambridge letters into the whole harmony of my text—the general purpose of which was to be a reflection of all the amenity and felicity of our young life at that time at the highest pitch that was consistent with perfect truth." James carried his case to the court of last resort, arguing that he seemed to feel William's presence guiding him as he worked and pleading with him " 'to do the very best for me you *can*.' " The alterations of the texts were sanctioned finally by James's conviction that these materials from the past were "*my* truth, to do what I would with." When, for example, James had changed William's reference to the assassinated Lincoln, he observed, "I could *hear* him say Abraham and couldn't hear him say Abe. . . ."[21] As the author of the letters, William might well be a historical personage, but, as Henry's brother, he was a living presence in the autobiographer's memory, and, created anew by the novelist's imagination, he would become a character in Henry's story. "Henry's story"—the ambiguity on my part is deliberate, referring alike to James's double role as author and protagonist. What these two Henrys share is an identity that manifests itself in acts of appropriation, feeding on the "life" in the lives of others.

The past, then, was James's "truth," and his letters about the project testify that even the seemingly most factual of materials—the text of a letter, the date of a trip—were subject to his shaping hand. The autobiographer was hardly self-effacing, and his acts of commemoration mostly served a distinctly autobiographical purpose, whatever nephew Harry may

[21] *Letters*, II, 346, 347, 348. Adeline R. Tintner quotes a more complete version of this letter, which restores deletions made by Lubbock, in her essay "Autobiography as Fiction: 'The Usurping Consciousness' as Hero of James's Memoirs," *Twentieth Century Literature*, 23 (1977), 242-44. As her title suggests, Tintner regards *A Small Boy* and *Notes* as examples of "a new kind of 'experimental' novel" (239).

have been led to expect earlier on. As Bosanquet pointed out, "an entire volume of memories [*A Small Boy*] was finished before bringing William to an age for writing letters,"[22] and no sooner had James arrived at this point (at the opening of Chapter 3) than he moved swiftly to shift to other shoulders the principal burden of whatever commemorative obligation he may have felt. "William," he wrote, "is from this season on . . . so livingly and admirably reflected in his letters . . . that I feel them particularly plead . . . for the separate gathered presentation that happily awaits them" (267).[23] Most of the material about others in *Notes*—and William's case is no exception—develops the themes of James's story of himself.

If we set aside for the moment the four chapters (6, 7, 8, and 13) that feature Henry James's father and Minny Temple, which were expanded or added to incorporate sets of letters he received during the course of composition,[24] the outline of Henry's own story in *Notes* emerges much more clearly. It is the narrative of an identity crisis, posed in terms of vocation and developed in two distinct phases: the first of these concerns William James as he faces the choice of a career (Chapters 3-5, covering the years 1860-1862), and the second places Henry in a parallel position (Chapters 9-12, covering the years 1861-1866). I am being deliberately schematic in order to throw into relief what I take to be the essential drama of *Notes* and indeed of the entire autobiography, and I do so all the more because James has never quite received credit for having had the insight and the courage to probe his memories of the troubled period preceding his total public commitment to the life of art. The climactic episode of the "obscure hurt" in Chapter 9 has, to be sure, generated an enormous amount of controversy over the years, but it has become customary to treat it

[22] Bosanquet, p. 252.

[23] Harry James performed this office in the two-volume edition of William's letters that he published in 1920.

[24] See Edel, *The Master*, p. 457, and Rosenbaum, 53.

independently of the rest of the autobiographical narrative to which it is so intimately and decisively related.[25]

## V. "What we were to do instead
### was just to *be* something, something unconnected
### with specific doing"

Nowhere does *Notes* follow William's movements more closely than in Chapters 3-5; William's decision in 1860 to become a painter (Chapter 3) and his subsequent decision a year later to abandon painting for science (Chapter 5) provide the chronological framework for this section of the narrative. The treatment of this material, however, is clearly a response to autobiographical considerations. Thus James does not investigate William's motivation for choosing these two callings—these moves are "natural" if not "logical" (300). Instead it is his father's reaction to them that receives analysis. Looking back on his father's response to William at this critical moment in his brother's development, James saw prefigured the problems of vocation that he would face "when I myself, later on, began to 'write' " (269). The elder Henry James was clearly the pivotal figure in the drama of vocation as the autobiographer understood it, and the father's views on this subject are given an extended presentation in three of the thirteen chapters of *Notes* (3, 5, and 9). His father had told William that the " 'ca-

---

[25] Nowadays, the typical student of James's novels is apt to satisfy his curiosity about their author by consulting the massive Edel biography, rarely undertaking to read the autobiography. Proceeding the other way around, as Edel himself, of course, was obliged to do, we cannot help but be struck by the extent to which not merely the themes but also the dramatic structure of the first volume of the biography, *The Untried Years*, are derived from the autobiography. Both conclude with the death of Minny Temple and James's first mature experience of Europe. The biographical insights that reward close study of the autobiography are exemplified in a fine essay by William Walsh. "A Sense of Identity in a World of Circumstance: The Autobiography of Henry James," in *A Human Idiom: Literature and Humanity* (New York: Barnes and Noble, 1964), pp. 52-73.

reer of art' " (268) was "narrowing" (269); "what we were to do instead," son Henry recalled, "was just to *be* something, something unconnected with specific doing" (268). The father's idiosyncratic concept of identity, together with the rather abstract conditions he envisaged for its fulfillment, had created no little embarrassment and perplexity for his sons even when they were children. "Under pressure of the American ideal in that matter," they had "felt it tasteless and humiliating" that their father was "*not* in business," and they would plead—in vain—for a more demonstrable version of selfhood, one that would be consonant with the American values of doing and success: " 'What shall we tell them [their schoolmates] you *are*, don't you see?' " (278). As the boys reached manhood, they had to answer for the Jamesian condition of inwardness in their own right, and they became increasingly restive with their father's hopelessly un-American indifference to vocation. James concedes that the atmosphere of his father's house was "doubtless delightful," but he emphasizes that however hospitable it was to the life of the imagination, it did not promote "the act of choice—choice as to the 'career' for example, with a view of the usual proceedings thereupon consequent" (302).

William is presumably included in the autobiographical "we" of these exchanges with their father, but that is as close as he comes to occupying the foreground of James's commentary. When the family leaves Europe for Newport so that William can study painting with William Morris Hunt, it is Henry's state of mind on the eve of departure that is featured (Chapter 3). And once they are in Newport, William's story is largely pre-empted by Henry's (Chapter 4). The autobiographer makes his excuses, observing that he takes the risk "of appearing to make my own scant adventure the pivot of that early Newport phase" (284), but take the risk he does, willingly and at length.

Henry, too, studied for a time with Hunt, and so he found himself temporarily in the temple of Art with no questions asked, even though he had entered it "by the back door" (285).

The solitude of the studio in which he worked alone afforded him a sheltering environment in which he could explore his creativity undisturbed, "indulged yet ignored." He emphasizes that his separation from the other "real" studio where William and the "serious" pupils worked kept him "somehow the safer" (286), safe to pursue an artistic vocation without his fitness for it becoming subject to judgment. Only the shadows on the "blank-eyed faces" of the plaster casts he copied waited for Henry "to prove myself not helpless" (284). Significantly, his brief interlude as a painter comes to an end one day when the separation that had kept him safe is breached. Crossing into the "larger" studio, he beholds the other pupils drawing his cousin Gus Barker from "life." Dazzled by William's mastery and overwhelmed by a sense of his own inadequacy, he is moved to renounce his pursuit of drawing for good.

Counterpointed against this setback is Henry's ecstatic pursuit of literature under the guidance of John La Farge. The autobiographer's moving tribute to this friend and mentor of his Newport youth emphasizes La Farge's serene confidence in his own abilities and his generous encouragement of James's. Seven years older than Henry, La Farge seemed to possess precisely those qualities which James wished for himself at that time: he had a knowledge of the world, a European cultivation, and he had been initiated into the mysteries of art. James presents him as a kind of priest of experience, and the depth of feeling registered in the portrait of La Farge, the most beautifully realized of any in the volume, expresses James's grateful discovery of an attractive alternative to his father's view that the " 'career of art' " was "narrowing."

## VI. Father

Three long chapters (6-8) devoted to Henry's father separate William's departure from Newport for Cambridge and the Harvard (Lawrence) Scientific School in the fall of 1861 (Chapter 5) and Henry's own departure from Newport for Cambridge and the Harvard Law School in the fall of 1862

(Chapter 9). These three chapters, which occupy almost a third of the volume, can be criticized as an interruption of the narrative movement and concerns of the earlier chapters, and James himself came to do so, especially in the discursive and disjointed commentary of Chapter 8, where the narrator speaks repeatedly of his need to maintain control over his materials. In certain obvious respects these chapters do differ markedly from the rest of the narrative. The concentrated chronology of the first five chapters (1860-1861) opens up here to reach back to the early 1840s in Chapter 6 and to extend to the early 1870s by the end of Chapter 8. The dates are those of the letters presented, and these are organized by correspondent: first, James gives his father's letters to Emerson (Chapter 6), then those to Caroline Sturgis Tappan (Chapter 7), and finally those to a series of other figures, including Mrs. James T. Fields and Charles Eliot Norton (Chapter 8). Nowhere in *Notes* is James's commemorative impulse more clearly in the ascendant, and his earliest letters about the project show that he had intended from the first to " '*do*' " his father as tenderly and beautifully as he could.

The themes of his commentary on his father and his father's philosophy in Chapters 6 and 7 (there is very little in Chapter 8), however, have an unmistakable relevance to the more distinctly autobiographical focus of the chapters that precede and follow them. James himself makes the connection between his father's views on religion and on vocation (which he presents in Chapters 3, 5, and 9) when he speaks of his father's philosophy as meeting "the whole question of the attitude of 'worship' " with the same "good faith" and "easiest sufficiency" that it had met the other familiar American questions of "education, acquisition, material vindication, what is called success generally" (336). James recalls that he was "troubled" by "our being so extremely religious without having . . . anything in the least classified or striking to show for it" (337). For the son who craved something to show, the father was hardly a satisfactory model. The "selfless detachment" (334) of the father's inward life had brought him only "thin consolations and broken rewards" (333); his voice and his works were little heeded beyond the immediate family circle. If we judge by these conventional measures of success, it is hard to escape the implication that the elder Henry James was a failure, and the autobiographer struggles repeatedly to dismiss the negative assessment of his father's career that keeps rising to the surface of his account.

James was clearly ambivalent about the value of " 'Father's Ideas' " (330). He acknowledges with embarrassment his "inattention" (333) to them, yet he rather defensively repudiates the possibility that he might ever have thought of his father as inhabiting "a fool's paradise" (372). It is nonetheless true that he maximizes the difference between his own views of reality and his father's. The "novelist *en herbe*" (373) confesses: "I couldn't have framed stories that would have succeeded in involving the least of the relations that seemed most present to *him*; while those most present to myself . . . were the ones his schemes of importances seemed virtually to do without. Didn't I discern in this from the first a kind of implied snub to the significance of mine?" (339). James does not permit himself to wish for a different father, but he does wish that he "might have caught him sooner or younger, less developed" (340). The phase of the father's career to which the son was especially drawn was that of his spiritual crisis in England in 1844 and his Swedenborgian conversion—one more story of illness and recovery. Significantly, James concludes his most extended analysis of his father[26] with a tribute to his mother. He honors her not only for her support of his father throughout the long years during which public recognition continued to elude him but also for her support of himself in his difference from his father.

## VII. "The indefinable shining stigma"

At the opening of the last of the three chapters on the elder Henry James, the autobiographer announces his decision to

[26] Pp. 334-44, which he added to Chapter 6 as the typescript revisions indicate.

pursue the illustration of his father's character even though the letters in question should carry him "to points beyond my story proper" (385). The chronological limits James alludes to offer a clue to his sense of his "story" in *Notes*. The key years of the narrative, which takes Henry from his return to America in 1860 (Chapter 3) to the period of his first creativity at Ashburton Place in 1864-1866 (Chapter 12), are the years of the Civil War, so much so that *Notes* is in a profound sense James's Book of the War. James makes the most of every opportunity to talk about the war in *Notes*, and he observes of this propensity that it is "impossible . . . not in some degree to yield on the spot to *any* brush of the huge procession of those particular months and years" (382).[27] In the second of the chapters on his father, James does so yield, anticipating the drama of his identity crisis that is the subject of the final, climactic chapters of the autobiography (Chapters 9-12). The occasion is a letter of his father's concerning Wilky's wound in the attack on Fort Wagner and his return to Newport on a stretcher. Young Cabot Russell, Wilky's companion, was killed in the battle, and Russell's father had brought Wilky home to the Jameses after unsuccessfully searching the battlefield for the body of his own son. James's commentary on these events formulates with a dreamlike clarity the existential problem of his quest for identity as a young American artist in wartime.

In the Cabot Russell episode the war and its world of death and wounds emerge as the quintessential form of experience, ennobling each of the four characters in the passage—James, Russell's father, Russell himself, and Wilky—in direct proportion to the degree of their contact with it. James's situation, *mutatis mutandis*, is that of the small, sick boy in an upper room in Geneva all over again, and he presents his " 'relation to' the War" with the same elaborate mixture of qualification and assertion that characterizes his discussion of the small boy's practice of "taking in." He had, he writes, "under stress, to

[27] See also pp. 276 and 282 of the autobiography for further examples of James's sentiments on the war years.

content myself with knowing it [the war] in a more indirect
and muffled fashion than might easily have been," and yet he
claims that "the whole quite indescribably intensified time"
remains with him "as a more constituted and sustained act of
living, in proportion to my powers and opportunities, than
any other homogeneous stretch of experience that my memory now recovers" (382-83). The lines that immediately follow
this statement confirm that even fifty years afterward James's
state of mind about the war remained unsettled; unresolved
and conflicting feelings rise and shift on the surface of the
autobiographical discourse:

> The case had to be in a peculiar degree, alas, that of
> living inwardly—like so many of my other cases; in a
> peculiar degree compared, that is, to the immense and
> prolonged outwardness, outwardness naturally at the very
> highest pitch, that was the general sign of the situation.
> To which I may add that my "alas" just uttered is in the
> key altogether of my then current consciousness, and not
> in the least in that of my present appreciation of the same
> —so that I leave it, even while I thus put my mark against
> it, as I should restore tenderly to the shelf any odd ro-
> coco object that might have slipped from a reliquary. (383)

Evocation of his limited experience of the war seems quite
naturally to elicit from the autobiographer a spontaneous
expression of sympathy for his earlier self, yet the narrator
moves swiftly to explanations as though to correct some lapse
in the psychological decorum presumably governing the autobiographical act. Significantly, although James does not
disavow the "alas," he makes it clear that feeling, slipping
from the grasp of form, must be restored to its appointed
place in a work of art serving a private religion of experience.
Something of the strain involved in the performance of this
redemptive work of autobiography, as James struggles to
demonstrate his distance from, and his mastery over, his "then
current consciousness," is suggested in his strange designation

of his most "sustained act of living" as "any odd rococo object."

Such as it is, however, James's claim to a share in the war is totally eclipsed by his evocation of Wilky and Cabot Russell in the rest of the passage. The central image of his "quasi-twilight vision" (383)—and I am tempted, given the circumstance, to call it an icon—is that of the dead hero:

> . . . the image that hovers to me across the years of Cabot Russell himself, my brother's so close comrade—dark-eyed, youthfully brown, heartily bright, actively handsome, and with the arrested expression, the indefinable shining stigma, worn, to the regard that travels back to them, by those of the young figures of the fallen that memory and fancy, wanting, never ceasing to want, to "do" something for them, set as upright and clear-faced as may be, each in his sacred niche. They have each to such a degree, so ranged, the strange property or privilege—one scarce knows what to call it—of exquisitely, for all *our* time, facing us out, quite blandly ignoring us, looking through us or straight over us at something they partake of together but that we mayn't pretend to know. We walk thus, I think, rather ruefully before them—those of us at least who didn't at the time share more happily their risk.

Next to this haunting image of life in death, James places that of his wounded brother Wilky, and he makes a point of referring in the text to the accompanying illustration, William's drawing of their "poor lacerated brother's aspect" (384) as he lay on the stretcher. Even "lost Cabot Russell's stricken father," while not in the war, shares an immediacy of its experience that lies beyond James's grasp, and he is remembered "clear as some object presented in high relief against the evening sky of the west" (383).[28] To the James who could claim

---

[28] Exclusion from "life," especially from the experience of deep suffering, is one of James's most pervasive themes. John Marcher's overwhelming vision

in the rhetorical shuttling of the first part of the passage that his "small scraps of direct perception . . . were all but touched in themselves as with the full experience," the arresting figures of the fallen in his private war memorial seem to reply, "*Noli me tangere.*"[29] The fallen possessed a knowledge "that we mayn't pretend to know," and now younger brother Wilky, whom James established in *A Small Boy* as the type of the active participant in "life," was one of their number, having earned "the indefinable shining stigma." The war placed James's problem of vocation in a new perspective, for the notion of a link between personal and national history must have been inevitable in his case, if we accept the autobiographer's portrait of himself as a small boy troubled by his sense of having nothing to show. Not only were young Americans to be identified by their choice of a career; now, in wartime, they had something still more tangible to display, the marks of their wounds.

## VIII. "AN OBSCURE HURT"

When James finally halts his sprawling tribute to his father, he observes that he has "dropped too many of those threads

---

of an unknown mourner's ravaged face at the end of "The Beast in the Jungle" is perhaps the most striking of the countless examples that could be cited. This story offers a tragic view of the sense of personal inadequacy that James records in a different vein in the autobiography. Young Henry's abortive foray into the "larger" studio at Newport would be a characteristic instance of the more balanced if rueful acquiescence of the small boy, son, and brother in his passive nature, an acquiescence sustained, as Marcher's was not, by a compensatory confidence in the value of his own imagination.

[29] In *The Bostonians* (1886) James uses the heroic experience of the war to measure the moral impoverishment of all of American life in the years that followed. John Goode argues that this novel "is controlled by the visit of Ransom and Verena to the Harvard Memorial [for the Union dead], and is dominated therefore by the catastrophe of the Civil War." "The Art of Fiction: Walter Besant and Henry James," *Tradition and Tolerance in Nineteenth-Century Fiction*, ed. David Howard et al. (New York: Barnes and Noble, 1967), p. 268. See also Paul John Eakin, *The New England Girl: Cultural Ideals in Hawthorne, Stowe, Howells and James* (Athens: Univ. of Georgia Press, 1976), p. 211.

of my rather niggled tapestry that belong but to the experience of my own weaving hand" (410). Resuming the narrative he had shelved at the end of Chapter 5, he opens Chapter 9 with his entrance to Harvard Law School in the autumn of 1862. His effort to explain this "oddest" of "errands" involves him in the most intricate and sustained investigation of his own motives to be found anywhere in the autobiography. The manifest complexity of both the narrator's behavior and the design of the text signal that we enter here the critical phase of James's youth. Going to law school, as he well knew, was a stopgap measure, a provisional strategy intended, as he puts it, to gain him time until he should be ready to "brandish" in public "the flag" (411) of that commitment to the life of the imagination which had been the vital principle of his existence since the days of small boyhood. The autobiographer's retrospective analysis stresses the wholly symbolic aspect of the law-school gesture. It offered "the positive saving virtue of vagueness," for the nineteen-year-old Henry was obliged "to be vague *about* something"; "just staying at home when everyone was on the move couldn't in any degree show the right mark" (412).

James is rather sensitive, however, to the possibility that any speciousness or deception may seem to have been involved, and he proceeds in a long and involuted paragraph to identify three determining influences on his behavior in the autumn of 1862. We are to understand first of all—and, I think, rightly—that symbolic flags and standards of identity are "hoisted sooner or later by all of us . . . somehow and somewhere." Nevertheless, the familiar predicament of late adolescence, the hesitation before the total commitment demanded by adult life, was clearly exacerbated by a second factor, "the outbreak of the War" (411). The insistent imagery of martial display underlines the fact that the war established the norm ("the conventional maximum") for definitive, public masculine assertion of identity against which James then and now would have to measure his own variety of selfhood. The inveterate issue of vocation fused now with the call to arms.

Finally, to make matters still more complicated, James's father surfaced in the midst of this tangled drama of self-definition. After James's account of the fits and starts of William's search for his true calling, we are not surprised to learn that Henry James the elder is just as heavily implicated in his younger son's dilemma. Only the year before, the father had emphatically rejected the idea of any connection with Harvard; now he acquiesced "in the most offhand and liberal manner" in the idea of Harvard Law School. James concludes the passage by criticizing his father for this inconsistency, in which the son now beholds "the ugly grin" of "that irony of fate" (412) which clouded the whole affair.

"All of which would seem to kick up more dust than need quite have hung about so simple a matter as my setting forth to the Cambridge scene with no design that I could honourably exhibit" (413). It is not easy to distinguish between narrator and protagonist here, for if the autobiographer has been kicking up dust in his analysis, the dust seems to have hung there because his younger self needed to be vague. The simple matter of Henry's going to Cambridge becomes a charged field in which restless particles—vocation, father, and the war— spin and collide. The prose seems to take on the very coloration of its subject, suggesting an extremely close identification between Jameses past and present, so much so that the behavior of the one seems to be a re-enactment of the other. For all the apparent detachment of the autobiographer's comment on his sense of something excessive and obscure about the giant preliminary paragraph concerning his problematical decision to attend law school, he cannot prevent himself from going over the ground a second time, with not a little obscurity and at twice the length. We are given explanations about explanations, and so James returns to his father, backtracking to the year before, when his father had rejected the idea of his attending Harvard College.

James had found it relatively painless to accept this earlier prohibition, since it sanctioned a prolongation of the beneficent moratorium of his Newport period. The importance of this phase of his development is underscored when James makes it the occasion of his first explicit, if extremely tentative, statement of his artistic vocation in the autobiography. He says of himself at the time, "What I 'wanted to want' to be was all intimately, just *literary*" (413), and he felt free to cultivate the life of the imagination "under the rich cover of obscurity" of his private world. It is, therefore, all the more understandable that the father's willingness a year later to have the son do as he pleases was apprehended as a problem rather than as an opportunity, inconveniently terminating the security of the Newport equilibrium. As long as the youth felt himself unready to make any public display of his inward commitment, the instruction not to pursue a course of action was, more or less, what he wanted to hear. When his father did not repeat this message a year later, the about-face caught the son off guard. James's difficulty was precisely that "there was no difficulty about anything, no intrinsic difficulty" (414); he was thrown back on his own devices.

Significantly, no sooner has the autobiographer related this cessation of the parental prohibition than he reports that two fresh difficulties had arisen for him, "the breaking out of the War" and "a passage of personal history the most entirely personal, but between which, as a private catastrophe or difficulty, bristling with embarrassments, and the great public convulsion that announced itself in bigger terms each day, I felt from the very first an association of the closest, yet withal, I fear, almost of the least clearly expressible" (414). In point of fact, these two events date from the spring and fall of 1861 and can hardly be said, chronologically speaking, to have "come up" for James in any literal sense with regard to his decision to attend law school in 1862. It does seem probable, though, that they "came up" for him then psychologically: now that the father's original prohibition had ceased, the son required a new one in order to have a plausible rationale for his passive existence amid the patriotic fervor of wartime activity.

The unlikely law student of 1862 seems to have taught the autobiographer a lasting lesson in "the positive saving virtue

of vagueness," for James's account of "the most entirely personal" passage of his personal history, an injury sustained while
fighting a fire, communicates in its apparently circumstantial
detail an aura of precision, yet the episode remains tantalizingly incomplete or puzzling in at least three key respects.
James surprisingly refrains from specifying the nature of the
injury; his hints as to the date of the accident have been shown
to be misleading; and, most curious of all, he asserts that he
believed "from the first" in the duration and the "interest" of
his wound. Leon Edel has taken great pains to demystify these
troubling features of James's portentous account, and some
such attempt was probably inevitable since James's vagueness
about his "odious" "physical mishap" has left twentieth-century commentators free to imagine that the novelist suffered
some kind of castration. Edel suggests that the "obscure hurt"
itself was probably a back injury, to which James referred
many times over the years and which he usually dated as of
1862. The upshot of Edel's speculation, however, is to substitute one kind of injury for another, whereas James simply
leaves us in the dark. As to James's immediate conviction of
the lasting effects of the injury, Edel proposes an unconscious
identification with his father at the moment of the accident,
since the elder Henry James had lost a leg putting out a stable
fire in his youth. Clearly the autobiographer does have a parallel between two fires on his mind, but this is not the one he
brings up in the passage. Finally, Edel tests James's dating
against the historical record, establishing the time of the Newport fire as October 28, 1861, some six months after the outbreak of the war, whereas James presents the two events as
occurring simultaneously. Edel reads these manipulations and
omissions of fact as part of a deliberate strategy of obfusca-
tion, inferring that the autobiographer "seems to have felt that
by vagueness and circumlocution he might becloud the whole
question of his non-participation in the Civil War."[30] If, how-

---

[30] Edel, *The Untried Years*, p. 175. For Edel's commentary on "the obscure
hurt," see pp. 175-83. Edel's interpretation, especially his emphasis on Hen-

ever, James had truly sought to becloud the issue, he would hardly have mentioned "trump[ing] up a lameness at such a juncture" (415) even as a possibility to be deprecated. In fact, James makes his "non-participation" in the war and, by extension, in "life" the major theme of his narrative.

Accordingly, the autobiographer maximizes the confusion and embarrassment of his earlier state of mind, reiterating his fear that his readers may find it hard to credit his reconstruction of this critical moment of his development as man and artist. Thus he stresses the peculiarity of the link he made *at the time* between his injury and the war: "the queer fusion or confusion established in my consciousness during the soft spring of '61 by the firing on Fort Sumter, Mr. Lincoln's instant first call for volunteers and a physical mishap, already referred to as having overtaken me at the same dark hour." This felt connection is not only "queer" and "unnatural"; it is "beyond all present notation," "least clearly expressible," "scarce at all to be stated" (414). That is to say that if the autobiographer blurred the chronology of the events of 1861, his doing so is to be valued for its psychological verisimilitude to the extent that the injury—of whatever sort—became associated in his mind in 1861 with the "shining stigma" of those wounded in the war. James goes out of his way to underline the distortions that Edel is concerned to document, so much so that it makes more sense to interpret the blurring, vagueness, and circumlocution involved not as evidence of the autobiographer's deliberate manipulations of fact but rather as a genuine testimony to the involuntary confusion of his earlier self.

What the autobiographer actually reconstructs for us with no little precision is the curious way in which the young non-combatant became in his own eyes a veteran. These are the critical "twenty minutes" that established for the young James

ry's unconscious identification with his father at the moment of the injury, was anticipated by Saul Rosenzweig, in "The Ghost of Henry James: A Study in Thematic Apperception," *Character and Personality*, 12 (1943-1944), 79-100.

"a relation to everything occurring round me not only for the next four years but for long afterward":

> I must have felt in some befooled way in presence of a crisis—the smoke of Charleston Bay still so acrid in the air—at which the likely young should be up and doing or, as familiarly put, lend a hand much wanted; the willing youths, all round, were mostly starting to their feet, and to have trumped up a lameness at such a juncture could be made to pass in no light for graceful. Jammed into the acute angle between two high fences, where the rhythmic play of my arms, in tune with that of several other pairs, but at a dire disadvantage of position, induced a rural, a rusty, a quasi-extemporised old engine to work and a saving stream to flow, I had done myself, in face of a shabby conflagration, a horrid even if an obscure hurt; and what was interesting from the first was my not doubting in the least its duration—though what seemed equally clear was that I needn't as a matter of course adopt and appropriate it, so to speak, or place it for increase of interest on exhibition. (415)

James's skirmish at Newport is juxtaposed against the attack on Fort Sumter in a kind of psychological double exposure, perfectly captured here in the first sentence, which could apply with equal justice to either of the two events. In this mysterious vision we see the young James facing fire and fire, making a symbolic response to "Mr. Lincoln's instant first call for volunteers" as he helps to extinguish the Newport blaze. So totally did he appropriate the war experience that he found it hard to distinguish afterward whether the "huge comprehensive ache" he felt came most "from one's own poor organism" or "from the enclosing social body . . . rent with a thousand wounds" (415).

If James felt, as he insists he did, a tremendous pressure to make some public gesture in the early years of the war, and if the injury in the Newport fire somehow stood for his share of the experience in the field, why was it clear to him then—

and now—that he need not place his "obscure hurt" "for increase of interest on exhibition"? Because James never specifies the nature of the wound (although he could have, Edel argues, and did on other occasions), we can only conclude that the episode and passage are still more complicated than anything I have suggested about them so far. James's commentary on the "interest" of the "obscure hurt" bears this out, quite overshadowing his report of the physical symptoms, such as they were; it opens up a whole new dimension of the episode:

> The interest of it [the obscure hurt], I very presently knew, would certainly be of the greatest, would even in conditions kept as simple as I might make them become little less than absorbing. The shortest account of what was to follow for a long time after is therefore to plead that the interest never did fail. It was naturally what is called a painful one, but it consistently declined, as an influence at play, to drop for a single instant. Circumstances, by a wonderful chance, overwhelmingly favoured it—*as* an interest, an inexhaustible, I mean; since I also felt in the whole enveloping tonic atmosphere a force promoting its growth. Interest, the interest of life and of death, of our national existence, of the fate of those, the vastly numerous, whom it closely concerned, the interest of the extending War, in fine, the hurrying troops, the transfigured scene, formed a cover for every sort of intensity, made tension itself in fact contagious— so that almost any tension would do, would serve for one's share. (415-16)

The insistent, almost obsessive, repetition of the word "interest," the cheerful ring of such phrases as "wonderful chance" and "tonic atmosphere," the general air of vital excitement generated by the expansive rhetorical energy—all these features of the prose throw the "obscure hurt" into an altogether different perspective. The apparently disabling injury is presented, paradoxically, as an enabling event, associated with health and growth, and forming "a cover for every sort of intensity." James gives us a clue to his meaning here, perhaps, when he speaks earlier in this same mammoth paragraph of his literary activity at Newport in 1861-1862 in precisely the same way: his father's rejection of his proposal to attend Harvard College had left him free to cultivate "the life of the imagination" "under the rich cover of obscurity." To the extent that we read James's remarks on the "interest" of his injury literally, they may seem hardly comprehensible as a response to a set of physical symptoms; to the extent, however, that he may be regarded as describing the life of his imagination, they make a good deal more sense, especially in the context of the autobiography up to this point. As we have seen, James always apprehended his fundamental condition of inwardness both as a limitation or incapacity and as a compensatory resource that promoted creativity. Illness and imaginative activity are characteristically linked in the small boy's practice of "taking in"—indeed the one could be said to foster the other; James describes this process, moreover, as "deeply dissimulative."

This line of interpretation would seem to be confirmed, presently, when, in the aftermath of the "shabby conflagration," Henry reluctantly breaks his silence, confides his "state" to his father, and consults "a great surgeon" in Boston about his case. We could almost take the doctor, who made light of "the bewilderment exposed to him" and treated his patient "but to a comparative pooh-pooh" (416), as the prototype for the uncomprehending audiences that James was destined to confront in the two great crises of his artistic career later on. In any case, James's summation of the surgeon's diagnosis sounds the familiar refrain of all his early years: "the inconvenience of my state had to reckon with the strange fact of there being nothing to speak of the matter with me" (417). Readers of *A Small Boy* will inevitably recognize the episode of the wound and the anticlimactic interview with the doctor as a heightened, possibly morbid, restatement of the perplexing condition of the inward life that has been James's theme from the beginning of the autobiography: the plight of the imaginative small boy who, having nothing to " 'show' " in the years before his emergence as an artist, could "but pass for a fool while other exhibitions [went] forward" (8).

Following the emphases of James's own account—the uncanny nature of the link between the two fires (at Newport and at Fort Sumter) and the inexhaustible "interest" of the injury—I am proposing that his experience in the "shabby conflagration" was principally a psychological event in which the young man earned for himself the right to be what he had always been, one of life's noncombatants, and he did so, paradoxically, in the most heroic terms available to him at the time, those of the Civil War. In an uncharacteristic burst of violent physical action—there is nothing remotely like it anywhere else in the autobiography—Henry rose to the occasion—of the fire, of the war, of the private life of his own embattled imagination—and in so doing he made himself the cause of his inveterate and increasingly problematic passivity: "I had done myself . . . a horrid if obscure hurt."[31] If we assume that the discourse operates simultaneously in a double frame of reference, physical and psychological, we can say that the account of the wound captures the fundamental ambiguity of James's inwardness: it is both something to show (hence the painful physical reality of the hurt, which led to the visit to the doctor) and nothing to show (hence the obscurity and "irrelevance" of the hurt, which result in the doctor's pooh-pooh). In this view the importance of the Newport fire is that it supplied a convenient occasion for James to act out his "befooled" belief that he was "in presence of a crisis." In the deepest sense the "crisis" here would be one of his identity itself, the parallel crises of Newport and Charleston Bay serving merely as conduits for its expression. If James was vague about the hurt, it was because the activity of his imagination,

[31] We must note, however, the presence in the passage of an ambiguously passive alternative: "one's own poor organism . . . had suffered particular wrong."

however real, was not something he could easily display; if he was vague about the date, it was because it would be hard to say when it "happened." The posture of the young man in the event would, then, be sharply analogous to that of the autobiographer who lived to re-create it: he was performing an essentially autobiographical task, providing himself with a demonstrable cause for his condition, making a statement about how he came to be the self he was.[32]


## IX. PORTSMOUTH GROVE

The doctor's failure to confirm James's experience of the wound was, needless to say, a devastating setback to the young man's quest for a serviceable contemporary identity. If he was forced to retreat from the treacherous publicity of the doctor's office, however, he could remain loyal to his working theory of his condition in the private world of consciousness and memory, the secure sanctuary of his "cabinet of intimate reference" (423). And so, in the second half of Chapter 9, which takes Henry— at last!—to law school in the fall of 1862, the autobiographer reverses the experiential pattern of the first half, moving this time from an embarrassed sense of having nothing to show

[32] Erik Erikson's analysis of the drive that motivates the process of identity formation places James's behavior both as a young man and as an autobiographer in a revealing perspective: "By accepting some definition as to who he is, usually on the basis of a function in an economy, a place in the sequence of generations, and a status in the structure of society, the adult is able to selectively reconstruct his past in such a way that, step for step, it seems to have planned him, or better, he seems to have planned *it*." By extension, the autobiographical act would be a special expression of a universal human need to cope with the "ego-chill . . . which comes from the sudden awareness that our nonexistence . . . is entirely possible." *Young Man Luther: A Study in Psychoanalysis and History* (1958; rpt. New York: Norton, 1962), pp. 112, 111.

In my commentary I have avoided saying whether or not I believe that James did in fact sustain some kind of injury while fighting a fire in Newport, because obviously no one—not even Edel—can speak definitively one way or the other. Moreover, what James came to believe about the event is the real issue, and readers of *A Small Boy* know that from early on James believed that his physical condition somehow set him apart from others.

for himself in wartime to a triumphant affirmation of his place among the heroes of the war. To be sure, Henry's initial stance in Cambridge was predictably inauspicious: in an image that possibly recalls his participation in the Newport fire, James speaks of "the felt . . . limits of *my* poor stream of contributive remark" to the frequent discussions of the war at Miss Upham's, the boarding house where he dined with brother William. Tapping the young man's "trickle" (421), however, the autobiographer causes "a saving stream to flow" (to use his earlier phrase), and the outpouring comprises some of the most remarkable and highly wrought pages in all of *Notes*.

To enumerate James's experiences of the war is to share his rueful sense of how easily any one of them might be dismissed at a dinner table of the period as merely a "scrap of a substitute for the concrete experience" (422); they include a visit to the wounded at Portsmouth Grove, two visits to Wilky and Cabot Russell in camp at Readville, the missed experience of Wilky's departure from Boston under Colonel Robert Shaw, and an anxious afternoon spent in a Newport garden during the Battle of Gettysburg. To this list should be added the return of the wounded Wilky to Newport, which James treated earlier, as we have seen, and which he alludes to here (423). It is truly a gathering of the minor and the missed, and the evocation of these memories is punctuated first, last, and throughout with professions of apology for so small an exhibition. The first of these, which prefaces his account of the central "flower" of his "queer cluster" (423), the visit to Portsmouth Grove, is typical: "If I had not already so often brazened out my confession of the far from 'showy' in the terms on which impressions could become indelibly momentous to me I might blush indeed for the thin tatter dragged in thus as an affair of record" (422). This is the perennial dilemma of the small boy and autobiographer, and, as so often in the autobiography, James readily imagines that his readers, placing his proffered display of experience in a distinctly diminishing perspective, may find it all too easy to conclude that such a life must have been "a dry desert" (423) indeed. James gives voice to such doubts so frequently in the autobiography that it is hard not to view them as, at least in part, expressions of his own misgivings about the value of the life of impressions.

In its way, then, the account of the visit to Portsmouth Grove covers in a general sense the ground of his old debate with William about their education in Europe, vindicating the richness of an apparently impoverished consciousness; it constitutes, moreover, a definitive reply to the Boston surgeon about the true status of his wound. As in the twenty minutes of the Newport fire, so in the "three or four hours" at Portsmouth Grove, Henry established "a relation" with the war, incarnate this time in the figure of the wounded American soldier, who seems not a little like James's own disabled self of the earlier part of the chapter. In a suggestive reversal of roles, Henry offered to the injured what the great Boston surgeon failed to offer Henry himself, "the last tenderness of friendship": "I drew from each his troubled tale, listened to his plaint on his special hard case . . . and sealed the beautiful tie, the responsive sympathy, by an earnest offer . . . of pecuniary solace" (424). So compelling is this vision of himself as the wound dresser that the autobiographer explicitly, self-consciously, and rather prolixly competes with Walt Whitman for pre-eminence as the great witness of America's tragic war.

In the conclusion of his narrative of Portsmouth Grove, James traces his identification with the heroic wounded and the no less heroic wound dresser to his own wounded state. He claims that the key to the entire memory of the hospital camp on the Maryland shore lies in his "perfectly distinct" recollection of the painful exaltation of his return to Newport that evening. In this celebration of his injury, the physical pain of his "impaired state" is accompanied by "a strange rapture . . . a realisation . . . that, measuring wounds against wounds, or the compromised, the particular taxed condition, at the least, against all the rest of the debt then so generally and enormously due, one was no less exaltedly than wastefully engaged in the common fact of endurance" (426). Here James spells out one of the fundamental principles informing the narrative in *Notes*, that of the felt connection between the most private area of personal history and the public history of the nation at war. The curious mixture of disability and sensitivity that characterizes the young man's state of mind aligns it with the painful pleasure of the small, sick boy's beloved practice of "taking in" and prepares us for the inevitable act of appropriation it involves. James's "obscure hurt," however pooh-poohed, was to serve as his "shining stigma" after all, earning him a rightful place beside Wilky and Cabot Russell among the heroes of the war. The metamorphosis of the malingerer is complete.

It would be hard to overstate the importance of this episode, for it is clearly the affective center of James's narrative in *Notes*. At Portsmouth Grove James found his way to a triumphant affirmation of his own mode of existence; his share in the glory of experience was equal, wound for wound, to that of any veteran. The autobiographer is admirably frank and determined about his double view of the claims he makes for his hours at Portsmouth Grove as at once apparently tenuous and really momentous:

> There are memories in truth too fine or too peculiar for notation, too intensely individual and supersubtle—call them what one will; yet which one may thus no more give up confusedly than one may insist on them vainly. Their kind is nothing ever to a present purpose unless they are in a manner statable, but is at the same time ruefully aware of threatened ridicule if they are overstated. Not that I in the least mind such a menace, however, in just adding that, soothed as I have called the admirable ache of my afternoon with that inward interpretation of it, I felt the latter—or rather doubtless simply the entire affair—absolutely overarched by the majestic manner in which the distress of our return drew out into the lucid charm of the night. To which I must fur-

ther add that the hour seemed, by some wondrous secret, to know itself marked and charged and unforgettable— hinting so in its very own terms of cool beauty at something portentous in it, an exquisite claim then and there for lasting value and high authority. (426-27)

That is to say that the position of the autobiographer vis-à-vis his readers is much the same as that of the young James vis-à-vis the doctor, but with a decisive difference. The special nature of the experience in question, an inward psychological reality, would seem to exceed the capacity of autobiographical discourse to express it; unalterably convinced of the truth of his strange relation to the war, however, the autobiographer draws on the manifold resources of his art and faces up to the doctor—and any other doubters—once and for all. He makes the elements conspire to prove him right: nature overarches "the entire affair," and the time itself is prescient with the very construction that he would one day place on the event.

What, then, are we to conclude when we learn that the biographical record contradicts the autobiographer's version of this critical episode of his life? According to Edel, the visit to Portsmouth Grove took place in August of 1861, which would place it some two months *before* the Newport fire in October; in *Notes*, on the other hand, the visit to Portsmouth Grove comes in August of 1862, *after* the Newport fire.[33] The issue is one of substance, for the two events are placed by the autobiographer in a causal sequence. Thus, when James speaks of his "impaired state" as the clue to the special significance he attached to Portsmouth Grove, we assume that he is referring to the "obscure hurt," an affliction that, if we follow Edel, can have occurred only later on. This distortion of his personal chronology forces us to sharpen our assumptions about James's performance of the autobiographical act. Is the autobiographer deliberately seeking to impose on the reader an

[33] Edel, *The Untried Years*, p. 169. Edel's source here, apparently, is the diary of Thomas Sergeant Perry.

elaborate exercise in apologetics? Or is his memory untrustworthy? Have states of mind belonging to other experiences been transferred unconsciously to the original recollections of Portsmouth Grove and the Newport fire? Clearly the account of the afternoon spent ministering to the wounded is in some deep sense a fiction, but it is crucial to discriminate the kind.

In the final weeks of his work on *Notes*, James himself dramatized the problematic relationship between autobiographical truth and biographical fact in an instructive exchange of letters with his old friend Thomas Sergeant Perry. On the one hand, there were occasions when he felt that he had to simplify the rather disjointed movements of the James family in Europe for the sake of coherent narrative and felicitous characterization, and he begged Perry "not publicly to question or disintegrate my chronology."[34] On the other hand, it would be misleading to suggest that James always gave precedence to aesthetic considerations, for the autobiographer could be scrupulous about the historical record, and he called on Perry to verify the accuracy of his memories about quite a number of details (names, dates, and so forth), most of them having to do with the Civil War. One instance in particular, however, dramatizes James's chastened awareness that more was involved in the re-creation of the past than conscious choice between the competing claims of art and history. He asked Perry whether the first day of the Battle of Gettysburg was a Sunday—"I kind of *need*, for my small context, that July 1st '63 *should* have been a Sunday."[35] Later, corrected by Perry, he mused: "how strangely one's *associations* with the far-off times & things get themselves twisted & turned. I have been thinking all my life, with an association, of the Gettysburg Sunday—& feel a kind of donkeyism in having been through the pages [ages?], so complacently out of it."[36] Measuring his

[34] James to Perry, January 11, 1914. Virginia Harlow, *Thomas Sergeant Perry: A Biography* (Durham: Duke Univ. Press, 1950), p. 344.

[35] James to Perry, September 17, 1913, Harlow, p. 341.

[36] James to Perry, October 12, 1913, Harlow, p. 343. Is "pages" a slip for "ages"? If so, the slip may suggest the extent to which the text and the past became fused and confused in the course of the autobiographical act.

intended shaping of the remembered past in his art against verifiable historical actuality, James was obliged to recognize that the content of his memories had already been shaped by the unpredictable workings of autonomous forces within his consciousness. The instance of the Gettysburg Sunday may serve, then, as a warning that the notion of a clear-cut opposition between fact and fiction suggested by the discrepancies between the autobiography and the biographical record is simplistic and must be discarded in favor of a more sophisticated formulation of experiential reality.

If James's memories of Portsmouth Grove and the Newport fire had gotten "twisted & turned," as Edel persuades that they probably had, the autobiographer himself provides us with a context in which the distortions in question were certainly natural and probably inevitable. Henry was, we might say, "accident prone" at the time, and the autobiographer's reconstruction of his earlier state of mind presents a subtle and persuasive picture of the complex mixture of the voluntary and involuntary in the young man's felt "relation" between the war and his disability. The story of his willed fusions and helpless confusions of private with public event in Chapter 9 is told with such frankness that the existence of the distortions of fact detected by Edel can come as no surprise; the motivation for them is if anything overdetermined. Far from discrediting the truth of the autobiographical narrative, these distortions confirm its essential authenticity. I use the words "truth" and "authenticity" advisedly, since to speak of "distortion" as I have been is to risk the implication that there is some primary *ur*-text of experience of which James's perception then and now would be corrupt variants, whereas it is the thesis of James's story that all experience is subjective, that what "really happened," autobiographically speaking, is what the self perceived. James himself, of course, was haunted in his moments of doubt by the thought that the impressions he took in were not equivalent to the real thing, that the gaper and dawdler was missing out on "life." Thus the mood of the autobiographer's rendering of the inward life alternates between celebration and apology, and it seems to have been one of the principal tasks of the autobiographical act to exorcise these doubts for good.

## X. "A *MODUS VIVENDI* WORKABLE FOR THE TIME"

When James speaks of his "relation" to his injury as "a *modus vivendi* workable for the time" (416), he captures in a phrase the most provocative feature of his narrative in Chapter 9: the explicitness with which he portrays his earlier self as engaged in making fictions about himself, fashioning the materials of his private experience into a story that he could exhibit not only to himself but to the world. To state the young man's case in this way is to see him as a proto-autobiographer and to interpret his behavior as a metaphor for the autobiographical act. Such a parallel is, of course, necessarily speculative, useful only to the extent that it helps us to understand why James found this particular phase of his career so compelling, requiring a complexity of analysis not to be found in any other part of the autobiography. In order to explore the interest of this parallel, we need first to establish the principal features of young James's fiction about himself in these years.

The theme of the ninth chapter, as we have seen, is Henry's urgent need for a "flag" that he could "brandish" to the world in wartime, his search for a covering fiction that could take up the fact of his inveterate sense of disability and adjust it to available patterns of acceptable contemporary behavior. After the story of his injury had failed to pass muster with the doctor in Boston, James relates that he spent "the second half of that summer of '62" selecting "the best" of the "hundred ways to behave" (417) that lay before him. He needed to perform a gesture that would, as he puts it, see him through, that would enable him to temporize until he would in his own good time be ready to unfurl the banner of his art to the world. For all the "oddness" of his decision to study law, it would be hard to fault this course of action as the "best" way to behave, for it squared his problematic situation ("my condition of having nothing to exhibit") in his own eyes and in others' simultaneously. To begin with, this all-purpose decision seemed to meet the American expectation that every young man should have a career, while it actually postponed an act of choice that he felt unready to make—"it was only I . . . who, ready as yet to assert nothing, hung back" (438). At the same time, study of the law placed him in circumstances in which he could continue to nurse his injury and, by extension, his view of his inward condition; "studious retirement and preparatory hours," he surmised, "did after all supply the supine attitude, did invest the ruefulness, did deck out the cynicism of lying down book in hand with a certain fine plausibility." Moreover, as far as James was concerned, law school served as the needed surrogate for military service, "a negative of combat, . . . something definitely and firmly parallel to action in the tented field." James does not state—and perhaps he did not anticipate—the most important of the many advantages of his strategic move to Cambridge: it provided this "queerest of forensic recruits" (417) with a perfect setup for the inward life as he had led it until then.

There was, of course, a cost involved in living under the auspices of the fiction that sanctioned his existence in Cambridge, and James presents "a black little memory" of his "exhibited inaptitude" for the law, a case he was obliged to argue in a moot court. James's evocation of this episode suggests the extent to which his pursuit of the law functioned as a "negative" of his artistic creativity, for he conjures up his failure on this occasion as an inadequate performance of an art in "a perfect glare of publicity," "the image of my having stood forth before an audience with a fiddle and bow and trusted myself to rub them together desperately enough . . . to make some appearance of music." His "luckless exposure" (438) here repeated the lesson of his encounter with brother William and Hunt's other pupils in the theater of the "larger" studio at Newport: to display himself and his creative powers in public was to risk humiliation, a risk that was fulfilled in the two major crises of his artistic career, the failure of *Guy Domville* in 1895 and the failure of the New York Edition of his work in 1909. As always, Henry's refuge and consolation was the secret richness of his inward life ("perceiving . . . kicked up no glare"), and he could draw on the fiction of his study of the law to provide a "plausible" cover for the private exercises of his imagination. The law student could be alone in his room on much the same terms as the small sick boy had been in London, Geneva, and Boulogne, but with a difference. There was an alcove in his room in Winthrop Square in which Henry, "even so shy a dreamer as I then had to take myself for," began "to woo . . . the muse of prose fiction" (439), taking the first tentative steps in the direction of his mature identity as an artist.

Going to law school restored an equilibrium to Henry's existence that had been missing since the breakup of the Newport phase, and his beloved practice of "taking in" dominates the narrative once more.[37] Attending lectures on the law, listening to conversation at the boarding-house table—these were opportunities to study types of the American character (Chapter 10), while reading Wilky's letters home from the front permitted Henry a "visionary 'assistance' at the drama of the War" (456) (Chapter 11). The autobiographer is acutely self-conscious about the disparity between the modest scale of his own activities in Cambridge and the heroic cast of his younger brother's participation in the Union campaigns. The contrast between the two brothers and between the two ways of "taking" life that each comes to symbolize is only a more intense version of the one that James presented in his Geneva period in *A Small Boy*; the autobiographer's commentary on Wilky's letters in Chapter 11 focuses on "the spirit of [his] own poor

[37] It is probably of some significance that at one point James formulates his decision to go to Harvard Law School as "my joining, in a sense, my brother at Cambridge" (412). The sibling rivalry between Henry and William has been so overplayed in recent criticism that another and equally important facet of their relationship has been obscured. William's stardom may have generated feelings of inferiority in Henry, but it also supplied a kind of cover for Henry's development of his own creativity without the family exposure that he found so inhibiting.

perusal of them" (461), sounding the perennial lament over the missed opportunities for experience. When the narrative takes up Henry's residence at Ashburton Place in 1864-1866 in Chapter 12, however, the autobiographer brings his story to a climax with an account of his public assertion of his identity as an artist.

The exuberant mood of this chapter is altogether different from the mood of the three preceding chapters, with their painful memories of the embarrassment and anxiety of the shy young man who had yet to prove himself as an artist. The autobiographer revels in this expansive phase of new-found confidence and brimming vitality; these are banquet years, and the text is profusely decorated with imagery of feasts and flowers. Henry had begun to exchange his habitually sedentary and reclusive posture for a more active and outgoing mode of existence, and James clearly finds the spectacle an exhilarating tonic: "I literally, and under whatever felt restriction of my power to knock about, formed independent relations—several" (476); "I literally came and went, I had never practised such coming and going" (481). What lay behind this sudden display of mobility and volition was an explosion of creativity, for at last the small boy, son, and brother had something to show, and the autobiographer speaks of his first short stories in a revealing phrase as "holding up their stiff little heads in such a bustle of life and traffic of affairs" (494). He proved to himself that he could hope to make a living as a professional writer, and he gloats over "the very greenbacks" he earned when Charles Eliot Norton published his "first fond attempt at literary criticism" (476) in the *North American Review*. This first "positive consecration to letters" (447) was soon confirmed when E. L. Godkin invited him to help launch *The Nation* in the summer of 1865, and presently William Dean Howells accepted "the most presuming as yet of my fictional bids" (494) for the *Atlantic*.

Pursuing the logic that governed his account of his injury, his visit to Portsmouth Grove, and his study of the law in the preceding chapters, James parallels his emergence as a writer with the return of the veterans from the war. The sense of "fusions" between personal and national history that colored the young man's consciousness at the time structures Chapter 12 as it does so much of James's story in *Notes*. At the beginning of the war Henry's unreadiness for "life" had put him at odds with his culture; now, however, he felt that the rhythms of his inward existence were in phase with the general "lift" and "push" (490) of the last days of the war. In his turn, the autobiographer fuses the young man's coming of age with the symbols of experience and achieved maturity that flooded the American scene in 1865, the "bronzed, matured faces and . . . bronzed, matured characters" (488) of the soldiers returning home. The war was over, and James's Book of the War was complete.[38]

It seems likely that James originally intended to conclude *Notes* at this point and that the addition of Chapter 13 represents a change in plan. He wrote to Henrietta Pell-Clarke on May 5, 1914, that he was "3 quarters done" when he received from Alice James a packet of letters from his cousin Minny Temple written to John Chipman Gray during the last year of her life.[39] He subsequently decided to "round off" (504) *Notes* with an extra chapter devoted to her memory. "Her death made a mark," he wrote on the last page, "that must stand here for a too waiting conclusion. We felt it together as the end of our youth" (544). This note of finality enhanced the moving story unfolded in the letters of a courageous young woman's losing battle with tuberculosis. Taken together with James's willingness in his letters to accept the portrait of Minny as "*the* success" of the book,[40] it has seemed to give James's autobiography something of the aura of a repressed, unhappy

[38] Hoffa has observed that James plays down the earliest evidence of his literary activity; if so, perhaps he did this to make the parallel between personal and national history more striking. "The Final Preface," 290. The testimony of James's brother Wilky and of his friend Perry suggests that Henry was a secret scribbler as early as 1858-1860.

[39] Rosenbaum, 53.

[40] See, e.g., James to Alice H. James, March 29, 1914, *Letters*, II, 362.

love story.[41] James's commentary, however, suggests that it is not his love *for* Minny but his identification *with* her that provides the clue to the significance of her portrait in *Notes*. "She had beyond any equally young creature I have known," he writes, "a sense for verity of character and play of life in others," but she was "launched" on the adventure of living "in such bedimmed, such almost tragically compromised conditions" (509). In the context of the autobiography the thematic affinities between Minny's story and James's are unmistakable: the character of the sensitive invalid yearning for and missing "the ampler experience" of life functions as a kind of alter-ego for James himself. Thus her fate at the last as one "beaten" (528) by life is doubly poignant for the autobiographer; the ending of her story could so easily have been the ending of his own.

In its broad outlines the pattern of James's experience in *Notes*, especially his account of the war years in Chapters 9-12, resembles the one studied by Erik Erikson in *Young Man Luther* (1958): an unusually gifted young man undergoes a period of neurotic suffering followed by a sudden breakthrough into creativity. Erikson cites the cases of Freud, Darwin, Luther, and Shaw as characteristic examples of this crucial phase of life history, which he terms the *"identity crisis."* This is "the major crisis of adolescence," which "occurs in that period of the life cycle when each youth must forge for himself some central perspective and direction, some working unity, out of the effective remnants of his childhood and the hopes of his anticipated adulthood." When Erikson goes on to say that the youth "must detect some meaningful resemblance between what he has come to see in himself and what his sharpened awareness tells him others judge and expect him to be," I feel that he has articulated the dynamic at work unconsciously in the episode of James's "obscure hurt" and consciously in his decision to go to law school. One could proceed to mount a full-

[41] James attempted to qualify the impact of Chapter 13 in the opening of *The Middle Years* by juxtaposing the story of his own year of initiation in Europe in 1869-1870 against the tale of Minny's defeat.

scale Eriksonian analysis of James's life in these years, for
most of the principal features of the identity crisis are to be
observed in his behavior during the war: the need for a *"moratorium"* as a way of "postponing the decision as to what one
is and is going to be"; the temporary choice of a *"negative
identity,"* which one "has been warned *not* to become, which
he can become only with a divided heart, but which he nevertheless finds himself compelled to become"; the experience of
"identity diffusion," which "leads to significant arrest and
regression" and is frequently characterized by quasi-catatonic
states; a shying away from intimacy with others; and "a tor-
tuous self-consciousness, characterized at one time by shame
over what one is already sure one is, and at another time by
doubt as to what one may become." Interestingly, Erikson
draws an analogy between his own conception of the identity
crisis and the notion of a " 'growth-crisis' " described by William James in his chapters on the sick soul, the divided self,
and conversion in *The Varieties of Religious Experience*.[42] What I
am suggesting is that the biographical materials James was
reconstructing contained latent within them a coherent experiential shape, that of the decisive phase of identity formation
described by Erikson and by William James. In the course of
the autobiographical act Henry James elucidated this shape in
his own fashion, and he exploited its contours to structure his
story of himself in *Notes*.

XI. "Locked fast in the golden cage
of the *intraduisible!*"

With the publication of *Notes* in March 1914, some basic task
that had supplied the motive force for the autobiographical
act had been accomplished. James himself seems to have sensed
this, for he wrote his nephew Harry on April 7, 1914, that,
although he probably would "perpetrate a certain number more
passages of retrospect & reminiscence" in the time to come,

---

[42] Erikson, pp. 14, 43, 102, 100, 101, 41.

they would be "quite disconnected from these 2 recent volumes [*A Small Boy* and *Notes*], which are complete in themselves & of which the original intention is now a performed & discharged thing."[43] This sense of an ending, confirmed in the event by James's failure to complete *The Middle Years* (published as a posthumous fragment by Percy Lubbock in 1917), poses the whole question of James's motivation for the autobiographical act, which had organized and sustained his existence during his final period of creativity.

Because the autobiographer portrays himself as the champion of the small boy in the years when he had had nothing to show, we could infer that, having brought the story of his earlier self to the threshold of his artistic career, James felt that further autobiographical narrative was superfluous. Such an explanation makes a good deal of sense, and we have seen that James himself, in a major statement at the beginning of Chapter 11 of *Notes*, was willing to strike a pose of considerable detachment about the autobiographical enterprise. He claimed that his purpose was aesthetic, the character of "the man of imagination" struck the novelist as an excellent opportunity for narrative, and he had merely taken himself as a conveniently representative instance of his chosen subject. Such a rationale, however attractive, hardly predicates the urgency of James's personal involvement in the undertaking that makes the text and the letters about it so compelling. Even in the first weeks of work on *A Small Boy* James knew that he was going to get in deep, and this was what he wanted. Thus he writes to nephew Harry on December 23, 1911: "the only thing is to *let* everything, even *make* everything, come and flow, let my whole consciousness and memory play into the past as it will, and then see afterwards about reducing and eliminating."[44] And a week or so later, on January 2, 1912, he wrote to Alice James, paradoxically, that "the only thing" that was interfering a bit with his progress on the project was

[43] MS in the James family collection at the Houghton Library.
[44] MS, Houghton.

"the positive muchness of the tide, of reconstruction . . . with which I have to struggle."[45] James had intended to produce a single volume, but by summer it was clear that there would have to be two; he had set in motion a process that seemed to have a will of its own. He wrote to Harry on September 23, 1912: "This whole record of early childhood simply *grew* so as one came to write it that one could but let it take its way."[46] James himself was clearly aware that more was involved in the autobiographical act than his literary talk of "the man of imagination" could account for, and so at the end of this same passage in Chapter 11 he confesses that the success of the project as far as he is personally concerned depends in the last analysis on its achievement in a distinctly non-aesthetic theater of action. Even if his reader should judge the autobiography as an artistic "defeat," James felt he could "fall back on the interest, at the worst, of certain sorts of failure": "I shall have brought up from the deep many things probably not to have been arrived at for the benefit of these pages without my particular attempt" (455).

The autobiographical act was itself a major psychological event, and I would argue that James derived strength for the present from the insight he acquired into the resources of his ego in meeting a life crisis during the Civil War so long ago. It is not hard to see why the autobiographer was drawn to the story of a young man who managed both in spite of and because of illness and disability to achieve a full realization of his creativity. James had reasons enough to need such support and inspiration in these years: the apparent failure of the New York Edition, the death of William, his own poor health, and, perhaps most of all, his fear that he might never make good his hope to return to the house of fiction. The autobiography is *about* the making of existential fictions, the contriving of "a *modus vivendi* workable for the time," and the autobiography itself, moreover, *is* such a fiction. This James himself well

[45] MS, Houghton.
[46] MS, Houghton.

knew. On March 21, 1914, in his moving reply to Henry Adams's "melancholy outpouring" occasioned by reading *Notes*, James affirmed that the autobiographical act had expressed his will to live: "It all takes doing—and I *do*. I believe I shall do yet again—it is still an act of life."[47]

In *A Small Boy* and *Notes* Henry James revisited the hiding places of the power of his imagination in preparation for a triumphant return to the house of fiction. What he could not have anticipated was that the preparation and the return itself were destined to be one and the same, that the great story he had to tell about American life and culture was not the saga of business and society that he tackled in the unfinished *Ivory Tower* but his story of himself. He had made himself a work of art—as he put it, "it does even partly exhilarate me to recognize that the small Boy, while yet so tame and intrinsically safe a little animal, is locked fast in the golden cage of the *intraduisible!*"[48] Next to the small boy, with his shrinking sensibility and his painful feeling of inferiority, the autobiographer positively towers, taking what history could offer to build himself a monument and memorial. If we recall that James attributes to the small boy a nagging misgiving about the morality of "spiritual snatching," it has to be said that the imperial imagination of the autobiographer, operating on a truly Napoleonic scale, knew no such constraint. He appropriated the Louvre as the stage for the small boy's imaginative visions, and he placed the son and brother in one of the hallowed niches reserved for the wounded in the Civil War. Haunted early and late by the thought of missing out on life, the autobiographer made himself by imaginative decree a member of the elect company of the experienced, those who have "the strange property or privilege" of "looking through us or straight over us at something they partake of together but that we mayn't pretend to know" (384).

[47] *Letters*, II, 360-61.

[48] James to Auguste Monod, September 7, 1913, *The Selected Letters of Henry James*, ed. Leon Edel (New York: Farrar, 1955), p. 107.

# CHAPTER THREE

## Jean-Paul Sartre:
## The Boy Who Wanted
## to Be a Book

A LITTLE BOY of seven sneaks on board a train bound for Dijon and falls asleep. Awakened by the ticket-collector, the child admits that he has neither ticket nor money, not even an identity card. To save himself, he reveals that his presence is urgently required in Dijon; the fate of France and even mankind itself hangs in the balance. Like Scheherazade, the child instinctively recognizes that his life depends on words: as long as he keeps on talking, the ticket-collector will not make him get off the train. He never learns, however, whether or not his claim to an indispensable role in the affairs of men is accepted, for the inscrutable ticket-collector remains silent.

In this fable of himself as the boy on the train in *The Words* (1964), Jean-Paul Sartre dramatizes the unfathered condition of his orphaned childhood and its lifelong consequences for his sense of identity. The mandate from the world, that alone could validate for the child a legitimate selfhood, is lacking, and the boy is, accordingly, thrown back on the resources of his imagination to supply it: "My sole recourse, at the age of seven, was within myself, who did not yet exist."[1] The circular logic of his lack, isolating him within the closed circuit of his mental system, is inescapable: "I had been born in order to fill the great need I had of myself" (69). Thus the fancied

[1] *The Words*, trans. Bernard Frechtman (Greenwich, CT: Fawcett, [1966]), p. 69. Subsequent references are to this edition and will appear in the text. Originally published in French under the title *Les Mots* (Paris: Gallimard, 1964).

encounter with the world, in which the child beguiles the
time on the train by spinning out words to the ticket-collector, is finally only an exercise in self-projection: "The train,
the ticket-collector, and the delinquent were myself. And I
was also a fourth character, the organizer, who had only one
wish, to fool himself, if only for a minute, to forget that he
had concocted everything" (70). The wish of "the organizer"
is that of the child and the autobiographer who came to write
about him—and doubtless that of the reader of autobiography, too—united as they are in their aspiration to pass through
language into the estate of an enduring and justified selfhood,
stable beyond solipsism, beyond the memory of the fictions
that alone can bring it into being. In Sartre's view, the child
he was and the autobiographer he is are equally given to this
quest, and so the unsparing anatomy of the sources and strategies of self-invention in autobiography emerges with a double intensity in *The Words*.[2] Here the plot of Sartre's autobiographical narrative mirrors the autobiographical act that creates
it:

> Everything took place in my head. Imaginary child that
> I was, I defended myself with my imagination. When I
> examine my life from the age of six to nine, I am struck
> by the continuity of my spiritual exercises. Their content
> often changed, but the program remained unvaried. I had
> made a false entrance; I withdrew behind a screen and
> began my birth over again at the right moment, the very
> minute that the universe silently called for me. (71)

[2] Recent discussions of *The Words* have emphasized the central place of self-
invention in the narrative. See, e.g., Dominick LaCapra on "the myth of self-
genesis" in *A Preface to Sartre* (Ithaca: Cornell Univ. Press, 1978), pp. 185,
193. LaCapra notes (p. 243) a similar focus in Jeffrey Mehlman's commentary, *A Structural Study of Autobiography: Proust, Leiris, Sartre, Lévi-Strauss* (Ithaca: Cornell Univ. Press, 1974), pp. 151-86. The best treatment of Sartre's
view of self-invention as a moral and metaphysical imperative is Victor Brombert, "Sartre et La Biographie Impossible," *Cahiers de l'Association Internatio-
nale des Études Françaises*, No. 19 (1967), pp. 155-66.

On the train, behind the screen, in the head, an existential urgency motivates both boy and autobiographer to cast life history into narrative.

After Sartre wrote the first version of *The Words* in 1954, he worked on the manuscript from time to time during the next ten years, revising it extensively in 1963 before it appeared in 1964. Sartre's comments about the project, both during the extended period of composition and still later, after publication, illustrate the range of purpose that can govern the writing of an autobiography. In 1955, for example, Sartre adopts the perspective of the historian, who understands his own story as an example of the ways in which the individual—in this case a man of fifty, son of *petits bourgeois*, who was nine years old on the eve of the First World War—is defined through his connection with the historical situation into which he is born. He traces this view of his biography to the pivotal experience of his conscription in 1939, which taught him that even the apostle of existentialist freedom could be the victim of circumstance.[3] In a second interview, in 1957, Sartre maintains this historical interpretation, suggesting the extent to which his own story represents the experience of an entire generation of bourgeois intellectuals. He now announces, however, that his primary intention in writing his autobiography is the elaboration of a biographical methodology designed "to determine the meaning of a life and the purpose that fills it."[4] In his study of Sartre's practice of biography, Douglas Collins confirms this motive, placing *The Words* in a context that includes Sartre's studies of Baudelaire, Genet, and Flaubert. It is the task of Sartrean biography to reveal the decisive moment of choice in which the individual selects

[3] Contat, Michel, and Michel Rybalka, *Les Écrits de Sartre: Chronologie, bibliographie commentée* (Paris: Gallimard, 1970), p. 386. See also Philippe Lejeune, *Le pacte autobiographique* (Paris: Seuil, 1975), p. 205, for the view that 1940 stands out as a turning-point in Sartre's career.

[4] "Jean-Paul Sartre on His Autobiography," interview with Olivier Todd, *The Listener*, 57 (6 June 1957), 915. See Contat, p. 386, for French version.

the project that will in turn constitute his essential totality as a person.[5]

What unites Sartre's four life-studies is their focus on literature as the source of self-definition. As Sartre put it in 1970, "I wrote *The Words* in order to answer the same question posed in my studies of Genet and Flaubert: how does a man become someone who writes? . . . What is interesting is the birth of the decision to write."[6] In *The Words* Sartre presents both his early decision to write and his recent decision to write his autobiography as the beginning and ending phases of a neurosis. As a child of seven he had embraced literature as an absolute in order to justify his existence, and his faith in literature served as the unexamined core of his identity for more than thirty years until his troubled relations with the Communist Party after the Second World War awakened him to the sickness of this state of mind. He had lived, as it now seemed, a life of illusion.[7] Infatuated with the glory of the great literary dead, the boy had been prematurely afflicted with a perverse and radical strain of autobiographical ambition: Sartre offers himself as an extreme instance of a child who proposed to himself nothing less than to transform the contingency of his existence into the permanence of a book. Proleptic autobiographer, the child stood the Romantic injunction of the life-writer on its head, as who should say, "This is no child,/Who touches this touches a book." Of the child who wanted to live his life in narrative terms from a posthumous perspective, Sartre observes, "I became my own obituary" (129). There is much to learn from Sartre's brilliant diagnosis of the child's literary disease, for the endless debate among critics today about the definition of autobiography and

---

[5] Collins, *Sartre as Biographer* (Cambridge: Harvard Univ. Press, 1980), pp. 20-21.

[6] Sartre, *Situations* (Paris: Gallimard, 1972), IX, 133-34 (my trans.). "Si j'ai écrit *Les Mots* c'est pour répondre à la même question que dans mes études sur Genet et sur Flaubert: comment un homme devient-il quelqu'un qui écrit? . . . Ce qui est intérèssant c'est la naissance de la décision d'écrire."

[7] See Lejeune, *Le pacte*, p. 206, on the stages of Sartre's awakening.

the boundaries of fact and fiction reflects a fundamental uncertainty about the relation between autobiographical narrative and the life it claims to record. Ironically, the text that could, perhaps, do more than any other to illuminate the truth of the relation has been discredited as autobiography precisely on the ground that it falsifies this relation.

## I. "The way things happen in actual experience"

Reviewing *The Words* shortly after its appearance in 1964, Paul de Man found the tightness and rigor of the composition, especially in the first part of the book, to be at odds with "the autobiographical genre," in which "narrative always remains open and seemingly erratic." "The people, events, and details that occur in an autobiography," he continues, "may well be reported inaccurately, distorted by lapses of memory or by the passions involved whenever a man speaks about himself, but they occur *without plan or interpretation, the way things happen in actual experience.*"[8] Given the assumption that human existence is essentially non-narrative or even anti-narrative in character, the concept of an autobiographical narrative would be a contradiction in terms. To require of an autobiography that it record a life in a narrative untainted by plan or interpretation would be to make it a virtual impossibility as a narrative kind, yet de Man begins his critique of Sartre by postulating the existence of an "autobiographical genre." Is it really the case, as this position assumes, that experience and narrative are antithetical categories, cousins of that troublesome pair, fact and fiction, which has hobbled so much of the discussion of autobiography over the years? De Man's objections to Sartre's autobiography fail to engage the central proposition of his story, the possibility that narrative itself could be a mode of experience rather than merely a literary form. Even though the relation of narrative to the fundamental structures of con-

---

[8] De Man, "Sartre's Confessions: *The Words* by Jean-Paul Sartre," *New York Review of Books*, 5 November 1964, p. 11, emphasis added.

sciousness remains unclear at the present time, the most constructive approach to Sartre's meditation on this problem in *The Words* is to place it in the context of parallel thinking by a good many others in various disciplines who have conceived of narrative both as a mode of perception and as a mode of cognition.

Attacking the view of narrative implied by de Man's position, that it is "used by artists to control, manipulate, and order experience," Barbara Hardy asserts that narrative is "a primary act of mind transferred to art from life." She believes that the qualitites of narrative in the novel are a manifestation of "that inner and outer storytelling that plays a major role in our sleeping and waking lives." "For we dream in narrative," she continues, "daydream in narrative, remember, anticipate, hope, . . . hate, and love by narrative. In order really to live, we make up stories about ourselves. . . ." Thus, novels are to be valued precisely for the insight they offer into "the whole range of psychic narratives"[9] that constitute our mental reality. The philosopher Stephen Crites echos Hardy's view when he urges, in a speculative essay entitled "The Narrative Quality of Experience," that "storytelling is not an arbitrary imposition upon remembered experience, altogether alien to its own much simpler form." This is not only because "consciousness has a form of its own, without which no coherent experience at all would be possible," but because "the form of active consciousness, i.e., the form of its experiencing, is in at least some rudimentary sense narrative." Although the purpose of the essay is to defend this thesis, Crites is the first

[9] "Towards a Poetics of Fiction: An Approach through Narrative," *Novel*, 2 (1968-1969), 5. Drawing on a recent essay by Paul Ricoeur, a Heideggerian exploration of "Narrative Time" which develops "a parallel between the generation of narrative in history and literature and the temporal structure of human existence," Avrom Fleishman entertains the possibility "that life—indeed, the idea of *a life*—is already structured as a narrative." See Fleishman, "Envoi: Life as Narrative," *Figures of Autobiography: The Language of Self-Writing in Victorian and Modern England* (Berkeley: Univ. of California Press, 1983), pp. 476, 478, and Ricoeur, "Narrative Time," *Critical Inquiry*, 7 (1980), 169-90.

to acknowledge the circularity of his argument: the form of the stories—sacred and mundane—that structure experience suggests that the structure of experience itself must be in some sense narrative; it is the narrative form of experience itself that generates the stories that structure it. For a measure of the plausibility of his argument, Crites, like Hardy, can only appeal to the phenomenological experience of consciousness as captured, this time, not in novels but in Saint Augustine's reflection on time and memory in the tenth and eleventh books of the *Confessions*. Defining *narrative* as a "cultural form capable of expressing coherence through time," Crites derives it from consciousness itself, which "grasps its objects in an inherently temporal way." Following Augustine, Crites celebrates memory as the source of order in human experience, for "it is memory that bestows the sense of temporal succession as well as the power to abstract coherent unities from this succession of momentary percepts." In tracing the origins of narrative form to the experience of consciousness preserved and shaped by memory, Crites is careful not to settle for a simplistic model of the relation between narrative and experience: "In principle, we can distinguish between the inner drama of experience and the stories through which it achieves coherence. But in any actual case the two so interpenetrate that they form a virtual identity, which, if we may pun a little, is in fact a man's very sense of his own personal identity." Thus, if narrative forms are constituted by experience, they also shape it, for the content and form of experience are mediated by the prevailing symbolic systems in a culture, and narrative forms are prominent among them. The dialectical interplay between experience and narrative is necessarily cultural as well as psychological: "the *way* we remember, anticipate, and even directly perceive, is largely social."[10]

Two recent attempts to develop a typology of narrative form lend support to the conclusion of Hardy and Crites that the

[10] "The Narrative Quality of Experience," *Journal of the American Academy of Religion*, 39 (1971), 300, 297, 294, 298, 305, 304.

structures of narrative reflect, and are derived from, the structures of consciousness. In an effort to understand how the narrative mentality is created, Brian Sutton-Smith and Gilbert J. Botvin have studied the development of storytelling competence in children. Using a system of classification derived from Vladimir Propp's analysis of Russian folktales in order to determine the structural complexity of the stories they collected, they note that a child's acquisition of narrative structures follows a temporal sequence that closely parallels the four stages of a child's cognitive development established by the research of Jean Piaget.[11] Similarly, Hayden V. White's investigation of the tropes of discourse has led him to see in Piaget's schema the possibility of an experimentally derived ontogenetic basis for the ubiquitous fourfold pattern of rhetorical figures employed by consciousness in its effort to order experience: "what Piaget's theories do suggest is that the tropes of figuration, metaphor, metonymy, synecdoche, and irony, which are used in conscious processes of poiesis and discourse formation, are grounded, in some way, in the psychogenetic endowment of the child, the bases of which appear sequentially in the fourfold phasal development which Piaget calls sensorimotor, representational, operational, and logical."[12] "In some way"—more than this neither White nor Sutton-Smith nor Crites nor Hardy can say, given the state of current knowledge. What they share is a conviction that the structures of narrative and discourse are more than arbitrary constructs imposed on the flux of experience to organize it; somehow these structures originate in—and hence mirror—the operational modalities employed by consciousness itself in the very process of experience to bring understanding, order, coherence, unity to its reality. To this extent experiential con-

---

[11] Botvin, Gilbert J., and Brian Sutton-Smith, "The Development of Structural Complexity in Children's Fantasy Narratives," *Developmental Psychology*, 13 (1977), 377-88.

[12] *Tropics of Discourse: Essays in Cultural Criticism* (Baltimore: Johns Hopkins Univ. Press, 1978), p. 12.

sciousness could be said to be narratively and discursively constituted.

In his assessment of history as discourse, however, White joins a prominent group of historiographers, including R. G. Collingwood, W. B. Gallie, and Louis O. Mink, who conceive of narrative not as a mode of perception but rather as a mode of cognition. "We do not *live* stories," White reminds us, "even if we give our lives meaning by retrospectively casting them in the form of stories." Affirming Collingwood's view of the historian as a storyteller, White nevertheless dissents from his belief that historical events could constitute a story in themselves: "Considered as potential elements of a story, historical events are value-neutral." It is the historian who, drawing on his knowledge of "the *types* of configurations of events that can be recognized as stories by the audience for which he is writing," emplots events and thereby endows them with meaning. To acknowledge this fiction-making operation of the historical enterprise, however, "in no way detracts from the status of historical narratives as providing a kind of knowledge, . . . [for] the encodation of events in terms of such plot structures is one of the ways that a culture has of making sense of both personal and public pasts."[13]

W. B. Gallie has given the most comprehensive elaboration of the central place of narrative in the concept of historical understanding. He defines "historical understanding" as "the exercise of the capacity to follow a story, where the story is known to be based on evidence and is put forward as a sincere effort to get at *the* story so far as the evidence and the writer's general knowledge and intelligence allow." He conceives of "following a story" as "a teleologically guided form of attention" in which "we are pulled along by our sympathies towards a promised yet always open conclusion."[14] Refining the work of Collingwood and Gallie on narrative as a mode of

[13] *Ibid.*, pp. 90, 84, 85.

[14] *Philosophy and the Historical Understanding* (New York: Schocken, 1964), pp. 105, 64-65.

historical understanding, Louis O. Mink criticizes Gallie's conception of narrative experience as a "phenomenology of 'following,' " stressing instead that it is the experience of "*having followed*" that is crucial for narrative to function as cognition: "to know an event by retrospection is categorically, not incidentally, different from knowing it by prediction or anticipation." "Experiences come to us *seriatim*" whereas our understanding of them requires the "grasping together in a single mental act things which are not experienced together."[15] Reversing Barbara Hardy's thesis that narrative is a primary act of mind transferred from life to art, Mink joins White in concluding that narrative qualities are transferred from art to life: stories are not lived but told. It is just at this juncture that *The Words* takes on its peculiar suggestiveness: if the autobiographer proposes to tell the story of himself as a child, the story told is that of a child who proposes in his turn to live his life as a story. Working from art to life and from life to art respectively, the child Sartre was and the autobiographer he is explore the constitution of selfhood through narrative.

## II. *The Childhood of Famous Men:* Jean-Jacques, Johann-Sebastian, and Jean-Paul

"Around 1850, in Alsace, a schoolteacher with more children than he could afford was willing to become a grocer. This unfrocked clerk . . ." (5). Sartre begins *The Words* in this vein, reviewing the vital statistics of his Schweitzer and Sartre ancestors which lead, step by step, to the death of his father and his own orphan birth a few pages later on: "In 1904, at Cherbourg, the young naval officer, who was already wasting away with the fevers of Cochin-China, made the acquaintance of Anne Marie Schweitzer, took possession of the big, forlorn girl, married her, begot a child in quick time, me, and sought

[15] "History and Fiction as Modes of Comprehension," *New Literary History*, 1 (1969-1970), 546, 547.

refuge in death" (9). The presence of this capsule family history, streamlined as it is, would seem to conform to standard biographical practice, presumably supplying an aetiology of the self the narrative proposes to exhibit. In Sartre's witty version of his genealogy, however, characterized by its fortuitous, sudden, and surprising begettings, the biological chain of causation unstabilizes the possibility of an orderly genetic identity. The child's orphanhood becomes precisely the sign of his causeless condition, his haunting sense of the gratuitousness of his existence. In this parody of the conventional biographical beginning, Sartre explodes naive historicism as the source of self-definition.[16] Unfathered by history, the disinherited child is left to his own devices to fashion a justified selfhood: "I keep creating myself . . ." (20).

The orphan's troubled sense of identity emerges only gradually, for his ego is nourished by the adulation of a doting family circle. Following his father's death, Sartre and his mother, Anne-Marie, return to the home of her parents, Charles and Louise Schweitzer, and it is here, in the hothouse atmosphere of sentimentalized domesticity of his grandfather's house, that Poulou, as he was called, lives out his childhood, "alone between an old man and two women" (52). For a time he is content to feed his hunger for importance by performing the role of the child as angel and prodigy in a bourgeois "Paradise" presided over by his patriarchal grandfather. The motive and model for the child's cultural histrionics is Charles Schweitzer, a tall, bearded pedagogue with a taste for magniloquent sublimity in the manner of Victor Hugo. Given the presuppositions of nineteenth-century culture, the old man is ideally suited to sustain the orphan's sense of self, for the historicism discredited by the autobiographer was an article of faith in the Schweitzer household: "My grandfather believes in Progress; so do I: Progress, that long, steep path which leads to me" (21).

Ironically, the security of a necessary existence is under-

---

[16] See LaCapra, pp. 184-85, for Sartre's use of parody in *The Words*.

mined by the very success of Poulou's performance as the
remarkable child. His mastery of the repertoire of poses and
attitudes that elicit confirmation of his valued presence from
the adults is subverted by the acute self-consciousness that it
entails: "How can one put on an act without knowing that
one is acting?" (52). Thus reality and identity elude the child:
"Play-acting robbed me of the world and of human beings. I
saw only roles and props." The price of his impersonations is
that he becomes "a fake child" (53), "a miniature adult" (43)
who knows "how to say things 'beyond my years' without
meaning to" (19). The child's insecurity is compounded by
his suspicion that the adults are only faking an interest in him:
"I would suddenly discover that I did not really count, and I
felt ashamed of my unwonted presence in that well ordered
world." Lacking a father to endow him with a reason for being,
Sartre comments wryly, "nobody, beginning with me, knew
why the hell I had been born" (55).

Oppressed by his own nothingness, Poulou imagines
M. Simonnot, his grandfather's colleague at the Modern Language Institute, to be the incarnation of the justified self, privileged to awaken daily to a Whitmanesque ecstasy of self-rec-
ognition: "Yes, it's I. I'm M. Simonnot all over" (56-57). When
grandfather Schweitzer, noting Simonnot's absence from a literary party, proclaims, "There's someone missing here: Simonnot" (57), the child envies Simonnot his possession of an
indispensable place in the universe, "a nothingness hollowed
out by universal expectation, an invisible womb from which,
so it seemed, one could suddenly be reborn" (57-58). Only in
literature could the boy be born on his own terms.

"I began my life as I shall no doubt end it: amidst books"
(25). For the child whose first encounter with the world is
circumscribed by the book-filled walls of his grandfather's
study, literature is not merely coextensive with reality, it precedes it in the order of being, so that books offer immediate
access to the ideal archetypes of the things beyond the study
walls. Better still, for this nothing of a boy, books permit him
to assume alternative identities at will, for when his mother

reads to him, he learns that words have the power to lift him out of himself: it is neither he who listens nor she who reads, "it was the book that was speaking" (29). And so Poulou turns to his bookish imagination to become the maker and master of his own logocentric universe. His first stories, crude as they are, anticipate the solution to his existentialist identity crisis that he was to pursue in literature for most of his adult career: the child emerges as the necessary hero called to the work of redemption—in this case to save frail young ladies from death at the hands of barbarous villains: "When the janissaries brandished their curved scimitars, a moan went through the desert and the rocks said to the sand: 'Someone's missing here. It's Sartre.' At that very moment I pushed aside the screen. I struck out with my sabre and sent heads flying. I was being born in a river of blood. Oh, blessed steel! I was where I belonged" (72). It was in words that Sartre could give himself the substance of a Simonnot, and *The Words* is the story of the boy's search for a beginning in language that could serve as his end in life.

Like Don Quixote, Tom Sawyer, and Emma Bovary, the Poulou of the first section of the autobiography, "Reading," is predestined to a confusion of literature with life. How could it have been otherwise, Sartre asks, for a lonely child with only books for companionship? Grandfather Charles initiates the boy into the solemn mysteries of the temple of literature, and it is inevitable that the illustrious dead from Hesiod to Hugo who line the study walls should become his "friends," for these authors "had been metamorphosed into books": "Corneille was a big, rugged, ruddy fellow who smelled of glue and had a leather back" (40). Content to fake an interest in the formidable Corneille as an adjunct to his role as the precocious child, it is only in the synopsis of the action at the end of the heavy volume that the boy finds genuine pleasure, and soon he is reveling in the plot summaries of plays and novels in the Larousse. This growing addiction to plot is compounded when his mother and grandmother conspire to introduce him to the literature of adventure in popular magazines, newspaper serials, and children's books as an antidote to the taxing seriousness of the grandfather's diet of classics. Poulou's clandestine indulgence in trash is an ecstatic exercise in alterity: "From my annihilation there immediately sprang up natives armed with spears, the bush, an explorer with a white helmet" (46). It is also an unconscious assimilation of the teleology of narrative, worked out in the relentless predictability of conventional plots: "I noted that the return to order was always accompanied by progress; the heroes were rewarded; they received honors, tokens of admiration, money; thanks to their dauntlessness, a territory had been conquered, a work of art had been protected from the natives and taken to our museums; the girl fell in love with the explorer who had saved her life; it all ended with a marriage" (47). Complementing his delight in the purposeful structures of reality in the literature of adventure is Poulou's love for the cowboys, musketeers, and detectives of the early cinema. Like M. Simonnot, these heroes are "expected" by the girl in danger, by the general, by the traitor lurking in the forest" (78), and the dangers they confront—"the accidents of the duel" which partake of "the rigor of the musical development"—are understood by the boy as "fake accidents which ill concealed the universal order" (78-79).

The vicissitudes of his fantasy life, however, manifest the ambiguities that living a life according to the specifications of fiction entails. Poulou discovers that a necessary corollary of his escapist practice of negative capability in his identification with the heroes of pulp and screen is the depressing experience of nothingness, of superfluity, that overtakes him once more after the end of the film or story. Thus it is that Sartre observes of his waking fantasies, "I remained a future hero and longed for a consecration which I continually postponed" (81). This complication of the ending is illustrated in his ritualized re-enactment of the exploits of his heroes in the darkened study to the strains of Chopin or Schumann from his mother at the piano. Imagining himself in the role of some

Byronic outcast, Poulou transfers to his own aimless existence the emplotted purpose of a hero's career:

> Sometimes I would skim through my life, I would skip two or three years to assure myself that all would end well, that the King would restore my titles, my lands, and a fiancée almost intact and that he would ask my forgiveness. But I would immediately jump back to my unhappy situation of two or three years earlier. That moment charmed me; fiction merged with truth. As a heartsore vagabond seeking justice, I resembled, like a twin brother, the child who was at loose ends, a burden to himself, in search of a reason for living, who prowled about, to a musical accompaniment, in his grandfather's study. Without dropping the role, I took advantage of the resemblance to amalgamate our destinies; reassured as to the final victory, I would regard my tribulations as the surest way to achieve it. I would see through my abjection to the future glory that was its true cause. (80-81)

Here, as so often in *The Words*, when both Poulou and Sartre rewrite their lives as fiction, there is a willed blurring of the boundaries between realms of experience: the "heartsore vagabond" of fantasy and the child "at loose ends" of memory are twins as long as the fantasy lasts. As fiction merges with truth, it becomes impossible to distinguish between the "my life" of the one and the "my unhappy situation" of the other. This blurring of boundaries between literature and life, this fictionalization of reality, is woven into the very texture of a consciousness devoted to the realization of fiction in fantasy. The conscious textuality of Poulou's daydreams of heroism, his skimming and skipping, is repeated in the daring deeds of his bedtime fantasies: major shifts in plot are achieved by "crossing out," and he always verbalizes the invariable anti-ending with the formula, " 'Continued in the next installment' " (73). No wonder, then, that Sartre recalls his instinct to defer the ending, for "the final victory," "the future glory"

(81) that confirms the necessity of the hero's existence, brings with it as well the child's return to despair over his own plotless and hence unnecessary life: "All my exploits, laid end to end, were only a string of random events." Repetition of the fiction of the hero never yields "an actual future" (82) for the boy.[17]

Nevertheless, Poulou's reading of Jules Verne's *Michael Strogoff* confirms his belief in the possibility of the destiny that eludes him in his practice of fantasy. "Justified as soon as he made his first appearance" (82), Strogoff's beginning is the antithesis of Sartre's. His secure possession of a future guarantees the integrity of his existence, preserving it from the blight of contingent reality, the random accidents and fruitless repetitions that poison the child's days. Poulou may envy Strogoff his destiny, yet his republican sympathies, heightened by his fascination with Pardaillan, the proletarian hero of Michel Zévaco's popular serial, repudiate the authoritarian origin of Strogoff's mission in the command of the czar: "I could neither produce from myself the imperative mandate that would have justified my presence on this earth, nor recognize anyone else's right to issue it to me" (84).

Sartre's division of *The Words* into two parts, "Reading" and "Writing," highlights the decisive shift in Poulou's development that opens an exit from this existential impasse. Turning author himself, the child begins to write his way out of his conflicted stance toward authority. To be sure, Poulou's first novels, *For a Butterfly* and *The Banana-seller*, represent a continuation of the fantasy life he pursued in "playing moving-

---

[17] In his autobiography, *Stop-time* (New York: Viking, 1967), Frank Conroy recalls a similar impression as a boy of eleven of life's formlessness: "I waited, more than anything else, waited for something momentous to happen. Keeping a firm grip on reality was of immense importance. My vision had to be clear so that when 'it' happened I would know. The momentous event would clear away the trivia and throw my life into proper perspective. As soon as it happened I would understand what was going on, and until then it was useless to try. (A spectacularly unsuccessful philosophy since nothing ever happened.)" (p. 19).

pictures" (87). Their content, shamelessly plagiarized from the literature of popular adventure, is equally derivative, and the boy's new posture as "the writer" is an extension of his inveterate family role as the child prodigy. Sartre's analysis of these early fictions, however, stresses a new complication in this latest practice of self-invention. The hero of these tales, like the hero of the movie fantasies, is still Poulou, but "he did not have my name, and I referred to him only in the third person": "I split myself in two" (91). In this way the child begins to experiment with a structure capable of mediating between his resistance to authority (this would be the role of the hero) and his need for it (this he would supply himself), becoming the *causa causans* of his own world.

If, as Sartre argues throughout the autobiography, he regarded words as "the quintessence of things" (87), Poulou's embrace of *poesis* is the logical consequence of his search for reality. Anticipating the privilege of the autobiographer, the boy-novelist contrives to be both agent and witness of his own birth:

> I was beginning to find myself. I was almost nothing, at most an activity without content, but that was all that was needed. I was escaping from play-acting. I was not yet working, but I had already stopped playing. The liar was finding his truth in the elaboration of his lies. I was born of writing. Before that, there was only a play of mirrors. With my first novel I knew that a child had got into the hall of mirrors. By writing I was existing, I was escaping from the grown-ups, but I existed only in order to write, and if I said "I," that meant "I who write." In any case, I knew joy.

In this remarkable passage Sartre shows the orphan in the act of becoming father to himself, consciously re-enacting the advent of reflexive consciousness and emergence of self that accompany the infant's decisive passage through the *stade du miroir*.[18] The acquisition of language and the formation of

---

[18] See Jacques Lacan, "The mirror stage as formative of the function of the

identity are inextricably linked. In this sense Sartre can imagine the lost "novels" of those early years as containing the autobiography he is in the process of writing: "If it had occurred to me to lock them up, they would reveal to me my entire childhood" (95).

Ironically, the child's destiny as a writer is confirmed by his grandfather's strategy to dissuade him from it. Having seen Verlaine enter a bar in 1894 " 'as drunk as a pig' " (96), the old man determines to provide the boy with a suitable alternative to the decadent self-destruction of the *poète maudit*. In a "man to man" talk with his grandson, Charles Schweitzer maps out a decorous bourgeois career in which Poulou would become a conventional schoolmaster like himself with genteel scholarly and literary interests to be dabbled in on the side. In Sartre's rendering, the culminating moment in its dreary desiccation achieves a perfection of the banal worthy of Flaubert: "Upon my death, unpublished works would be found among my papers, a meditation on the sea, a one-act comedy, a few sensitive and scholarly pages on the monuments of Aurillac, enough to fill a thin volume that would be edited by former pupils" (97). It is the very dullness of this vision of writing that persuades the boy of its verisimilitude to adult reality. Given a future, located in a culturally sanctioned plot, Poulou now has an answer to the riddle of identity, a ticket for the ticket-collector demanding his reason for existence. "Depicting real objects with real words that were penned with a real pen, I'd be hanged if I didn't become real myself!" (99). Sartre refers Poulou's decision to become a writer back to the circumstances of his orphan condition, arguing that the child heard in the grandfather's "man to man" advice about the literary vocation the accents of authority, the voice of "the absent father who had begotten me" (98).

It is only when the boy succeeds in transferring to the persona of the writer the glamor of the swashbuckling heroes of his reading that he can bring himself to embrace with enthu-

---

I," in *Écrits: A Selection*, trans. Alan Sheridan (London: Tavistock, 1977), pp. 1-7.

siasm the plodding security of his grandfather's bourgeois model
of the literary vocation. He would be "a writer-knight" (108),
"whose exploits would be real books" (106) which would speak
to the deepest needs of humanity. The Simonnot-like solidity
and necessity that the boy associates with the writer's identity
is captured in the shock of recognition he experiences when
he comes across a drawing of the crowds thronging the piers
of Manhattan to witness the arrival of Dickens: "There's
someone missing here. It's Dickens!" (105). When it comes to
substantiating the need upon which his own existence as the
"writer-knight" is predicated, however, Poulou is at a loss for
want of "hydras and dragons" (109). Stifled by the idea of a
future in which "he teaches Greek and describes the monuments of Aurillac in his spare time" (110), the boy reshapes
his new-found identity again, transforming the "writer-knight"
into the "writer-martyr." Drawing on his grandfather's hu-
manistic practice of literature as a surrogate religion, the child
translates the vexing obscurity of his grandfather's version of
the writer's life into the tribulations of a saint devoted to the
redemption of mankind through the creation of works of art.
The "filthy twaddle" of Charles Schweitzer's humanism provides the germ for his grandson's conception of the book as
the ideal model of identity, for if works of art really were
"metaphysical events, the birth of which affected the universe" (111), then they enjoyed that necessary existence the
orphan was seeking for himself.

All of Poulou's fantasy life, early and late, revolves around
the question of origins, and the central metaphor of birth and
beginning always refers back to his orphan condition. In his
earlier projections of the adventure paradigm the hero is characteristically a solitary figure, "a lonely adult, without father
and mother, without home or hearth, almost without a name"
(72-73), who requires the fathering need of the heroine-to-be-
rescued to generate the longed-for mandate to exist. Unpro-
vided with a generative story of his own, the child preys on
the plots of popular literature and film to narrativize and hence
justify his otherwise pointless living: "I would walk on a flam-

ing roof, carrying in my arms an unconscious woman" (73).
If Poulou plays the savior, it is because his own existential
salvation is at stake, and it is in this sense that he can say of
Charles Schweitzer's instrumentality in his decision to become a writer, "I was saved by my grandfather" (85). This
motif of the rescue is a prominent feature of the boy's fantasies, and Sartre assigns to it a decisive role in the child's discovery of the shape of his life at the age of eight, for he identifies a recurring anxiety dream about a little girl facing an
unknown danger as the source of his decision to become a
writer. Associating her with another girl who had died the
year before, Sartre writes: "in order to save that dead little
girl, I launched out upon a simple and mad operation that
shifted the course of my life: I palmed off on the writer the
sacred powers of the hero" (104). And so the orphan super-
man is supplanted by the equally solitary writer, and the effect is decidedly incongruous, as in Sartre's summary of the
new model fantasy in which the inevitable innocent in jeop-
ardy is rescued not by some daring physical exploit but metaphorically, by the writing of a book:

> During the period in which I was protecting female or-
> phans, I had already begun to get rid of them by sending
> them into hiding. As a writer, my manner did not change:
> before saving mankind, I would start by blindfolding it;
> only then would I turn against the black, swift little
> henchmen, against words; when my new orphan dared
> untie the blindfold, I would be far away. Saved by a lone
> deed, at first she would not notice, shining on a shelf in
> the National Library, the brand new little volume that
> bore my name. (112-13)

As in the earlier scenarios of adventure, the resourceful Poulou emplots his orphanhood by dividing himself in two, playing both savior and saved, father and child, cause and effect,
but with a difference. Now that the hero as author contains
by definition his own generative principle, the heroine becomes a figure of secondary importance; no immediate contact

between the two is required for the writer's solitary exercise of power to bear its fruit. In this way Poulou remakes the boring scholar of Aurillac fashioned by his grandfather into a veritable demiurge whose powers of language establish reality itself, transforming "idle heaps of whiteness" into "incorruptible substance, the *text*" (114).

In these ontological imaginings, to write is to begin, to originate, and in the child's creation myth the *telos* of the tale is now the text. In the days when he lacked the sense of a future that father and destiny could provide, he deliberately lingered *in medias res*, endlessly postponing the ending. Now, however, in his new cycle of daydreams about the writer as hero and saint, the body of the narrative interests him only insofar as it leads to the conclusion he securely anticipates. Faithful to his romantic notion that the writer's glory can be achieved only through suffering, Poulou fabricates the requisite difficulties by casting himself as the rejected artist, persecuted by a hostile public. It is the conclusion which absorbs him, and the boy shifts back and forth between two favorite alternatives. In one ending glory arrives too late, for he is already dying "on an iron cot," despised and alone. In the other, at the age of fifty he becomes an overnight success when his hitherto unpublished work is accidentally discovered and printed; secret witness to his fame, " 'Jean-Paul Sartre, the masked writer, the bard of Aurillac' " (118) prefers to maintain his incognito and disappears once more into obscurity. As far as Sartre is concerned, "the two dénouements come to the same thing: . . . the eagerness to write involves a refusal to live" (119).[19] In his exploration of this fundamental paradox posed by the inextricable linkage between death and glory,

---

[19] In Sartre's *Nausea*, trans. Lloyd Alexander (New York: New Directions, 1964), Antoine Roquentin comments in his diary, ". . . you have to choose: live or tell" (p. 39). Subsequent references are to this edition and will appear in the text. As we have seen in Chapter Two, Henry James makes of this choice one of the great themes of his autobiography. See Brombert, "Sartre et la Biographie Impossible," for a discussion of the metaphysical dimension of this dilemma, the choice between existence and being.

the autobiographer moves to the heart of his inquiry into the relation between narrative and experience in *The Words*.

Sartre provides a clue to the strangely end-focused, death-centered drift of these latest fables of birth and beginning when he notes the thematic continuity of Poulou's fantasy-life: "great writers are akin to knights-errant in that both elicit passionate signs of gratitude" (104). If this recognition from others is the *sine qua non* of the necessary self, in the child's fabulation the story of the obscure writer's belated achievement of fame posits delay as a precondition of success. Sartre identifies a prototype for this myth of the writer's life in Poulou's fascination at this time with an anecdote he read about a chance encounter in a wayside station in Siberia between an aging author and a beautiful countess who has admired his work. In Sartre's reconstruction of the child's interpretation, " 'The Countess was death' ": when she kisses the writer, he dies into glory, for he is no longer a man; "all that was left of him was the list of his works in flaming letters" (120). Henceforward, death itself plays the role of the damsel-in-distress in the dramatic economy of Poulou's existential romances. So closely linked are death and glory that the child instinctively interprets the relation as one of cause and effect. Thus, when Sartre goes back "to the origins" of his life as a writer, he concludes, "it was death that I was seeking" (121).

Paradoxically, the death he earlier feared as a confirmation of his nothingness he now prizes as the source of a transcendent identity, as rebirth into a non-contingent existence as a text. In a startling inversion of the Incarnation, the Word made flesh, the child proposes to himself nothing less than to "appear to the Holy Ghost as a precipitate of language," the flesh made word. In this bold conception of the literary vocation as an *imitatio dei*, writing becomes the medium of Poulou's "transfiguration," a second birth in which he exchanges the spirit for the letter, the soul for the body, his mortal flesh for a "glorious body in words." The author's lifework is himself, his identity the fruit of a proto-autobiographical act in which the contingency of the self, the subject of indeterminate origins, is redeemed by its transmutation into the necessity of matter, becoming "a pure object":

> Around 1955, a larva would burst open, twenty-five folio butterflies would emerge from it, flapping all their pages, and would go and alight on a shelf of the National Library. Those butterflies would be none other than I: I, twenty-five volumes, eighteen thousand pages of text, three hundred engravings, including a portrait of the author. My bones are made of leather and cardboard, my parchment-skinned flesh smells of glue and mushrooms, I sit in state through a hundred thirty pounds of paper, thoroughly at ease. I am reborn, I at last become a whole man, thinking, talking, singing, thundering, a man who asserts himself with the peremptory inertia of matter. (121)

"Around 1955," moreover, Jean-Paul Sartre began to write his autobiography.

Poulou discovers in a book of biographies for children, *The Childhood of Famous Men*, the prototype for the book of his own life. From Sartre's account of it, this little volume with its edifying message that "good conduct and filial piety lead to everything, even to becoming Rembrandt or Mozart," sounds very much like the Algeresque literature of self-help that was a staple of children's reading in the United States of this period:

> The author recounted, in the form of short narratives, the very ordinary occupations of no less ordinary but sensitive and pious boys who were called Johann-Sebastian, Jean-Jacques or Jean-Baptiste and who gave joy to their families as I did to mine. But the poison was this: without ever mentioning the name of Bach, Rousseau, or Molière, the author made a point of constantly inserting allusions to their future greatness, of recalling casually, by means of a detail, their most famous works or deeds, of contriving his accounts so artfully that it was impossible to understand the most trivial incident without re-

lating it to subsequent events. He introduced into the tumult of everyday life a great, fabulous silence which transfigured everything: the future. (127)

Replacing chance with destiny, the emplotted life manifests the true identity of the individual as a principle of historical necessity. The child intuitively realizes that to look at the past "through future eyes" (124) is to understand "the end . . . as the truth of the beginning" (125), and so he can say of these biographies, "I read the lives of those falsely mediocre children as God had conceived them: starting at the end" (127). When his infatuation with this book with its appropriately "corpselike smell" (126) gives way to deliberate imitation, however, when he chooses as his own future "the past of a great immortal" and attempts "to live backwards" (124) in the manner of his reading, he finds the hoped-for significant existence eludes his conscious grasp:

> I would find myself on the other side of the page, *inside the book*: Jean-Paul's childhood resembled that of Jean-Jacques and of Johann-Sebastian, and nothing happened to him that was not broadly premonitory. But this time it was at my grandnephews that the author was winking. *I* was being seen, from death to birth, by those future children whom I did not imagine, and I was sending them messages which to me were undecipherable. I shuddered, paralyzed by my death, which was the true meaning of all my gestures. (128)

Ironically, Poulou's efforts to enact the myth of the childhood of the great man only heighten his sense of alienation. Purchasing a future at the price of the present, his project founders on the ineluctable disjunction between being and knowing, and he finds his quest for an ending slipping back toward the insincerity of the old world of play-acting and illusion he sought to escape. "A little faker" once more, Poulou great-author-to-be shams for his alter-ego, "a light-haired little boy of the thirtieth century who was . . . observing me through a book":

I concocted double-edged remarks which I let fall in public. Anne Marie would find me at my desk, scribbling away. She would say: "It's so dark! My little darling is ruining his eyes." It was an opportunity to reply in all innocence: "I could write even in the dark." She would laugh, would call me her little silly, would put on the light; the trick was done; we were both unaware that I had just informed the year 3,000 of my future infirmity [his blindness]. . . . My mother had left the room, I was alone, I repeated to myself, slowly, above all without thinking about it: "In the dark!" There was a sharp crack: my great-grand-nephew, out there, had shut his book; he was dreaming about the childhood of his great-grand-uncle, and tears were rolling down his cheeks. "Nevertheless, it's true," he would sigh, "he wrote in the dark!" (128-29)

As before, the upshot of these literary exercises is a disheartening sense of failure; Poulou's ambition to "write" his life according to the specification of his chosen narrative never yields self-discovery: "I was always before or after the impossible vision that would have revealed me to myself" (130).[20] As reader, as the writer, as the great-man-as-child, the boy is doomed to perpetuate his inauthenticity by his struggle to free himself from it. There is no exit from the ontological trap of childhood in *The Words*.

When Poulou proposes to perform his own biography by appropriating the past he will eventually have to serve as the

[20] In "Un rapport illisible: *Coeur des ténèbres*," trans. Vincent Giroud, *Poétique*, No. 44 (1980), Peter Brooks give a nice formulation of the elusiveness of self-knowledge in autobiographical narrative: "La logique du récit autobiographique ne reçoit jamais la connaissance de cette fin qui pourrait lui donner une finalité et un sens. Toute la connaissance qu'on en peut avoir est toujours prise dans un processus de suspens et de retard, si bien qu'elle arrive trop tard. Marlow, en tant que successeur attardé de Kurtz le précurseur, vient trop tard, et le conte implique que tel est toujours le sort de celui qui cherche à connaître plutôt que de vivre la fin. Les dénouements sont introuvables— ou peut-être ne sont plus trouvables" (483).

model for his future, he embarks on a peculiar program which illustrates the elusiveness of self-knowledge experienced by any practicing autobiographer. Sartre identifies the child's determination "to live backwards" (124) as "a state of retrospective illusion" which destroys the temporal structure of experiential reality: "An old defunct is dead by nature; he is dead at the time of baptism, neither more nor less than at the time of extreme unction; his life belongs to us; we enter it at either end or in the middle; we go up and down the course of it at will. . . . His existence has the appearance of an unfolding, but as soon as we try to restore a bit of life to it, it relapses into simultaneity" (125). Commenting on Moritz Heimann's observation that "a man who dies at the age of thirty-five is at every point of his life a man who dies at the age of thirty-five," Walter Benjamin confirms the truth of Sartre's meditation on the discontinuity between the underlying synchrony of retrospect and its narrative structures, on the one hand, and the diachronic unfolding of life in time, on the other: "Nothing is more dubious than this sentence [of Heimann's]—but for the sole reason that the tense is wrong. A man—so says the truth that was meant here—who died at thirty-five will appear to *remembrance* at every point in his life as a man who dies at the age of thirty-five. In other words, the statement that makes no sense for real life becomes indisputable for remembered life. The nature of the character in a novel cannot be presented any better than is done in this statement, which says that the 'meaning' of his life is revealed only in his death."[21] In this view, the "I" of autobiographical discourse, with its double reference to the self of the present and the self of any moment from the past, is by definition a split or discontinuous personality. How is it possible, then, to achieve the knowledge of identity and of the significance of a life that constitutes autobiography's *raison d'être*, when death

[21] "The Storyteller," in *Illuminations*, trans. Harry Zohn (New York: Harcourt, 1968), pp. 100-101. Peter Brooks directed my attention to this fine essay in his study of Conrad (see note 20).

and the meaning it alone confers lie beyond the pale of existence in time? The logic of such reflections leads both the child (intuitively) and the autobiographer (by design) to a posture of proleptic death; Sartre speaks for both (literally and figuratively) when he observes of the child's "posthumous" vantage point toward reality: "I became my own obituary" (129). Any autobiographer, like Sartre's Poulou and Tolstoi's Ivan Ilych, is devoted to "living backwards" from death in the pursuit of the meaning of a life.[22] "In my end is my beginning."

### III. "THE RETROSPECTIVE ILLUSION
### HAS BEEN SMASHED TO BITS"

There are a good many autobiographies of lives devoted to mistaken beliefs, and these are almost invariably written from the perspective of some subsequently discovered truth. Narratives of religious conversion—from the *Confessions* of Saint Augustine to *The Autobiography of Malcolm X*—with their two-part, before-after schemes of revelation offer the clearest and most numerous examples of this model of life history. Sartre's *The Words* is one of the comparatively rare instances of an autobiography that inverts this pattern, moving as it does from the discovery of belief to the eventual loss of conviction *without* at the same time affirming an alternative vision of the truth.[23] Having reconstructed in elaborate detail the psychological and cultural circumstances that lead Poulou in his ninth year to find salvation in his grandfather's faith in literature as an absolute, Sartre proceeds to relate his repudiation a generation later on of the nineteenth-century religion of secular humanism that structured his mature identity and adult career. According to Sartre, the radical nature of this experience of deconversion, which motivates the writing of the autobiography,

[22] Two essays that have deepened my own understanding of death as the great primary source of life's meaning are James Olney's "Experience, Metaphor, and Meaning: 'The Death of Ivan Ilych,' " *Journal of Aesthetics and Art Criticism*, 31 (1972), 101-14, and Benjamin's "The Storyteller."

[23] Cf. Lejeune, *Le pacte*, p. 206.

accounts for the polemical cast of the first version of *The Words* composed in 1954, the intemperance of its indictment of bourgeois values, and the violence of its self-condemnation. In his revision of the manuscript in 1963, the autobiographer sought a more balanced portrait of his childhood: "If I didn't publish this autobiography sooner and in its most radical version, it's because I judged it to be excessive. There's no reason to drag an unfortunate through the mud simply because he writes."[24]

Sartre's analysis of the shape and shaping of his life takes the form of the case history of an illness in which the cherished myth of the writer as hero and saint is the principal symptom. To be sure, the paralyzing self-consciousness of the nine-year-old's obsession with *The Childhood of Great Men* is followed by what Sartre recalls as the happiest period of his childhood, two years in which he finally forgets about his writing and his mandate, losing himself in absorbing friendships with Paul Yves Nizan, Norbert Meyre, and other classmates at the Lycée Henri IV: "We played ball between the Hotel of Great Men and the statue of Jean Jacques Rousseau; I no longer envied M. Simonnot. To whom would Meyre have tossed the ball after making a feint at Grégoire if I hadn't been present, *I, then and there?*" (139). Sartre argues, however, that the apparent resolution of the child's existential identity crisis, his passage from a morbid and reclusive inwardness to the healthy give-and-take of normal life with other boys his age, actually masks the onset of a "neurosis" (Sartre's term) that was to last for more than thirty years. His thesis is that "between the summer of 1914 and the autumn of 1916" (144) Poulou, ostensibly "cured" (130) of his literary malady, "had gone completely mad" (131). That is to say that during these years the boy wholly internalized the fantasy of a literary mandate for his existence. No longer consciously dreaming of female orphans, gallant knights, and the rest of the hero-mar-

---

[24] "Jean-Paul Sartre s'explique sur *Les Mots*," *Le Monde*, 18 avril 1964, p. 13 (my trans.). "Si je n'ai pas publié cette autobiographie plus tôt et dans sa forme la plus radicale, c'est que je la jugeais excessive. Il n'y a pas de raison de traîner un malheureux dans la boue parce qu'il écrit."

tyr-saint baggage, "living backwards" into greatness and glory became second nature to him: "my mandate became my character; my delirium left my head and flowed into my bones" (144).

The most striking consequence of this latest phase of Poulou's development is the pervasive transformation of his existence into narrative. In a game he plays with his mother, for example, they relate the most trivial incidents of their lives to each other in "an epic style," referring to themselves in the third person: "We would be waiting for a bus; it would go by without stopping; one of us would then cry out: 'They stamped their feet and called down curses,' and we would burst out laughing" (136-37). As the boy moves from narrative as a mode of cognition in the self-conscious plots of his fantasies to narrative as a mode of perception in the unfolding of his daily life, his behavior, as recreated by Sartre, enacts *in his present* that "teleologically guided form of attention" that Gallie postulates as the central dynamic of historical understanding of the past. In this way the most banal episodes of his quotidian existence become charged with the significance that retrospective emplotment alone—or so it would seem—is privileged to confer. For Poulou, age ten, to kill time in a china shop while his grandmother hunts for plates is really to kill time, for despite the appearance of being only a "minor character" "relegated to a corner," narrative conditioning teaches the boy that he is really "the hero of a long story that ended happily." His grandmother, the china shop, and the rest of reality are eclipsed in a spectacular Sartrean epiphany of narrative consciousness in which the self witnesses the alpha and the omega of its own identity and existence:

> . . . I was the beginning, middle, and end gathered together in a tiny little boy already old, already dead, *here*, in the shadow, among piles of plates taller than he, and *outside*, far far away, in the great dismal sun of glory. . . . Boxed in, pulled together, touching my tomb with one hand and my cradle with the other, I felt brief and splen-

did, a flash of lightning that was blotted out by darkness. (152-53)

From the "posthumous" perspective of the child, experiential reality becomes indistinguishable from its reflection in narrative form. Such a moment, at once in and out of time, "*here*" and "*outside*," offers a model of perfect autobiographical truth, in which life and life story are one and the same.

One of the consequences of this narrative state of mind is the boy's failure to share the anxiety of his peers about dying. So deeply ingrained is the sense of ending required by the story of the writer's death and glory that the boy instinctively believes that he enjoys a "providential guarantee" (124) against an accidental or premature death; Poulou is, after all, under contract with the Holy Ghost to perform his life for the purpose of narrative. The sober logic of the boy's literary mission yields a singularly austere form of the familiar interdependency of life and art that was a commonplace of Romantic organicism (as in the presentation to Walt Whitman on his deathbed of the final and inevitable "Deathbed Edition" of *Leaves of Grass*): "I was going quietly to my end, having no hopes or desires other than what was needed to fill my books, certain that the last burst of my heart would be inscribed on the last page of the last volume of my works, and that death would be taking only a dead man" (123-24).[25] In this way, vampire fashion, the boy's ultimate identity as immortal text is sustained.

According to Sartre, the boy's false view of his literary vocation governed his adult life for more than thirty years, and in this sense the question of the incompleteness of the auto-

---

[25] Anticipating the imminent publication of his novels in the Pléiade series of classic literature, Sartre commented in an interview in 1975: "it is true that I am eager to see this Pléiade published. I think the feeling comes from my childhood, in which fame consisted of being published in a large, carefully prepared edition that people would discuss." He went on to acknowledge that his appearance in the Pléiade represented a "closing" of his work. In *Life/Situations: Essays Written and Spoken*, trans. Paul Auster and Lydia Davis (New York: Pantheon, 1977), p. 73.

biography may be set aside as irrelevent, since the autobiographer has identified to his own satisfaction the nature and origin of the structuring principle of his life history.[26] Given the limitations of life in time, it is impossible to test the truth of autobiographical retrospect against the biographical reality of the past as it was lived. Nevertheless, a comparison between *The Words* (1964) and Sartre's first and finest novel, *Nausea* (1938), offers some measure of the verisimilitude of his thesis about his literary neurosis. To begin with, the plot structure of each of these first-person narratives displays the aetiology of an illness. *Nausea* takes the form of a pseudo-autobiographical narrative in which Antoine Roquentin, the narrator and principal figure, confronts the apparent pointlessness of his existence. Haunted, like Poulou, by a sense of being *de trop*, Roquentin dreams of an alternative, justified existence as the necessary hero of an "adventure." Adventures, as Roquentin defines them, would redeem the plotless flux of temporal existence, in which there are neither beginnings nor ends ("nothing happens while you live" [39]), by endowing it with the permanence and order of the forms of art. The counterpart of Poulou's obsession with *The Childhood of Famous Men* as the ideal prototype for the emplotted life of the justified self is Roquentin's preoccupation with the recording of the song, "Some of these days," which exemplifies a possible alternative to the contingency of the human condition: "behind the existence which falls from one present to the other, without a past, without a future, behind these sounds which decompose from day to day, peel off and slip towards death, the melody stays the same, young and firm, like a pitiless witness" (176).

Thus Roquentin, who has never had any adventures, shares the boy's ambition to turn his existence into narrative, "to rid the passing moments of their fat, . . . twist them, dry them, purify myself, harden myself, to give back at last the sharp,

---

[26] For an instructive comparison between Sartre's autobiographical account of his life history and the known facts of his biography, especially for his omission of two key events, the remarriage of his mother and the discovery of his own ugliness, see Lejeune, *Le pacte*, pp. 204-206, 220-21.

precise sound of a saxophone note" (175). "I wanted the moments of my life," he writes, "to follow and order themselves like those of a life remembered" (40). The dynamic of the emplotted life or adventure is the same for both: what the autobiographer identified as a process of "living backwards" finds its parallel in Roquentin's argument that in an adventure, "the story goes on in the reverse"; only the invisible, transforming presence of the end can endow life or words with "the pomp and value of a beginning" (40). However, like the Sartre of *The Words*, Roquentin understands man's making of fictions as a deliberate practice of self-deception designed to insulate him from the terrifying recognition (experienced as *nausea*) of the incomprehensible reality of existence: "This is what fools people: a man is always a teller of tales, he lives surrounded by his stories and the stories of others, he sees everything that happens to him through them; and he tries to live his own life as if he were telling a story" (39). The conclusion of *Nausea* resembles the conclusion of *The Words* in its concern with the death of an illusion upon which a man's life has been founded. Toward the last, having abandoned his biography of the Marquis de Rollebon and with it history itself (and by implication the journal form in which he records this progressive abandonment), Roquentin observes, "Now when I say 'I,' it seems hollow to me. . . . the 'I' pales, pales, and fades out" (170). With the extinction of his former identity and chosen story, Roquentin can say, "I am going to outlive myself" (157); he faces a posthumous existence in a total present unshielded by comforting fictions of self, future, and past, an existence in which consciousness continues to bubble up gratuitously from moment to moment like gas.

If the Roquentin of the adventures resembles Poulou in the grips of his neurosis, the Roquentin who deconstructs them as illusions resembles the autobiographer composing *The Words*. Is it not the case, then, that already, in this early work, Sartre hardly shows himself to have been the victim of illusion that he says he was in *The Words*? The difference between the autobiographer of *The Words* and the disillusioned Roquentin of *Nausea* is that the latter, younger persona of Sartre still retains one final illusion, a vestigial belief in the possibility of creating a textual identity that could justify his existence "just a little" (177). So he dreams at the last, as he listens yet once more to "Some of these days," of writing a book "which would be above existence," "beautiful and hard as steel" (178). With surgical precision the Sartre of *The Words* lays bare the sustaining illusion of the disillusioned author of *Nausea*, the belief that his calling as a writer exempts him from the very limitations of the human condition it is his mission to proclaim:

> I *was* Roquentin; I used him to show, without complacency, the texture of my life. At the same time, I was *I*, the elect, chronicler of Hell, a glass and steel photomicroscope peering at my own protoplasmic juices. Later, I gaily demonstrated that man is impossible; I was impossible myself and differed from the others only by the mandate to give expression to that impossibility, which was thereby transfigured and became my most personal possibility, the object of my mission, the springboard of my glory. (158)

The parallels between *Nausea* and *The Words* are extremely suggestive from a biographical point of view, for they seem to corroborate the autobiographer's thesis about his neurosis; they cannot prove it, however, since the Poulou of *The Words*, for all his likeness to Roquentin (and to his author?), is, we must remember, the creation of the Sartres of 1954 and 1963. The thematic continuities of the two works can do no more than suggest the plausibility of Sartre's self-analysis.[27]

In any case, following the logic of his thesis, which postulates the neurosis of the boy of nine as the determining constant of the character of the man he became for thirty years, Sartre omits from *The Words* any detailed account of his life

---

[27] For discussion of the parallels between Roquentin and Poulou see Mehlman, pp. 155-63 passim. See Brombert on Roquentin "[qui] découvre l'impossibilité de 'se raconter' " (158).

beyond the end of his childhood. Skipping over his adult years, he presents himself at the last as "a man who's been waking up, cured of a long, bitter-sweet madness." Sartre's recovery entails at the same time the abandonment of the life-sustaining plot of his mission as a writer, for "the retrospective illusion has been smashed to bits" (158). In order to begin, the child had had to choose an ending, and with the end of this ending at the end of *The Words* the autobiographer can only return to the beginning to begin again, this time without an end in sight:

> I've again become the traveler without a ticket that I was at the age of seven: the ticket-collector has entered my compartment; he looks at me, less severely than in the past; in fact, all he wants is to go away, to let me finish the trip in peace; he'll be satisfied with a valid excuse, any excuse. Unfortunately I can't think of any; and besides, I don't even feel like trying to find one. We remain there looking at each other, feeling uncomfortable, until the train gets to Dijon where I know very well that no one is waiting for me. (159)

And so the autobiographer resumes the burden of his orphanhood once more, the plotless existence of those who are not "expected" by female orphans or by the world. It is altogether appropriate that the narrative of *The Words* should terminate following Sartre's disconfirmation of the narrative principle of his life history. The autobiographer has, as it were, outlived the possibility of his autobiography.[28]

In *The Words* Sartre takes his recovery largely for granted, devoting himself instead to an investigation of the reasons for his illness. As he put it much later on, "I felt a strong urge . . . to try and find out what could have made a nine-year-

[28] The case of Malcolm X offers a parallel instance of the autobiographer as witness to the obsolescence of his autobiography. See Paul John Eakin, "Malcolm X and the Limits of Autobiography," *Criticism*, 18 (1976), 230-42; rpt. in *Autobiography: Essays Theoretical and Critical*, ed. James Olney (Princeton: Princeton Univ. Press, 1980), pp. 181-93.

old boy slip into that 'neurosis of literature,' whereas other boys my age were normal."[29] Sartre's diagnosis of the boy's case opens up the fundamental issue of the origin and function of narrative in autobiography, especialy if we follow Sartre in thinking of narrative as a manifestation of self-definition in terms of plot: Simonnot, Dickens, and the heroes of movies and adventure stories are who they are because they are "expected"; their presence is required by the unfolding of Destiny (plot as a cosmic force). It may help to clarify this concept of emplotted identity if we understand plot, as Peter Brooks suggests we should, "less as a structure than as a structuring operation, used, or made necessary, by those meanings that develop only through sequence and succession: an interpretative operation specific to narrative signification."[30] By their plots ye shall know them, we might almost say, and in this sense the presence of chronological narrative in autobiography, far from representing the slavish adherence to the conventions of biography and the traditional novel that John Sturrock and Philippe Lejeune contend, is properly understood as a reflection of the inescapable narrativity of the process of self-definition in both the living of a life and the making of a life story. Before addressing the arguments of Sturrock and Lejeune against chronological narrative in autobiography, we may begin by reviewing Sartre's account of the sources, both psychological and cultural, of the plot he adopted for his life first as a child and later as an autobiographer.

It would, of course, be easy to set aside the testimony of Sartre's experience as altogether too abnormal to be considered representative of the problems that an autobiographer faces in attempting to render the content of a life history in

---

[29] *Sartre by Himself: A Film Directed by Alexandre Astruc and Michel Contat*, trans. Richard Seaver (New York: Urizen, 1978), p. 88.

[30] "Repetition, Repression, and Return: *Great Expectations* and the Study of Plot," *New Literary History*, 11 (1979-1980), 503. Brooks is probably the foremost student of plot at the present time. I shall be referring to several of his recent essays as I go along; his work has helped to clarify and confirm my own research on narrative in autobiography.

narrative form. Sartre's identification of his devotion to literature as a neurosis provides a precedent for such a position,
and Paul de Man, for one, has been willing to take him up on
it, judging *The Words* to be "an act of self-therapy which, as
such, does not belong to literature."[31] As we have seen, Sartre
himself attributes Poulou's sense of plotlessness to the deprivation of his orphan condition. In his reading, the instability
of the child's identity, his search for and his resistance to authority, is to be traced to his father's "early retirement" which
leaves him with "a most incomplete 'Oedipus complex' " (16).
Taking Sartre's interpretation as a point of departure, Douglas Collins offers the portrait of Poulou in *The Words* as a text-
book illustration of the "positive narcissist" identified by the
clinician Béla Grunberger. The absence of an oedipal conflict,
the hostility to the presence of foreign forces in the psyche,
and the concomitant view of the self as self-created are
the characteristic attributes of this variety of narcissistic
personality: "Because the child is either ignorant or willfully
oblivious of his father's determining role in the fact of his
existence, and because he is aware of an exclusive and over-
poweringly positive focus on his person, he sees himself as
divine and miraculous." Such a child easily imagines himself
to be a hero and requires an illusion of being indispensable to
others. The positive narcissist, moreover, like Sartre as autobiographer, has an ambiguous attitude toward his childhood:
"He is proud of his past because it is responsible for the fact
that he is divine, but he is ashamed because he detests the
notion of affiliation and finds it humiliating to be dependent
upon others for love and valorization."[32] As Sartre puts it, he
always preferred "to derive only from myself" (147). Collins's
hypothesis about the nature of Sartre's personality does provide a plausible explanation for the behavior of both Poulou
as a child and Sartre as an autobiographer. The point here,
however, is not to debate the validity of this analysis but to

[31] De Man, p. 13.
[32] Collins, pp. 189, 191.

suggest the extent to which Sartre's concepts of plot and identity may have been idiosyncratically determined.[33]

At the same time, however, Sartre's anatomy of Poulou uncovers a pattern of behavior that squares with other recent speculations about human conduct in general, and so his personal experience, for all its apparent eccentricity, may have a larger bearing on the relation between narrative and experience in autobiography than psychobiographical readings of Sartre's personality usually suggest. Poulou's childhood, strange as it is in its cerebral blend of neurotic brooding and literary fantasy, may nevertheless be truer to "the way things happen in actual experience" than most of the commentators have been willing to accept. As we have seen in Chapter One, Erik Erikson interprets man's emplotment of himself as the central figure in his life story as a defensive strategy designed to ward off his ego-chilling awareness that "nonexistence . . . is en-

---

[33] Commenting on Sartre's self-proclaimed "neurosis," Francis Jeanson wisely observes that "Sartre has never been greatly exercised about his own personal case, and it's much rather a question of a social neurosis that he has expressly undertaken to cure himself of." *Sartre dans sa vie* (Paris: Seuil, 1974), p. 20 (my trans.). See also pp. 25-41 for a sensitive and judicious psychological interpretation of the relation between the autobiography and the childhood it purports to record, especially his identification of *autocontestation* as a repeated behavioral pattern in Sartre's life history (pp. 20, 36-37). A. James Arnold and Jean-Pierre Piriou, in their monograph *Genèse et critique d'une autobiographie: Les Mots de Jean-Paul Sartre* (Paris: Archives des Lettres Modernes, No. 144, 1973), detect the profile of a sado-masochistic personality in the autobiography. Probing Sartre's preoccupation with the story of Griselda in *The Words*, they see in it a reflection of Poulou's incestuous identification with his mother, Anne-Marie. Sartre's curious attribution of sadism to the figure of the proverbial victim in the tale would be a manifestation of the child's fantasy of punishing the absent father, hated as the origin of the orphan's seemingly illegitimate condition (pp. 45-56 passim). Édouard Morot-Sir argues that the term "neurosis," which seems to him excessive as applied to Poulou's childhood, more aptly describes the psychological crisis of 1952-1953 in which Sartre became obsessed with his false identity as *fils de petits bourgeois*. Thus Morot-Sir interprets the writing of *The Words* as an attempt on the part of the fifty-year-old autobiographer to find himself by taking the lost child he had been for a guide. *Les Mots de Jean-Paul Sartre* (Paris: Hachette, 1975), pp. 19-20.

tirely possible."[34] Poulou's death-focused anxiety about his apparently ticket-less condition and his subsequent refuge in the shelter of a fathering fiction would be merely a special, perhaps extreme, instance of the Eriksonian thesis about the origins of the human quest for identity. In *The Sense of an Ending* Frank Kermode argues, in effect, that we are all orphans, living as we do "in the middest," equally removed from knowledge of our birth and our eventual death. "The retrospective illusion" of Poulou's teleological obsession which leads him to live his present "backwards" in terms of his chosen ending offers an exemplary illustration of the eschatological grounding of all human fiction-making in Kermode's view, the perennial attempt to bring closure and hence significance to the otherwise meaningless flux of human experience. As Sartre, Kermode, and Poe before them suggest, we write and we live with the end constantly in view.[35] Needless to say, Sartre's condemnation of his emplotted life and literary identity as a sickness challenges the very existence of autobiography, which depends on the possibility of negotiating some link between experience and narrative. It takes no stretch of the imagination to recognize that the autobiographical act itself could be guilty of "the retrospective illusion" that *The Words* is dedicated to smashing. Does the child's doomed project to perform his life as a narrative prefigure the hopelessness of the autobiographer's attempt—Sartre's or anyone's—to write the story of his life?

For Sartre, at any rate, the sources of "the retrospective illusion" upon which his identity and career were founded are as much social and historical as they are private and psycho-

[34] *Young Man Luther: A Study in Psychoanalysis and History* (1958; rpt. New York: Norton, 1962), p. 111.

[35] See Frank Kermode, *The Sense of an Ending: Studies in the Theory of Fiction* (New York: Oxford Univ. Press, 1968); Poe, "The Philosophy of Composition," and "Hawthorne's *Twice-Told Tales*" in *Literary Criticism of Edgar Allan Poe*, ed. Robert L. Hough (Lincoln: Univ. of Nebraska Press, 1965), pp. 20, 136; and Paul John Eakin, "Poe's Sense of an Ending," *American Literature*, 45 (1973), 1-22.

logical. When Poulou chooses as his future "the past of a great immortal" (124), he does so largely in response to a cultural fiction. *The Childhood of Famous Men* and its poisonous doctrine that "it was impossible to understand the most trivial incident without relating it to subsequent events" (127) infect the child with the nineteenth-century myth of progress. Grandfather Schweitzer and his library may be the repository for such a misguided belief, but as far as Sartre is concerned, the old man is no more to blame for it than his grandson; both are equally the victims of a "mirage . . . born spontaneously of culture." "The retrospective illusion" that governs the boy's fantasies was, Sartre believes, the muse of nineteenth-century history as well. Under its aegis, the causation and necessity that seem to structure events are retroactively imposed on the past, an "error of perspective" which Sartre illustrates as follows: "In the drawing-rooms of Arras, a cold, simpering young lawyer is carrying his head under his arm because he is the late Robespierre; blood is dripping from it but does not stain the rug; not one of the guests notices it, whereas we see nothing else; five years will go by before it rolls into the basket, yet there it is, cut off, uttering gallant remarks despite its hanging jaw" (125). The errors of history and biography show as the fruit of a cultural illusion, which Sartre reads as a response to "the slow movement of dechristianization that started among the Voltairian upper bourgeoisie and took a century to spread to all levels of society" (61). In this sense *The Words* records a pivotal moment in the secularization of Western culture: Sartre's life enacts, and his autobiography indicts, the pervasive function of nineteenth-century historicism as a surrogate religion. The lesson of *The Words* is the loss of narrative salvation; teleological history is dead.

In his seminal essay, "Fictions of the Wolfman: Freud and Narrative Understanding," Peter Brooks confirms Sartre's reading of cultural history, arguing that the "new importance" of "the life-history of societies, institutions, and individuals" in the post-Enlightenment West is a consequence of "the decline in belief in a sacred masterplot," "in a Providential history which subsumed all the errant individual human histories to some justified, if distant, end." This shift is manifested in the pronounced "narrativization of explanation" in nineteenth-century thought; whether it be history or detective story, "the authority of narrative derives from its capacity to speak of origins in relation to endpoints." Brooks concludes that the recourse to plot is inevitable in an uncertain, secular universe, for "telling the self's story remains the indispensable thread in the labyrinth of unauthored temporality."[36] The cultural context described by Sartre and Brooks helps to account for the rapid emergence of autobiography as a prominent literary genre in the nineteenth century. Thus Karl J. Weintraub argues that "autobiography assumes a significant cultural function around A.D. 1800," and he links this phenomenon to Western Man's adoption of the twin concepts of historicism and individuality. Autobiography became "the literary form in which an individuality could best account for itself," for "the only way to account for a specific person was to tell its story."[37] Similarly, Burton Pike suggests that in a post-Newtonian, mechanistic universe, with its burden of unredeemed temporal linearity, "History" came to serve the nineteenth-century autobiographer as "a cultural divinity," providing him with "an ideal external support for his individual problems with time and identity."[38]

With the rejection of the implicit teleology of the traditional

---

[36] Brooks, "Fictions of the Wolfman," *Diacritics*, 9 (1979), 74, 77, 81.

[37] "Autobiography and Historical Consciousness," *Critical Inquiry*, 1 (1975), 821, 847. See also his book-length treatment of these issues in *The Value of the Individual: Self and Circumstance in Autobiography* (Chicago: Univ. of Chicago Press, 1978). In *L'autobiographie en France* (Paris: A. Colin, 1971), Philippe Lejeune confirms Weintraub's assessment of the factors contributing to the rise of autobiography: "Si, après 1780, l'exemple de Rousseau a suscité tant de vocations, c'est que le terrain était propice, la plupart des esprits mûrs pour cette entreprise. Cette éclosion des différentes formes de la littérature intime, comme le préromantisme en général, est liée à la transformation de la notion de *personne*. C'est à cette époque qu'on commence à prendre conscience de la valeur et de la singularité de l'expérience que chacun a de lui-même. On s'aperçoit aussi que l'individu a une histoire, qu'il n'est pas né adulte. Cette découverte de l'historicité au sein même de la personnalité . . ." (p. 64).

[38] Pike, "Time in Autobiography," *Comparative Literature*, 28 (1976), 330.

chronological narrative as a false model of biographical explanation, autobiography has certainly reached a turning-point in its history. Philippe Lejeune and John Sturrock, however, do not read this subversion of chronological order in autobiography as a sign of terminal illness but rather of its renewed vitality. Lejeune suggests that the most cursory examination of the order of events supplied by memory will suffice to demonstrate that chronological order can hardly be said to be a "natural" representation of human experience. Yet most autobiographers have been content to accept it as such, preferring to conceptualize their uniqueness in terms of style or content rather than in terms of narrative structure. Only Sartre and Michel Leiris, he believes, among modern autobiographers, have invented new narrative structures and, in so doing, new models for the description and explanation of man. Lejeune's thesis is that the true narrative structure of *The Words* is that of an argument in dialectical philosophy; the rigorous unfolding of its logic is disguised as narrative through Sartre's skillful use of a chronological vocabulary. If *The Words* offers an Existentialist fable of man's free choice of his destiny, then his invention of his future can be said to constitute time itself, supplanting the deterministic causality implied by chronological order, the illusory logic of *post hoc, ergo propter hoc*.[39]

Lejeune takes great pains to demonstrate that Sartre violates calendar chronology in his account of his childhood. The effect of Sartre's presentation is synchronic, he suggests; the before-after schema implied by the two-part division of the text into a "Reading" phase followed by a "Writing" one is misleading since the two periods largely overlap in actual dat-

---

[39] Lejeune, *Le pacte*, pp. 198, 202, 204, 237-38. In Lejeune's discussion of form in autobiography it is not altogether clear whether he is proposing an alternative to chronological narrative or to narrative period. Complementing Lejeune's view that the narrative structure of *The Words* refers not to the chronological history of an individual but to the dialectical argument of Sartre's philosophical writings is Jose Huertas-Jourda's "The Place of *Les Mots* in Sartre's Philosophy," *Review of Metaphysics*, 21 (1967-1968), 724-44.

ing. Sartre's pseudo-chronological presentation, he argues, is an artful disguise for the true structure of the narrative, the dialectical logic of metaphysical argument.[40] It is just as likely in Sartre's case as it was in Henry James's, however, that the violations of temporal sequence are to be attributed to psychological verisimilitude, fidelity to the reality of remembered experience, than they are to deliberate programmatic manipulation on the part of the autobiographer. Reminding us of Freud's thesis that the unconscious knows no concept of time, Burton Pike would seem to validate the synchrony of *The Words* as a representation of biographical experience when he speaks of the child's "closeness to an undifferentiated sense of time."[41] Moreover, in *The Words*, if Sartre violates calendar chronology, he does so only to observe another chronology, the succession of states of mind that constitutes the aetiology of his illness, an illness, moreover, which he identifies as a diseased form of temporal perception ("the retrospective illusion"). It is, of course, beyond dispute that *The Words* gives us, as Lejeune points out, the existential ontology of Sartre's Existentialism. It is just as easy, however, to read the autobiography as tracing the sources of his philosophical thought to the circumstances of his childhood as it is to read the childhood as an Existentialist allegory. These two versions of the childhood years are not mutually exclusive but complementary, and I suspect that Sartre's inability to opt wholly for the one indicates that the truth claims of the other were simultaneously operative.

Like Lejeune, John Sturrock seeks to free autobiography from the constraints of chronological narrative. His call for "the New Model Autobiographer" is a plea for autobiography to recognize its affinities with fiction, abandoning its mistaken generic affiliation with biography. Sturrock reasons that chronological order in autobiography leads not to fidelity to

[40] Lejeune, *Le pacte*, pp. 207-209.
[41] Pike, 333. See also Christine Downing, "Re-Visioning Autobiography: The Bequest of Freud and Jung," *Soundings*, 60 (1977), 218, 220.

biographical truth but to its falsification: "We are reassured by believing that what follows after also follows from, a reassurance we are fully entitled to reading a fictional narrative, whose sequence has been dictated by its author; we are hardly entitled to it reading a chronological life story, which is largely a sequence of contingencies. A life story so organized is the counterfeit integration of a random life into a convenient fiction." Instead, he urges that autobiographers turn in their quest for an ordering structure for life history to psychoanalysis and "those obsessional structures of the mind that alone guarantee the consistency of a personality," a consistency obscured by conventional chronology. Sturrock joins Lejeune in celebrating Michel Leiris as the harbinger of the new dispensation of an autobiography organized not by chronology but by the association of ideas and words. Unlike biography, in which "the destination of [a] life story is . . . a single, terminal point in time—the moment of the biographee's death or retirement," the *telos* of autobiography is the autobiographical act itself, "a whole, unfinished series of points in time" which "grows longer as he writes." The "associative autobiography" has the merit of avoiding the distortion of biographical truth latent in chronological narrative, "the mistaken view that the process of narration is subsumed in the events narrated."[42]

Sturrock is not alone in appealing to psychoanalysis to supply an alternative to the chronological narrative of traditional autobiography. Christine Downing argues that the discovery of the unconscious by Freud and Jung has irrevocably disconfirmed "the conventional notion of a discrete individuality as subject of the autobiography." In its place "a radically new conception of self emerges," for psychoanalysis teaches that "there are connections in us different from the causal, chronological ones perceived by rational consciousness."[43] Because the unconscious has its own associational version of the self's

[42] Sturrock, "The New Model Autobiographer," *New Literary History*, 9 (1977-1978), 54-55, 54, 56, 61, 61-62.

[43] Downing, 213, 218.

history, Downing calls for a "revisioning" of autobiography that would give a new importance to primary process, dream material, fiction, and myth. The autobiographical quest for knowledge of the self can succeed only if its traditional reliance upon an historicist approach to life history is exchanged for a psychoanalytically informed act of *poesis*. Bruce Mazlish, however, remains skeptical about the possibility of the psychoanalytic autobiography. Like Sturrock and Downing, he draws a distinction between traditional autobiography and a psychoanalytically inspired alternative on the basis of narrative structure. In case history "it is from the *analysis* of the neurosis that the whole previous life of the patient is then unfolded," while in "normal" autobiography "such an unfolding generally takes place in a linear, narrative, and highly chronological fashion; and of course, its starting-point is not in a neurosis (or at least not an overt one)." The "normal" autobiographies of Freud and Ernest Jones lead him to conclude that "psychoanalytic autobiography at the best of hands may not be possible at all."[44] Interestingly, Lejeune concurs in this assessment, commenting that, for the most part, autobiographies are being written today as though psychoanalysis had never existed, with the notable exception of Leiris (and Conrad Aiken, he might have added).[45] Why is this the case, we are entitled to ask, especially since the testimony of Sturrock, Downing, Mazlish, Lejeune, and others suggests that psychoanalysis has decisively altered the way we read autobiography? Sturrock infers that autobiographers continue to toe "the chronological line" because they mistakenly believe that "a random order means no order at all."[46] This is only

[44] "Autobiography & Psycho-analysis: Between Truth and Self-Deception," *Encounter*, 35 (Oct. 1970), pp. 33, 36.

[45] Lejeune, *L'autobiographie en France*, pp. 95-98. The manuscript of Mark Twain's autobiography and the series of posthumously published versions (each varying according to the preferences of its editor) stand as a monument to the problems of the "associative" autobiography.

[46] Sturrock, 55.

part of the answer, based on Sturrock's appeal to the associative, non-narrative face of the psychoanalytic enterprise.

If psychoanalysis, with its technique of free association, has seemed to promote a nontemporal or spatial model of human experience, as Sturrock points out,[47] it also gives a prominent place to narrative in the working out of the clinical process. According to Stephen Marcus, Freud implied that "a coherent story is in some manner connected with mental health . . . , and this in turn implies assumptions of the broadest and deepest kind about both the nature of coherence and the form and structure of human life." From this perspective, "illness amounts at least in part to suffering from an incoherent story or an inadequate narrative account of oneself." Conversely, at the successful completion of analysis the patient comes into possession of his own story.[48] The Jungian clinician James Hillman takes a similar position on the role of narrative in psychoanalysis. Accepting E. M. Forster's definition of "plot" as an explanatory structure of causation, Hillman argues that the analyst's theory functions as the plot in an analysis. "*Poesis*" is the central activity of therapy, the "originating of significative imaginative patterns." In Hillman's view, analysis unfolds as a "battle of stories," a dialectical interplay between the analysand's symptomatic account and the analyst's imaginative revisioning of it into a second narrative or diagnosis: "Successful therapy is thus a collaboration between fictions, a revisioning of the story into a more intelligent, more imaginative plot."[49] In his study of Freud's Wolfman, Peter Brooks extends Hillman's view of analysis itself as an act of

[47] *Ibid.*, 61. See Kermode on "the questionable critical practice of calling literary structures *spatial*" (p. 52 and ff.).

[48] "Freud and Dora: Story, History, Case History," *Partisan Review*, 41 (1974), 92.

[49] "The Fiction of Case History: A Round," in *Religion as Story*, ed. James B. Wiggins (New York: Harper, 1975), pp. 130, 139-40. In *Sincerity and Authenticity* (Cambridge: Harvard Univ. Press, 1972), Lionel Trilling observes, "As I need scarcely say, psychoanalysis is a science which is based upon narration, upon telling" (p. 140).

*poesis* into the making of the case-history which records it. Brooks stresses the narrativity of the structure of explanation in case and case-history, the necessary emplotment of the material generated by free association: "The thematic material suggested by the dream, and the associations which the dreamer is able to articulate in reviewing the dream, can only begin to make sense when narrativized, ordered as a sequence of events." However, Freud, in Brooks's view, like Sartre in my own, radically problematizes narrative as a mode of cognition. Brooks summarizes the implications of Freud's convoluted emplotment of the Wolfman's story as follows:

> A narrative account which allows the inception of its story to be either event or fiction—which in turn opens up the potential for another story, anonymous and prehistoric—perilously unstabilizes belief in explanatory histories as exhaustive accounts whose authority derives from the force of closure, from the capacity to say: here is where it began, here is what it became. . . . As a result, "biography" and "character," the coherent, identifiable shape of the person—which Freud had of course been subverting from the beginning of his career—is here radically decentered from itself, the aetiology of its development assigned to an unspecifiable network of event and fiction.[50]

Nevertheless, despite its devastating polemic against "the retrospective illusion" of nineteenth-century bourgeois historicism, the testimony of *The Words* controverts Sturrock's rejection of biography and its characteristic chronological narrative as a structural model for autobiography. It sounds perfectly logical to distinguish, as Sturrock does, between the "single, terminal point in time—the moment of the biographee's death or retirement" and the "whole, unfinished series of points in time" that constitute the autobiographical act. In practice, however, the psychology of the autobiographical act is just as

[50] Brooks, "Fictions of the Wolfman," 76, 78.

likely to be borrowed from, indeed to be an extension of, the case of biography as it has been personally experienced. At any rate, the lesson of Poulou's childhood, as Sartre reconstructs it, is that the boy absorbed from the culture—specifically from the reading of biography—the available teleological structures for the emplotment of a life and the creation of an identity.

It is not my purpose to advocate chronological order in autobiographical narrative nor to dissolve the useful distinction between autobiography and biography. Rather, following *The Words*, I want to emphasize that chronological order, phenomenologically speaking, represents a great deal more than its familiar function as a literary convention suggests. To be sure, chronological order in a narrative—autobiographical or other—frequently does represent a failure of imagination, a mindless substitute for the difficult quest for form and meaning in human experience. As Sturrock would have it, "chronology invites the autobiographer to draw decently back from memories whose potency worries him,"[51] yet autobiographers of any distinction—Henry James, Mary McCarthy, Richard Wright, to name only a few—consistently refuse such an invitation without at the same time abandoning chronology. Lejeune's and Sturrock's attack on chronological order in autobiographical narrative is misguided in its failure to understand chronology as a manifestation of the ineluctable temporality of human experience.

Investigating "the phenomenology of narrative," Janet Varner Gunn concludes that "narrative experience . . . characterizes our actual experience in two ways: first, in its manifest representation of temporal succession, the surface level of day-after-day temporality that is most immediately available to reading, and second, in its latent dimension of depth that constitutes the more significant grounding for the fittingness between narrative and being in the world." For Gunn, the decisive feature of the autobiographical act is "its anchorage in the phenomenon of temporality."[52] In this sense, perhaps, chronological order, often dismissed for its simplistic reduction of the complexity of human experience (a complexity to which the non-chronological, associational networks of memory testify), may nevertheless, in its mimesis of the sheer successiveness of life in time, be said to be deeply implicated in the motivation to cast life history into narrative form. Even when autobiographical narrative seems to espouse some alternative to the principle of chronological order, it is quite possible that it is informed by a distinctly temporal consciousness. Thus Sturrock asserts that it was Leiris's "intense fear of death and the extinction of his ego which led him away from chronology and to the belief that he might, through his alternative method of recovering the past, immunize himself against the fatal passage of time."[53] Identifying such a fear as a determining factor in autobiographical motivation in general, Burton Pike speculates that the characteristic preoccupation with childhood in so many autobiographies is to be attributed to the adult's fascination with "the apparent permanence of life before full development of the ego makes clock time the time of our lives." Interestingly, the issue of chronology in *The Words*, which for Lejeune, as we have seen, was distinctly secondary in the narrative, emerges for Pike as a matter of primary thematic importance: "Much of the book is concerned with the child's discovery of the chronology of time in life and fiction, and the adult's despair over it."[54]

If readers detect an acute consciousness of temporality at work even in the supposedly non-chronological, experimental narratives that Sturrock and Lejeune make out respectively in Leiris and Sartre, this consciousness is also at work in the chronological narratives of the mainstream of conventional autobiography. In this respect there is a latent paradox in the phrase "chronological order" that merits investigation. I mean

[52] "Autobiography and the Narrative Experience of Temporality as Depth," *Soundings*, 60 (1977), 195, 197-98, 199.

[53] Sturrock, 62.

[54] Pike, 334, 341.

to suggest that no autobiography is *merely* chronological to the extent that pure chronology is the symbol not only of order but of dissolution as well, that unredeemed successiveness of ticking time that destroys life and meaning; even Christ, for Faulkner's Quentin Compson, like Sartre's Poulou sick unto death with time, "was worn away by a minute clicking of little wheels."[55] It is this darker aspect of chronology that Frank Kermode addresses when he distinguishes between two kinds of time: "*chronos* is 'passing time' or 'waiting time'—that which, according to Revelation, 'shall be no more'—and *kairos* is the season, a point in time filled with significance, charged with a meaning derived from its relation to the end." That the "chronological" could become a principle of "order," that *chronos* could yield *kairos*, this is one of the most profound of human fictions. It may well be that the persistence of chronological narrative in autobiography confirms its status as the archetypal form for human experience in and of time. As Kermode would have it, books are "fictive models of the temporal world," "humanly serviceable as models only if they pay adequate respect to what we think of as 'real' time, the chronicity of the waking moment."[56] Lejeune, for example, expresses surprise at the entrenched conservatism of autobiographical narrative in contrast to the formal experimentation of the modern novel,

---

[55] *The Sound and the Fury* & *As I Lay Dying* (1929; rpt. New York: Random, Modern Library ed., [1946]), p. 96. In "On *The Sound and the Fury*: Time in the Work of Faulkner," Sartre identifies in Quentin Compson a "posthumous" consciousness that resembles his recreation of Poulou's state of mind in *The Words*: "Quentin thinks of his last day in the past, like someone who is remembering. But in that case, since the hero's last thoughts coincide approximately with the bursting of his memory and its annihilation, who is remembering? The inevitable reply is that the novelist's skill consists in the choice of the present moment from which he narrates the past. And Faulkner, like Salacrou in *L'Inconnu d'Arras*, has chosen the infinitesimal instant of death. Thus, when Quentin's memory begins to unravel its recollections . . . *he is already dead*." Originally published in 1929; rpt. in *Faulkner: A Collection of Critical Essays*, ed. Robert Penn Warren (Englewood Cliffs, NJ: Prentice-Hall, 1966), p. 92.

[56] Kermode, pp. 47, 54.

yet we should note that he concedes a primacy to chronology even as he contests it: "And isn't it perfectly possible that a text, even as it refers in the last analysis to the chronological order of classical biography, could be organized itself in a different order?"[57] Similarly, even as he exhibits Leiris as a model of the alternative to chronological narrative, Sturrock notes Leiris's concession to an "inferred standard of rectilinearity" in his account of his method of composition, and he points out, moreover, that "fairly lengthy episodes from the past are narrated chronologically."[58] If *The Words* suggests that the paradigm of traditional autobiography is moribund now that "the retrospective illusion is smashed to bits," it is not at all clear that the alternative narrative structures proposed by Sturrock (associative) and Lejeune (dialectical) are viable solutions to bridging the widening gap between life and life story.[59]

## IV. NULLA DIES SINE LINEA

We have seen how narrative functions for the boy Poulou as a mode of perception and for Sartre the autobiographer as a mode of cognition: the anticipation of the one and the retrospect of the other are mirror images of a common quest for an emplotted, "ticketed" identity. Following the death of "the retrospective illusion," what remains for Sartre in his new, post-narrative mode of existence? Sartre has been emphatic in speaking of *The Words* as his farewell to literature, and his capsule formula for his huge, unfinished biography of Flau-

[57] Lejeune, *Le pacte*, p. 199 (my trans., emphasis added). "Et n'est-il pas parfaitement possible qu'un texte, tout en se référant en dernier ressort à l'ordre chronologique de la biographie classique, soit construit lui-même dans un autre ordre?"

[58] Sturrock, 61.

[59] In *The Forms of Autobiography: Episodes in the History of a Literary Genre* (New Haven: Yale Univ. Press, 1980), William C. Spengemann argues that the evolution of autobiography as a form was virtually complete by the middle of the nineteenth century. For a critique of this view, see my review of the book in the *Notre Dame English Journal*, 14 (1981), 71-76.

bert may serve with equal justice as a summation of his autobiography: "it really is the story of an apprenticeship that led to the failure of an entire life."[60] Nevertheless, he reports at the end of *The Words*: "I still write. What else can I do? *Nulla dies sine linea*." Arguing that "one gets rid of a neurosis, one doesn't get cured of one's self" (159), Sartre suspects himself of perversely continuing to believe in the discredited ideal of progress that *The Words* consigns to the rubbish heap of nineteenth-century bourgeois historicism: "I sometimes wonder whether I'm not playing winner loses and not trying hard to stamp out my one-time hopes so that everything will be restored to me a hundredfold" (160).

Sartre presents himself, his character and his views, as an insolvable bundle of contradictions. Even though he knows that the child is father of the man, that "all of the child's traits are still to be found in the quinquagenarian" (159), he deliberately devalues the past in favor of the future, stressing his sense of discontinuity with his earlier selves: "in 1936 and 1945, the individual who bears my name was treated badly: does that concern me?" So, to the man prepared to assert that Sartre is "the *same* person he has always known," Sartre imagines leaving him "an inert corpse for the pleasure of feeling like *a new-born babe*" (150). Barrett John Mandell interprets the autobiographical act as a "symbolic killing of one's fullest reality," the performance of a ritual death in order "to stave off non-being."[61] Both Poulou and Sartre the autobiographer prefer to conceptualize the autobiographical act as a process of birth and creation: "each and every moment repeated the ceremony of my birth. . . . it was I, rising from my ashes, who plucked my memory from nothingness by an act of creation which was always being repeated. Each time I was reborn better . . ." (148). Even as Sartre relegates "impossible Salvation to the proproom" (160), he continues to practice

[60] Sartre, *Life/Situations*, p. 112.

[61] " 'Basting the Image with a Certain Liquor': Death in Autobiography," *Soundings*, 57 (1974), 186, 181.

writing as a form of auto-resurrection. Paradoxically, even as the autobiographer unmakes the possibility of Poulou's ambition to live his life in narrative terms, he makes the boy into a book, and a book, we might add, to be classed with *The Childhood of Famous Men*, the prototype of the existence elected by the child. *The Words* is an anti-narrative narrative, an anti-autobiography.

Whether it be Roquentin's biography of the Marquis de Rollebon or his cherished song "Some of these days," *The Childhood of Famous Men* or *The Words*, narrative structure functions for Sartre as a refuge from the threatening contingency of the present. In his account of an "undated" childhood memory of the Luxembourg Gardens, the autobiographer captures the precariousness of his sense of identity, dependent as it is on the sustaining fiction of the narrativity of his existence. When his mother interrupts his play, asking him to rest beside her on a bench, Poulou seeks to dispel his boredom by discovering a latent necessity in an apparently random and pointless moment: "Everything leads to the bench, everything *has* to lead to it. What is its role?" The recourse to "the retrospective illusion" is both irresistible and unsatisfactory:

> I am not asking for sensational revelations, but I would like to sense the meaning of that minute, to feel its urgency, to enjoy something of the obscure, vital foreknowledge which I attribute to de Musset, to Hugo. Naturally I see only a haze. The abstract postulation of my necessity and the raw intuition of my existence dwell side by side without conflicting or blending.

Then, "in the nick of time," fiction and its formulas come to his rescue, redeeming him from the existential horror of the plotless moment; "Heaven charges me with a new mission; it's of the highest importance that I start running again." Poulou jumps to his feet and runs to the end of the lane. However, "nothing has happened," and once more the boy appeals to the narrative of fantasy, his vocation as the great writer, to work the emplotment of his otherwise unjustified existence:

"I hide my disappointment behind a screen of words: I assert that, around 1945, in a furnished room in Aurillac, this running will have untold consequences" (154). As the memory unfolds, Poulou oscillates between being and nothingness, now inside, now outside, the containing structures of self, of plot, of causation. In this pendulumlike movement of the child's struggle for significance, Sartre expresses the existential rhythm of all human experience in its gravitation toward the meaning that only the death-driven dynamic of narrative can supply.

Thus it is that when Poulou returns home from the park and enters his grandfather's library, he finds that even in the sanctuary of his faith in literary salvation he is face-to-face once more with contingent reality, "alone and without a future in a stagnant moment." Self and plot are curiously suspended, for "this moment is not in the program, . . . nothing will come of it this evening, or later, Aurillac will never know about this cloudy eternity," and "the illustrious writer . . . happens to be out." Since the drift of Sartre's argument here excludes the possibility of destiny, we can only attribute it to the uncanny that the child in his boredom should encounter a fly, that familiar emblem of the vanity of human wishes, and gratuitously kill it. This wanton sport, which Sartre interprets as an impersonation of "destiny," backfires, for Sartre reads the "insecticide" as a symbolic suicide: "I'm a fly, I've always been one. This time I've touched bottom. The only thing left for me to do is to pick up *The Adventures of Captain Corcoran* which is lying on the table. . . ." And so the cycle begins once more, and the entire Sartrean machinery of the teleologically governed existence resumes: "my glory" returns "to its abode"; "Mankind . . . calls me to the rescue"; "the Holy Ghost whispers its staggering words in my ear"; and "the Ilustrious Writer reappears on the scene." The redemptive transformation of his days into narrative is now complete:

> . . . the blond head of a grand-nephew is bent over the
> story of my life; his eyes fill with tears; the future dawns;
> an infinite love envelops me; lights whirl about in my

heart. I don't move; I don't even look at the great event.
I quietly continue reading; the lights finally go out; I no
longer feel anything except a rhythm, an irresistible impulse; I drive off, I have driven off, I keep going, the
engine purrs. I feel the speed of my soul. (155-56)

As long as the engine of plot "purrs," the heart beats, for life
as a structure of meaning and literature are one; the alternative to narrative motion is death. The "undated" memory of
the Luxembourg Gardens offers a fitting summation of the
themes of *The Words*, expressing in a paradigm of brilliant
compression the existential imperatives motivating the child
to "write" his life and the autobiographer to write about him.

In the case of a man who traces his origins to words, the
writer's motto, *Nulla dies sine linea*, takes on a special import:
to write is to constitute reality. Following the logic of his self-
analysis in *The Words*, Sartre observes in an interview eleven
years later that the advent of his blindness destroyed his chosen identity as "a man who writes," obliging him to live out
in his old age the posthumous existence that was the premise
of his selfhood in the first place: "In a sense, it robs me of all
reason for existing: I was, and I am no longer, you might
say."[62] The metaphysical rigor of Sartre's concept of himself
has tended to obscure the extent to which his case, special—
even prodigious—as it is, is nonetheless representative of the
human condition in general. Sartre himself best expresses this
representative dimension of his own experience in an interview in 1960 where he articulates as well as anyone ever has
the motive for writing an autobiography:

What I mean is that people—everyone—want this lived
life of theirs, with all its obscurities (they have their noses
in it) to be also a *presented* life, so that it stands free of
everything that blots it out and becomes, through expression, essential, by reducing the reasons for its obscurity
to the inessential conditions of its appearance. Each wishes

[62] Sartre, *Life/Situations*, p. 4.

179

to write because each needs to be *significant*, to *signify* what he *experiences*. Otherwise, everything goes too quickly, one has one's nose to the ground, like the pig that is forced to dig up truffles, there is nothing.[63]

Informing the act of self-revelation in *The Words* is Sartre's moral ideal of becoming wholly transparent to others. Sartre's vision of a new social order in which men would enjoy a footing of equality, solidarity, and mutual self-respect turns on the achievement of transparency, of absolute truth in interpersonal relations. As for Sartre himself, however, he concedes that "there is a depth of darkness within me that does not allow itself to be expressed."[64] The eloquent acceptance of the human situation that the autobiographer voices in the final lines of *The Words*, the definition of possibility in a matrix of limitation, recalls the unillusioned self-reliance of Wallace Stevens's Existentialist snowman who "nothing himself, beholds/Nothing that is not there and the nothing that is": "If I relegate impossible Salvation to the proproom, what remains? A whole man, composed of all men and as good as all of them and no better than any" (160).

---

[63] Sartre, *Situations*, IX, 37-38 (my trans.). "Ce que je veux dire, c'est que les gens—tous—voudraient que cette vie vécue, qui est la leur, avec toutes ses obscurités (ils ont le nez dessus), soit aussi vie *présentée*, qu'elle se dégage de tout ce qui l'écrase et qu'elle se fasse, par l'expression, essentielle, en réduisant les raisons de son écrasement aux conditions inessentielles de sa figure. Chacun veut écrire parce que chacun a besoin d'être *signifiant*, de *signifier* ce qu'il *éprouve*. Autrement, tout va trop vite, on a le nez contre terre, comme le cochon qu'on force à déterrer les truffes, il n'y a rien."

[64] Sartre, *Life/Situations*, p. 13.

# CHAPTER FOUR

# Self-Invention in Autobiography:
# The Moment of Language

In *The Words* Jean-Paul Sartre presents the two opposing views of the nature of the self and its relation to language that have been the principal subject of debate among theorists of autobiography in recent years: is the self autonomous and transcendent, or is it contingent and provisional, dependent on language and others for its very existence? In the fable of the train we are shown a Poulou whose ticketless condition exemplifies his initial lack of justified selfhood, his alienated sense of exclusion from the closed system of pre-existing reality—the Simonnot-like solidity of other selves—into which he has been born. In the narrative that follows, the boy reverses the balance of power, acquiring the ticket—identity, role, and mandate—that the exercise of language can confer; he embraces an heroic model of the literary self, becoming a demiurge with unlimited power to constitute reality in words. Despite the adult Sartre's subsequent disconfirmation of the child's dreams of autonomy, a disconfirmation which leaves the autobiographer without a ticket at the last, the ontological trick of traditional autobiography is played out in exemplary fashion in the boy's creation myth, and replayed in the autobiographer's reconstruction of his childhood illusions: the self exists (" 'Someone's missing here. It's Sartre.' " [72]), and it creates the world through language: "For centuries, in Aurillac, idle heaps of whiteness had been begging for definite contours, for a meaning; I would make real monuments of them. As a terrorist, I was concerned only with their being: I would establish it by means of language" (114).

When it comes to determining the relative positions of self and language in the order of being, students of autobiography align themselves variously, some on the side of the child with his ticket, some with the ticketless adult. When an "I" speaks, and especially in autobiographical discourse, is its language in effect an original speech, a self-validating testimony to the uniqueness of the self? Or is such speech always fatally derivative, like Poulou's faking a plagiarism of the language of the tribe? Whatever may be the case in biographical reality, the autobiographies of Mary McCarthy, Henry James, and Sartre, as we have seen, reveal the part of fiction in the self and its story in language which they set before the world. In all three cases the autobiographical act is deliberately presented as but the latest instance of an inveterate practice of self-invention which is traced to a determining set of biographical circumstances, the orphan condition of Sartre and McCarthy, the adolescent crisis of confidence unleashed for James by his choice of vocation. The fictive nature of selfhood, in other words, is held to be a biographical fact. Sartre further unstabilizes the very idea of autobiographical narrative when he demonstrates even as he performs it that the dynamic of retrospect is rooted in illusion.

With autobiographers themselves pointing the way, it is not surprising that the ontological status of self in autobiography has become the focal inquiry for theorists of autobiography in the last few years. Critical debate has been conducted with considerable passion, for at least some of the commentators involved believe that the future of autobiography itself is at stake.[1] The exact nature of the threat to the life of the genre, however, is variously perceived. In his wise survey of the contemporary theoretical and critical literature about autobiography, "Autobiography and the Cultural Moment," James Olney contemplates—with, I think, a certain light irony—the possibility that structuralist, poststructuralist, and deconstructionist critics of a distinctly French inspiration will succeed in dissolving "the self into a text and then out of the text into thin air," reducing the discourse of autobiography to "a

---

[1] Arguing that autobiography is a product of cultural conditions and assumptions, Elizabeth Bruss speculates that "autobiography could simply become obsolete if its defining features, such as individual identity, cease to be important for a particular culture." *Autobiographical Acts: The Changing Situation of a Literary Genre* (Baltimore: Johns Hopkins Univ. Press, 1976), p. 15.

mere stuttering" and the discourse of the criticism devoted to it to "a babbling about stuttering."[2] Michael Sprinker's incisive essay, with its appropriately apocalyptic title, "Fictions of the Self: The End of Autobiography," offers a nice illustration of the "French" challenge to the theory and practice of autobiography. It is Sprinker's thesis that "the gradual metamorphosis of an individual with a distinct, personal identity into a sign, a cipher, an image no longer clearly and positively identifiable as 'this one person' " is "a pervasive and unsettling feature in modern culture." Sprinker's readings of Foucault, Lacan, Vico, Kierkegaard, Nietzsche, and Freud all point to the same lesson, that "the self can no more be author of its own discourse than any producer of a text can be called the author—that is the originator—of his writing." In a characteristic and provocative quotation from *The Will to Power*, Sprinker underlines Nietzsche's radical view that "the 'subject' is not something given, it is . . . the fiction that many similar states in us are the effect of one substratum: but it is we who first created the 'similarity' of these states."[3] Nevertheless, despite the "bravura" of the "French" denial of the reality of the self, Olney is not about to despair of autobiography, for he reminds us that what these doubters "are still troubling about is the self and consciousness or knowledge of it."[4]

Janet Varner Gunn, for her part, perceives the threat to autobiography as coming not from the left (so to speak) in any (new, "French") deconstruction of the self but rather from the right in the traditional, Cartesian (old, "French" again) hypostasis of the privileged and transcendent self, "absolute, ineffable, and timeless," "beyond the reach of language." This self of "classical autobiographical theory"—a rubric under which she includes Wilhelm Dilthey, Georg Misch, Georges Gusdorf, and Olney—is in her view "*anti*-autobiographical" since

[2] Olney, "Autobiography and the Cultural Moment," in *Autobiography: Essays Theoretical and Critical*, ed. James Olney (Princeton: Princeton Univ. Press, 1980), pp. 22, 23. Hereafter this volume will be referred to as *Autobiography*.

[3] Sprinker, in *Autobiography*, pp. 322, 325, 333-34.

[4] Olney, "Cultural Moment," in *Autobiography*, p. 23.

"this self cannot be said to have a past at all: it never *was*, it simply *is*." For Gunn, the self is "the *displayed self* . . . who speaks, who lives in time," and it is her mission to formulate a "poetics of experience" in order to rescue autobiography from its quarantine in "some sterile corner outside of culture," restoring it to full participation in the life in time that is the only life we know. Despite her oversimplification of Olney's and Gusdorf's views of the relation between self and culture, a reduction which reading in Olney's *Tell Me Africa* (1974) and Gusdorf's *La découverte de soi* (1948) could serve to correct, Gunn's understanding of the relation between the self and language is instructive. "The self, then," she writes, "displays, not distorts, itself by means of language."[5] Sprinker, on the other hand, summarizes his inquiry into the textualization of the modern self by concluding that "the self is constituted by a discourse that it never completely masters."[6] In order to explore these opposing views of the self, of language, and of the relation between them in autobiography, we may turn to two representative works of the 1970s, James Olney's *Metaphors of Self: The Meaning of Autobiography* (1972), and a more recent essay by Paul de Man, "Autobiography as Defacement" (1979).

## I. AUTOBIOGRAPHICAL DISCOURSE: METAPHORS OF SELF OR THE LANGUAGE OF PRIVATION?

In Chapter One I discussed the determining role of reference in the recognition of any text as an autobiography, the principal reference, of course, being the identity explicitly posited

---

[5] *Autobiography: Toward a Poetics of Experience* (Philadelphia: Univ. of Pennsylvania Press, 1982), pp. 8, 9, 25, 19, 9-10. Although Gunn's principal emphasis is on "the *displayed self*," she also suggests that "the *displayed self*" represents only a beginning, a point of departure, in the quest for selfhood: "Only by moving out from the intersubjective world *where one already is* can one reach the destination of selfhood: from *bios* to *autos*; from *autos*, however, to solipsism" (p. 22). As to Gunn's presentation of her differences from Olney and Gusdorf, I think their views are much closer to her own notion of a poetics of experience than she seems to suspect.

[6] Sprinker, in *Autobiography*, p. 342.

between the central character and the narrator in the text on the one hand and the author of the text on the other.[7] It is precisely such a narrative's claim to be a version of the author's own life, anchored in verifiable biographical fact, that distinguishes an autobiography for the reader from other kinds of texts which it may closely resemble in other respects. In his searching essay on autobiographical discourse, Paul de Man mounts a frontal attack on the assumption that autobiography belongs "to a simpler mode of referentiality" of this sort, that it "seems to depend on actual and potentially verifiable events in a less ambivalent way than fiction does":

> But are we so certain that autobiography depends on reference, as a photograph depends on its subject or a (realistic) picture on its model? We assume that life *produces* the autobiography as an act produces its consequences, but can we not suggest, with equal justice, that the autobiographical project may itself produce and determine the life and that whatever the writer *does* is in fact governed by the technical demands of self-portraiture and thus determined, in all its aspects, by the resources of his medium? And since the mimesis here assumed to be operative is one mode of figuration among others, does the referent determine the figure, or is it the other way round: is the illusion of reference not a correlation of the structure of the figure, that is to say no longer clearly and simply a referent at all but something more akin to a fiction which then, however, in its own turn, acquires a degree of referential productivity?

In de Man's epistemology, the aspiration of autobiography to move beyond its own text to a knowledge of the self and its world is founded in illusion, for "the specular model of cognition," in which "the author declares himself the subject of his own understanding," "is not primarily a situation or an event that can be located in a history, but . . . the manifes-

---

[7] See Philippe Lejeune, *Le pacte autobiographique* (Paris: Seuil, 1975), pp. 13-46.

tation, on the level of the referent, of a linguistic structure." The referential basis of autobiography is, then, inherently unstable, an illusion produced by the rhetorical structure of language. Both critics (e.g., Philippe Lejeune) and autobiographers (e.g., Wordsworth) try in vain to "escape" the constraints of language; their "reinscription"[8] within the textual system is necessary and inevitable.

Examining Wordsworth's *Essays on Epitaphs* to illustrate the poet's understanding of the failure of all autobiographical discourse, de Man focuses on the figure of prosopopeia, the dominant trope of epitaph and autobiography alike, "by which one's name . . . is made as intelligible and memorable as a face." Tracing Wordsworth's treatment of this "fiction of the voice-from-beyond-the-grave," which supports the poet's cherished idea of the epitaph (and, by extension, of autobiography) as "a discourse of self-restoration" sustained in the face of death, he notes Wordsworth's curious and repeated counsel against the use of prosopopeia. De Man reads the apparent contradictions in Wordsworth's attitude toward prosopopeia as a manifestation of his (probably unconscious) recognition that the language of restoration he would perform is, paradoxically, a language of deprivation. De Man concludes:

> To the extent that language is figure (or metaphor, or prosopopeia) it is indeed not the thing itself but the representation, the picture of the thing and, as such, it is silent, mute as pictures are mute. . . . To the extent that, in writing, we are dependent on this language we all are, like the Dalesman in the *Excursion*, deaf and mute—not silent, which implies the possible manifestation of sound at our own will, but silent as a picture, that is to say eternally deprived of voice and condemned to muteness.

The deconstruction of autobiographical discourse is now complete; stripped of the illusion of reference, autobiography is reinscribed once more in the prison-house of language: "Death

[8] De Man, "Autobiography as De-facement," *MLN*, 94 (1979), 920-21, 923, 921, 922, 923.

is a displaced name for a linguistic predicament, and the restoration of mortality by autobiography (the prosopopeia of the voice and the name) deprives and disfigures to the precise extent that it restores."[9] As with Sartre and many another theorist and practitioner of the genre, death presides for de Man in the house of autobiography.

In *Metaphors of Self* James Olney proposes a radically different perspective on the rhetorical representation of the self in autobiography. To be sure, his working assumption about the part of fiction in human knowledge of both the self and the world resembles de Man's view of "the specular moment that is part of all understanding."[10] Olney writes, ". . . man explores the universe continually for laws and forms not of his own making, but what, in the end, he always finds is his own face: a sort of ubiquitous, inescapable man-in-the-moon which, if he will, he can recognize as his own mirror-image." Meaning is a specifically human invention, imposed on our experience, for "in the given, whether it be external reality or internal consciousness, there is nothing to be called meaning: the world means nothing; neither does consciousness per se."[11]

For Olney, the dominant trope of autobiography is metaphor, a term which in his extended usage includes all the "order-produced and order-producing, emotion-satisfying theories and equations," "all the world views and world pictures, models and hypotheses, myths and cosmologies . . . by which the lonely subjective consciousness gives order not only to itself but to as much of objective reality as it is capable of formalizing and of controlling." Even de Man's deconstructive view of autobiography as "de-facement," for example, would be such a metaphor—by implication, moreover, a metaphor of self; even his orderly disconfirmation of received ideas about the order of autobiographical discourse could be construed as a characteristic instance of Olney's "metaphorizing imagination," an attempt in this case to create knowledge of the true

[9] *Ibid.*, 926, 927, 925, 930.

[10] *Ibid.*, 922.

[11] Olney, *Metaphors of Self: The Meaning of Autobiography* (Princeton: Princeton Univ. Press, 1972), pp. 4, 30.

nature of language. In Olney's view language is a theater of possibility, not privation, through which both the writer and the reader of autobiography move toward a knowledge—albeit mediated—of the self.[12] To pass judgment on the ontological status of the self is "beside the point when one is speaking of metaphoric creation in autobiography and poetry." Instead, Olney's definition of the self is experiential and operational:

> The self expresses itself by the metaphors it creates and projects, and we know it by those metaphors; but it did not exist as it now does and as it now is before creating its metaphors. We do not see or touch the self, but we do see and touch its metaphors: and thus we "know" the self, activity or agent, represented in the metaphor and the metaphorizing.[13]

Again, de Man's anatomy of "de-facement," ostensibly designed to illustrate an altogether different, even antithetical, understanding of autobiographical discourse, seems curiously to confirm the agency of the "metaphorizing imagination" as Olney describes it. Thus de Man identifies the "figures of deprivation," the "maimed men, drowned corpses, blind beggars" who recur in Wordsworth's pages with disturbing frequency, as "figures of Wordsworth's own poetic self." A rhetorical detective of exemplary thoroughness, de Man scrutinizes the poet's "system of metaphors" in order to read a psychological portrait of the self between the lines, unveiling Wordsworth's ambivalence toward the dark underside of language, its insistent if latent "threat"[14] of death. De Man's conclusion, we may recall, is a demonstration of the privative nature of

[12] In a related essay on Tolstoi, Olney presents his metaphoric perspective on art as follows: "The composite metaphor of the work is a presentational image, or an expression, of the personality of its maker and of the meaning of his life." "Experience, Metaphor, and Meaning: 'The Death of Ivan Ilych,'" *Journal of Aesthetics and Art Criticism*, 31 (1972), 106.

[13] Olney, *Metaphors*, pp. 30, 31, 34.

[14] De Man, "De-facement," 924, 925, 928.

language, yet how eloquently both Wordsworth and de Man's analysis of him are made to speak it.

The point, however, is not to desconstruct a deconstruction of autobiographical discourse. Whether or not de Man's practice corroborates his theory, his stated view of autobiographical discourse in particular and of language in general controverts the traditional conception of autobiography as a theater of self-expression, self-knowledge, and self-discovery. In his view, the balance of power in the relation between self and language in autobiography shifts decisively to the side of language: the writer is as it were written by the discourse he employs; the self is displaced by the text, with the result that the portrait of the self is eclipsed, supplanted instead by knowledge of the trope of self-reference and its structural function in a rhetorical system.[15] One consequence of this shift is de Man's transference of agency from the author to the text itself, which "counsels" and "constructs" and so forth (the *Essays* "speak out" and "plead eloquently"—prosopopeia is catching!). What emerges from de Man's austere theory of language is a belief that "we are deprived of . . . the shape and the sense of a world accessible only in the privative way of understanding."[16] For Olney, on the other hand, language is not a mode of privation but an instrument of possibility and power to be placed at the service of self-definition. The self as we know it in autobiography does come into being through language, yes, as his concept of the metaphor of self suggests, but Olney celebrates man as "a great shape-maker impelled forever to find order in himself and to give it to the universe." For Olney, the exercise of autobiographical discourse is to be valued in the spirit that Socrates adopts toward his myth of the earthly paradise in the *Phaedo*: " '. . . either this or something very like it is a true account of our souls

[15] In *Blindness and Insight: Essays in the Rhetoric of Contemporary Criticism* (New York: Oxford Univ. Press, 1971), de Man writes: ". . . it follows from the rhetorical nature of literary language that the cognitive function resides in the language and not in the subject" (p. 137).

[16] De Man, "De-facement," 928, 925, 928, 930.

and their future habitation . . . this, I think, is both a reasonable contention and a belief worth risking; for the risk is a
noble one.' " Olney's comment on this passage may stand as
his rejoinder to de Man's bleak view of man as "eternally deprived of voice and condemned to muteness": "If we agree
with all the philosophers, scientists, and artists who tell us
that order and meaning are of ultimate importance, then it is
not only 'noble' but also peculiarly human, this will to believe
and this risk we run in maintaining faith in our own crea-
tions."[17]

Olney's invocation of Plato here is indicative of the fundamental ground of belief that divides the two views of the self,
of language, and of their interrelation in autobiographical discourse that I have been describing. It is certain, moreover,
that no appeal to the experience of writing autobiography is
going to settle the ontological question of the priority of self
or language in the order of being, although it is worth noting
that practice of writing the self tends to lead autobiographers,
as we have seen, to understand the self they sought to express
as necessarily a product of self-invention. Speaking of the autobiographical quest for the self, Mary McCarthy put it this
way: "It's absolutely useless to look for it, you won't find it,
but it's possible in some sense to make it."[18] De Man's critique
of the familiar assumption of autobiographical discourse suggests that its apparently referential basis fosters the illusion
that there is, to begin with, such a thing as the self, and that
language, following after, is sufficiently transparent to express
it. That is to say that the specular nature of autobiographical

[17] Olney, *Metaphors*, pp. 17, 18. In the last chapter of *The Rhizome and the
Flower: The Perennial Philosophy—Yeats and Jung* (Berkeley: Univ. of California
Press, 1980), Olney asks whether man's building of systems is not merely a
wishful projection of his need for order. The answer he gives comes in the
form of a *credo*: "All varieties of system—whether philosophical, psychological, theological, cosmological, aesthetic, musical, or poetic—are all, by their
structural order, hierarchical imitations of the prevailing harmony that is the
creative principle behind and throughout the universe" (p. 368). See also Paul
John Eakin, rev. of *Rhizome*, *Criticism*, 22 (1980), 394-96.

[18] "The Art of Fiction XXVII: Mary McCarthy," *Paris Review*, No. 27
(1962), 94.

discourse tends to posit the self as the cause of language rather than its most profound effect. [19] If the metaphor of self can be said finally to be only a metaphor, should we then cast off autobiography as an exercise in self-deception (if self there be to be deceived)? I would suggest that the most appropriate response to this disturbing insight is not that we should regret the erroneous perception involved but rather that we should acquiesce precisely in the power of language to create one of the most enduring of human illusions: if autobiographical discourse encourages us to place self before language, cart before horse, the fact of our readiness to do so suggests that the power of language to fashion selfhood is not only successful but life-sustaining, necessary to the conduct of human life as we know it. Some such belief as this seems to me to be intrinsic to the performance of the autobiographical act. The alternative, as expressed by Sprinker and de Man, is clearly disabling. While I see no way to adjudicate definitively between these conflicting views of the relation between self and language in autobiography, some further light on this issue can be derived from a review of the thinking devoted to the ontological status of the self, both as an entity and as a concept. Then we must turn to autobiographers themselves.

## II. The Origins of the Self:
### " 'Ego' is he who *says* 'ego' "

Much of the controversy about the ontological status of the self in autobiography has tended to polarize into a self-before-language or a language-before-self set of positions, whereas

[19] In "Eye for I: Making and Unmaking Autobiography in Film," Elizabeth Bruss gives a nice formulation of the traditional transcendentalist conception of autobiography: "We were apt to take autobiography, for all its local variations of design and reticence, as at least expressive of a common underlying reality—a self existing independently of any particular style of expression and logically prior to all literary genres and even to language itself." She goes on to suggest the alternative, anti-Cartesian conception of the relation between self and autobiography as follows: "Perhaps subjectivity takes shape by and in its language rather than using language as a 'vehicle' to express its own transcendental being." In *Autobiography*, p. 298.

the most promising contemporary treatments suggest that the self and language are mutually implicated in a single, interdependent system of symbolic behavior. There does seem to be a tendency in addressing great questions—the origin of the self, of language, of society—to reduce complex reality to the simplicity of either/or propositions, doubtless an instinctive preference for the single cause as the most powerful form of explanation. If we are to understand "the condition of man in language," however, Emile Benveniste warns that we must abandon "the old antinomies of 'I' and 'the other,' of the individual and society":

> It is a duality which it is illegitimate and erroneous to reduce to a single primordial term, whether this unique term be the "I," which must be established in the individual's own consciousness in order to become accessible to that of the fellow human being, or whether it be, on the contrary, society, which as a totality would pre-exist the individual and from which the individual could only be disengaged gradually, in proportion to his acquisition of self-consciousness. It is in a dialectic reality that will incorporate the two terms and define them by mutual relationship that the linguistic basis of subjectivity is discovered.[20]

We do well, accordingly, to note at the outset the problematical nature of any inquiry into human beginnings. Interestingly, ontogenetic development remains as clouded in some of its most important phases, especially the acquisition of language, as the predictably more tenuous accounts of phylogenetic prehistory; in both, fictions—scientific or other—are necessarily considerable. Thus Paul de Man reminds us that both Jean-Jacques Rousseau's *Essay on the Origin of Languages* and Jacques Derrida's commentary on it in *Of Grammatology* are "pseudo-historical" narratives in which the argument about

---

[20] Benveniste, *Problems in General Linguistics*, trans. Mary Elizabeth Meek (Coral Gables: Univ. of Miami Press, 1971), p. 225.

origins unfolds in the guise of "consecutive, historical process" for rhetorical purposes.[21] Similarly, Benveniste repudiates as "pure fiction" "that naïve concept of a primordial period in which a complete man discovered another one, equally complete, and between the two of them language was worked out little by little"; "we can never get back to man separated from language and we shall never see him inventing it."[22] Jean Laplanche goes to the heart of the matter when he formulates succinctly the epistemological problem posed by any hypothetical reconstruction of origins: "we never have at our disposal anything but what is presently observable. The constitutive is reconstructed from the constituted or, in any event, from a constitutive process which is not primal but derived; and that, of course, is the definitive impasse in every quest for origins."[23]

Despite the privative strain of these criticisms by Benveniste, de Man, and Laplanche, scientific investigation of origins in many fields—geology, paleontology, cosmogony—has never been livelier than at the present moment, and it is inevitable that students of the self should seek to locate their inquiries in the larger context of human evolution. Karl R. Popper is one of these, and in his recent collaboration with John C. Eccles, *The Self and Its Brain* (1977), he gives a privileged and determining role to language in the gradual emergence of the human self and the creation of human culture: ". . . I conjecture that only a human being capable of speech can reflect upon himself." It is through language and the development of imagination in language that man achieves the self-reflexive dimension of consciousness that distinguishes his mental life from the conscious experience of other animals: "That is to say, only if we can imagine ourselves as acting bodies, and as acting bodies somehow inspired by mind, that is to say, by our selves, only then, by way of all this reflexiveness . . . can

---

[21] De Man, *Blindness and Insight*, p. 137.

[22] Benveniste, p. 224.

[23] *Life and Death in Psychoanalysis*, trans. Jeffrey Mehlman (Baltimore: Johns Hopkins Univ. Press, 1976), pp. 128-29.

we really speak of a self." Popper argues accordingly that the invention of language is likely to be the oldest of humanity's great achievements, "the one most deeply rooted in our genetic make-up," heading a list which also includes "the use of artificial tools for making other artefacts; the use of fire as a tool; the discovery of the consciousness of self and of other selves, and the knowledge that we all have to die." Both the discovery of the self and the discovery of death, he reasons, depend on the invention of language, although awareness of death, judging from recent archeological findings on the burial customs of Neanderthal man, seems also to be very old and to have exerted a reciprocal influence on the development of self-consciousness in man.[24] It is suggestive that the concepts of self and death, which pair so largely in the theory and practice of autobiographical discourse, as we have seen, should be linked in Popper's view of human evolution, determined alike by the exercise of man's capacity for language. Adopting a Darwinian perspective, Popper supposes that "it was the emerging human language which created the selection pressure under which the cerebral cortex emerged, and with it, the human consciousness of self."[25]

When we shift from the shadowy speculations of phylogenetic prehistory to the comparative immediacy of developmental psychology, it is again the acquisition of language that functions as the decisive event in the ontogenetic history of the human individual. That this should be so is hardly surprising, if we are prepared to accept, with Benveniste, that "it is literally true that the basis of subjectivity is in the exercise of language." Benveniste defines "subjectivity" as "the capacity of the speaker to posit himself as 'subject,' " "the psychic unity that transcends the totality of the actual expe-

[24] Jacques Lacan writes that "the first symbol in which we recognize humanity in its vestigial traces is the sepulture." *Écrits*, trans. Alan Sheridan (London: Tavistock, 1977), p. 104.

[25] Popper, *The Self and Its Brain* (New York: Springer International, 1977), pp. 144, 553, 153, 30. Eccles agrees with Popper's view of the connection between knowledge of death and knowledge of the self (pp. 453-54).

riences it assembles and that makes the permanence of the consciousness." He proceeds to argue that this "subjectivity" is "only the emergence in the being of a fundamental property of language"; " 'ego' is he who *says* 'ego.' "[26] (The corollary of this view, I might add, is that without speech there can be no self. This is a proposition to which many autobiographers— Maxine Hong Kingston, Helen Keller, Saul Friedländer— subscribe, as we shall see.) This is not to say that language is the only or even the earliest mode of self-reference but rather that it is the most important. Joseph Church, for example, summarizing the evidence of three elaborate life histories of babies from birth to age two, notes that they "behave reflexively, toward themselves, from an early age."[27] With the advent of language, however, the gradual emergence of the self accelerates. It is not a question of language endowing a hitherto mute self with the capacity for self-expression, but, quite possibly, of language constituting the self in its very makeup. Perhaps the most radical view of the relation between language and the subject is Jacques Lacan's belief that language creates the unconscious, opening up an altogether new dimension of the human personality.[28] Karl Popper captures the anti-Cartesian, anti-Kantian drift of such speculations as they bear on the self when he emphasizes his sense of the self as an emergent rather than a pure or absolute entity, determined by intersubjective experience. He is willing to grant to the newborn child "a tendency to develop into a person conscious of himself," but this development of self is contingent on interaction with "the other selves and with the artefacts and other objects of his environment." "All this," Popper concludes, "is deeply affected by the acquisition of speech."[29]

[26] Benveniste, pp. 226, 224.

[27] *Three Babies: Biographies of Cognitive Development*, ed. Joseph Church (New York: Random, 1966), p. 291.

[28] See Malcolm Bowie, "Jacques Lacan," in *Structuralism and Since: From Lévi-Strauss to Derrida*, ed. John Sturrock (1979; rpt. New York: Oxford Univ. Press, 1981), p. 126.

[29] Popper, pp. 111, 49.

The connection between the development of language and the development of self-awareness, suggested by Popper and Benveniste and implicit in much of the research on child development, has been systematically investigated by David Bleich in his recent book, *Subjective Criticism* (1978). Building on the work of Ernst Cassirer and Susanne Langer, which posits the formation of symbols as the basis for all human knowledge and art, and which accords to language "a special status in the array of symbolic forms," Bleich argues that inquiry into language holds the key to understanding the motivation for the symbolic activity that creates not only human culture but the self as well: ". . . *language is the means and agency of our characteristic human self-awareness.*" The originality of Bleich's approach to symbolic activity resides in his attempt to correlate cognitive and affective development, to conceptualize "the onset of representational thought in terms of motivation."[30]

Thus, while most of the recent child-language studies, under the influence of Noam Chomsky, study structure at the expense of the semantic or expressive aspects of the collected language samples, Bleich emphasizes that the child's naming of objects "is almost always connected with an experience of social interaction": "the child learns to name things *to* someone [usually the mother]." Drawing on recent studies of "the pre-verbal infant's special attentions to appearance and disappearance of objects and people and his development of sensorimotor naming schemata in coordination with the mother figure," he formulates the explanation for the child's simultaneous achievement of language and self-awareness as follows: "The motive for this development is an accumulation of circumstances, cognitive and affective, in which the child's sense of loss of both particular objects and people, and of a sense of well-being, can no longer be handled by any sensorimotor means, and the full resources of consciousness available to human beings have at last to be activated."[31]

[30] Bleich, *Subjective Criticism* (Baltimore: Johns Hopkins Univ. Press, 1978), pp. 43, 44, 50.
[31] *Ibid.*, pp. 50, 53.

Reserving for later discussion Bleich's analysis of the case of Helen Keller as a demonstration that "the capacity for syntactical language and for self-awareness are parts of the same act of growth," I would like to emphasize here his reasoning for making this link between the advent of self-awareness and the acquisition of language and representational thought: "only because the self has become both a subject and an object may an 'object' be an experience and a concept"; conversely, "without language, it is not possible to distinguish between awareness and self-awareness." It is worth noting that Bleich's ontogenetic account of the motivation for the simultaneous acquisition of language and self-awareness squares with the phylogenetic speculations of Popper discussed previously. Adopting a broad Darwinian perspective, he extends the concept of *motive* to signify the organizing principle of all animal behavior, "part of the adaptational teleology of living things." Restated in evolutionary terms, *"the acquisition of language and representational thought transforms goal-directedness* [of all behaviors] *into the organ of consciousness."*[32]

The acquisition of language, in Bleich's analysis, emerges as a focal activity for the interpersonal experience that is the *sine qua non* of selfhood. In this emphasis on the affective, social dimension of nascent self-consciousness, his thinking accords with Freudian understanding of this process, especially Erik Erikson's stress on the basic trust between the nursing infant and the mother as the foundation for human identity.[33] Similarly, Popper writes, "a consciousness of self begins to develop through the medium of other persons: just as we learn to see ourselves in a mirror, so the child becomes conscious of himself by sensing his reflection in the mirror of other people's consciousness of himself."[34] Indeed, Lacan suggests that in this moment of the infant looking at himself in the mirror (*le stade du miroir*) we behold the earliest phase of the ontogenesis of the self, the very dawn of the "I": "This

[32] *Ibid.*, pp. 53, 61, 53, 64.

[33] See, e.g., Erikson, *Young Man Luther: A Study in Psychoanalysis and History* (1958; rpt. New York: Norton, 1962), pp. 117-18.

[34] Popper, p. 110.

jubilant assumption of his specular image by the child at the *infans* stage, still sunk in his motor incapacity and nursling dependence, would seem to exhibit in an exemplary situation the symbolic matrix in which the *I* is precipitated in a primordial form, before it is objectified in the dialectic of identification with the other, and before language restores to it, in the universal, its function as subject."[35] Despite elaborate studies of behavior in the first two years of life, however, knowledge of the child's consciousness in this period before language is likely to be problematic at best. Lois Bloom observes that "one cannot know the mind of a child with anything even approaching certainty or conviction."[36]

If both the ontogenetic and phylogenetic accounts that I have presented are correct, the origin of the self as the reflexive center of human subjectivity is inextricably bound up with the activity of language. The history of the self, then, would be coextensive with discourse itself and with the institutions of human culture. If we distinguish, however, between the self as existent, an entity, and the self as concept or idea, its origins appear to be both historically limited and culture specific. The idea of the self, of course, has been around for a long time, and it would be possible to argue that defining it has been a principal concern of Western philosophy since antiquity, appearing variously in the debate between idealists and materialists, in the "mind-body" controversy between interactionists and epiphenomenalists, and in the inquiry into "personal identity" at the present time.[37] Interestingly, belief in the existence of the self does not necessarily entail that belief in the value of the individual which is the premise, *ipso facto*, of autobiography as we know it today.

What, then, are the origins of the idea of the self that the

[35] Lacan, p. 2.

[36] Quoted in Bleich, p. 45.

[37] See, e.g., "Historical Comments on the Mind-Body Problem," in Popper, pp. 148-208; John Perry, ed., *Personal Identity* (Berkeley: Univ. of California Press, 1975); and Amelie Oksenberg Rorty, ed., *The Identities of Persons* (Berkeley: Univ. of California Press, 1976).

writing and reading of autobiography presuppose? In the light of the decisive importance attributed to the interpersonal experience of "the other" in the ontogenetic and phylogenetic speculations about the self that we have considered, it would be reasonable to expect that cultural models of human personality would determine the history of the self as an idea. Historians of autobiography, however, have been slow to capitalize on this insight even though it was adumbrated some twenty-five years ago in a brilliant and truly seminal essay by Georges Gusdorf, which James Olney justly regards as the harbinger of the theory and criticism of autobiography in our time.[38] What Gusdorf proposed in "Conditions and Limits of Autobiography" (1956) seems simple enough, but it is radical in its implications about the idea of the self: namely, that autobiography is not a universal phenomenon, and that the "conscious awareness of the singularity of each individual life" which autobiography assumes "is the late product of a specific civilization." Gusdorf reminds us that in the life of so-called primitive societies, the individual exists not in distinction to but as a function of the community; similarly, the "mythic structures" of "more advanced civilizations" generally subscribe to "theories of eternal recurrence" that promote an "unconsciousness of personality" and a comparative lack of interest in the transient phenomenon of the individual life. By contrast, when humanity enters into history in the wake of the Copernican Revolution, it exchanges the notion that its development is "aligned . . . to the great cosmic cycles" for the characteristically modern Western view that it is "engaged in an autonomous adventure." Gusdorf links the emergence of autobiography to this spiritual shift: "the man who takes the trouble to tell of himself knows that the present differs from the past and that it will not be repeated in the future."[39]

The only work I know of that does full justice to the broad

---

[38] Olney, "Cultural Moment," in *Autobiography*, pp. 8-9.
[39] Gusdorf, "Conditions and Limits of Autobiography," in *Autobiography*, pp. 29, 30, 31, 30.

anthropological perspective that Gusdorf enjoins is Olney's *Tell Me Africa: An Approach to African Literature* (1973).[40] In the light of Gusdorf's view of autobiography as a distinctly Western phenomenon, the very idea of African autobiography sounds paradoxical, and so it is. If we reflect, for example, on the implied audience for Camara Laye's *L'enfant noir* (1953), the problematical, transcultural nature of his autobiographical discourse becomes clear. In France and in French, Laye composes an account of his growing up in Guinea, climaxing in the circumcision rites of his initiation into manhood and adult membership in the life of his tribe. Clearly Laye's fascinating and detailed revelation of the ceremonies involved is not intended for members of his own tribal community since it would be patently gratuitous to remind them of what they already know (in addition to constituting a transgression of the secrecy enjoined on the initiates). As Olney formulates it, "the effect of such communal ritual throughout Africa [is] to merge individual identity with group identity so that the part represents the whole, the whole is embodied and personified in the part, and the linear immortality of either is assured in the birth, reincarnation, and perpetuation of the common spirit."[41] In the case of tribal man with his ritual institutions, the very idea of an autobiography, which Gusdorf reads as a manifestation of Western man's "desire to endure in men's memory,"[42] would necessarily be a work of supererogation. Laye's story is at once, then, that of an insider and an outsider: the recollected past does indeed present the reciprocity of his own identity with that of the group; the act of autobiographical recollection, however, testifies to his separation from this community in the present. The simple plot of *L'enfant noir*, as Olney's fine analysis of it suggests, is a beautifully tensioned structure of union and separation, departure and return. Laye's

---

[40] For Olney's account of the interrelationship between his own work and Gusdorf's, see "Cultural Moment," in *Autobiography*, pp. 10-11.

[41] *Tell Me Africa: An Approach to African Literature* (Princeton: Princeton Univ. Press, 1973), p. 67.

[42] Gusdorf, "Conditions and Limits," in *Autobiography*, p. 31.

narrative and Olney's history of African autobiography provide ample evidence of the truth of Gusdorf's view of the
practice of autobiography as bound by culture, limited in space
and time.

Despite the wisdom of Gusdorf's position that the self is a
culturally determined concept and the eloquent illustration of
it in his first book, *La découverte de soi* (1948), progress in establishing the history of autobiography has been fitful and
selective. Looking for the origins of such inquiry, commentators often point to (but much less often read) the massive
volumes that Georg Misch devoted to the history of autobiography in antiquity and in the Middle Ages. Whatever merits
Misch's work may have, for Philippe Lejeune it illustrates one
of the principal pitfalls awaiting the would-be historian of autobiography, the retrospective illusion that persuades the scholar
to read the past against the grain, accepting any kind of first-
person discourse about the self as equivalent to *autobiography*
in the modern use of the term.[43] When Lejeune devoted a
chapter to the methodological problems confronting the historian of the genre in *L'autobiographie en France* (1971), he addressed a real need, for there was very little in the critical
literature devoted to autobiography that could be considered
truly historical. Lejeune might state that it would be absurd
"to reduce the history of autobiography to a series of mono-
graphs devoted to each important work of the genre,"[44] yet
something very like this was true of the existing surveys of
autobiography.[45] Inevitably, too, the historical approach was
impeded by uncertainty as to the definition and scope of the
object to be analysed. Accordingly, much of the early work,
and Lejeune's own *L'autobiographie en France* is no exception,
was devoted to hammering out definitions of autobiography
that would serve to distinguish it from similar work in adja-

[43] Lejeune, *L'autobiographie en France* (Paris: Armand Colin, 1971), pp. 42-
43.

[44] *Ibid.*, p. 48 (my trans.).

[45] See, e.g., Roy Pascal, *Design and Truth in Autobiography* (Cambridge:
Harvard Univ. Press, 1960), Chs. 2-4.

cent genres,[46] and to taking a bibliographical census of texts that could constitute a working corpus of the relevant literature.[47]

Meanwhile, piecemeal, various explanations have been proposed to account for the rise of autobiography and its development of the prominence that it enjoys today as a literary kind. Gusdorf himself traces the origins of the genre to a comparatively early date, citing the introduction of silver-backed mirrors from Venice at the end of the Middle Ages[48] and Montaigne's withdrawal into his tower with the unheard-of project of analyzing and describing himself[49] as two early milestones pointing towards the modern preoccupation with self-knowledge. Anglo-American scholarship has stressed the contribution of the Protestant Reformation to the literature of self-analysis,[50] while European scholars like Pascal and Lejeune have preferred to associate the flowering of autobiography with a cluster of cultural developments at the end of the eighteenth century, including the Enlightenment, the beginnings of the Industrial Revolution, the new social prominence of the bourgeoisie, the rise of the autobiographical novel, and the stirrings of Romanticism.[51] The point is not to determine

[46] See, e.g., Lejeune, *L'autobiographie*, Ch. 1 ("Définition"), pp. 12-41; and Pascal, Ch. 1 ("What is an Autobiography?"), pp. 1-20.

[47] See, e.g., Lejeune, *L'autobiographie*, "Répertoire," pp. 106-37; Louis Kaplan et al., *A Bibliography of American Autobiographies* (Madison: Univ. of Wisconsin Press, 1961); and Richard G. Lillard, *American Life in Autobiography: A Descriptive Guide* (Stanford: Stanford Univ. Press, 1956).

[48] Gusdorf, "Conditions and Limits," in *Autobiography*, p. 32.

[49] Gusdorf, *La découverte de soi* (Paris: Presses Universitaires de France, 1948), p. 29.

[50] See, e.g., Paul Delaney, *British Autobiography in the Seventeenth Century* (London: Routledge and Kegan Paul, 1969); Daniel B. Shea, Jr., *Spiritual Autobiography in Early America* (Princeton: Princeton Univ. Press, 1968); and Sacvan Bercovitch, *The Puritan Origins of the American Self* (New Haven: Yale Univ. Press, 1975).

[51] See, e.g., Pascal, pp. 52-53; and Lejeune, *L'autobiographie*, pp. 52, 65. By contrast, in *The Discovery of the Individual: 1050-1200* (New York: Harper, 1972), Colin Morris locates the rise of autobiography in a much earlier period (see, e.g., pp. 79-86).

the relative merits of these alternative explanations but rather to note that all historians of the genre, whether they begin with Augustine's *Confessions* or Rousseau's, confirm the truth of Gusdorf's insight that the phenomenon of autobiography is historically limited and culture specific, that in the period *ante quem*—however defined—neither the self nor autobiography was a meaningful concept.

Autobiography continues to await a historian prepared to meet the methodological requirements of the sophisticated program of genre research elaborated by Philippe Lejeune and Elizabeth Bruss.[52] Although it is more traditional in its approach, a combination of history of ideas and formalist analysis, Karl J. Weintraub's recent study, *The Value of the Individual: Self and Circumstance in Autobiography* (1978), marks a new maturity in the quest for the origins of the concept of self that the existence of the genre predicates. In a separate essay entitled "Autobiography and Historical Consciousness," which serves as a kind of prolegomenon to the book, Weintraub set forth his central argument, a thesis that the concept of the self is derived from models supplied by the ambient culture.[53] All cultures "compress the essential values and convictions in human models" that exercise an "intensely persuasive and attractive power" on the process of self-formation because they are "taken to be of more universal validity [than any merely idiosyncratic notion of the self]." As Weintraub puts it, "the all-important issue" in the commerce between the individual and the culture is "whether the prime value is seen to lie in the personal variegation or in the basic commitment to the model." The shift toward the former is decisive for the history of autobiography, for the genre acquires significance as a cultural form only when individuality becomes "the most dominant personality conception of modern West-

[52] See Lejeune, *Le pacte*, pp. 311-41; and Bruss, *Autobiographical Acts*, pp. 1-18.

[53] For a parallel argument, see William C. Spengemann and L. R. Lundquist, "Autobiography and the American Myth," *American Quarterly*, 17 (1965), 501-19.

ern man." It is the purpose of *The Value of the Individual* to document in detail the gradual emergence of this ideal since the Renaissance; here Weintraub assays each of the autobiographical narratives he treats for evidence of its commitment to the concept of individuality and hence to the idea of autobiography in the modern sense. The essay argues that "the modern mode of self-conception as an individuality" and "the recognition of a strong historical dimension of all human reality" emerged simultaneously at the end of the eighteenth century and were mutually re-enforcing; in the writing and reading of autobiography "the trust in the power of genetic explanation" and "the fascination with individual specificity"[54] were united.

What literary historians have termed the Romantic self offers an obvious and familiar instance of the idea of the self as socially derived, a product of the cultural circumstances of a

[54] *Critical Inquiry*, 1 (1975), 837, 838, 847, 846. For all the methodological distance that separates a traditional historian of ideas like Weintraub from the pursuit of "the archeology of knowledge" by Michel Foucault, it is suggestive that Foucault's large-scale demarcation of Western intellectual history into a sequence of periods or *epistèmes* supports Weintraub's emphasis on the late eighteenth century as a pivotal moment in the evolution of the idea of the self. Foucault seeks to delineate what he terms the *epistème* of an age, the underlying set of structures that organizes the discourses in which knowledge is articulated. In *The Order of Things* (1966) he argues that it is the presence of man as a concept that distinguishes the beginning of a new *epistème* in the nineteenth century from the classical *epistème* of the seventeenth and eighteenth centuries in which man as a concept was absent. Alan Sheridan summarizes Foucault's argument in a way that suggests the plausibility of Weintraub's linking of autobiography with the paired concepts of individuality and historicism: the new form of representation that characterizes biology, economics, and linguistics in this period derives "not from man's consciousness of the world or of himself operating in the world, but rather from a sense of something taking place in himself, often at an unconscious level, in his subjectivity, in his values, that traverses the whole of his action in the world." *Michel Foucault: The Will to Truth* (New York: Methuen, 1980), pp. 82-83. Similarly, Foucault's speculation that we ourselves may now stand at the end of an *epistème* parallels the thinking of Brooks and Sartre (discussed in Chapter Three) that the narrative structures of explanation that we inherited from the nineteenth century have reached the point of exhaustion.

particular period of human history. In *Versions of the Self: Studies in English Autobiography from John Bunyan to John Stuart Mill* (1966), John N. Morris seeks to trace the decisive role played by certain versions of selfhood—both religious and secular—in the emergence of a distinctively modern sensibility. The model of self that Morris celebrates in Bunyan, Wordsworth, Mill, and others instructs us in the fortitude requisite to triumph in the struggle against the religious despair inspired by the idea of a meaningless universe. While it is unique among book-length studies of autobiography, Morris's predisposition to locate the sources of modern sensibility in the Romantic reaction against the metaphysical legacy of the Enlightenment, together with the decidedly moral vision that informs his approach to his material, finds its counterpart in three books on literary and cultural history by Robert Langbaum, Eugene Goodheart, and Wylie Sypher. All of them map out more or less the same spiritual itinerary, beginning with Wordsworth or Rousseau, who exemplify the plenitude of the self, and concluding with Beckett, who represents the self in an ultimate phase of exhaustion. The section titles of Robert Langbaum's *The Mysteries of Identity* (1977) give this sequence in outline form: "The Romantic Self" (Wordsworth) is succeeded by "Loss of Self" (Arnold, Eliot, Beckett), which in turn is followed, out of phase, by a cautiously hopeful concluding section, "Reconstitution of Self" (Yeats and Lawrence). Langbaum's decision to violate the chronology of his subject matter, concluding with Yeats and Lawrence and their attempts to create religions of art and love respectively, rather than with Beckett, whom he acknowledges as the "low point" and latest period of his history of the self, testifies to his wishful desire to reverse the death of the self that the unfolding of modern literature seems nevertheless to record. Langbaum hesitates before the example of Yeats and Lawrence, wondering whether they are "prophets of a new reconstructed ego" or only " 'the last romantics.' "[55]

---

[55] (New York: Oxford Univ. Press, 1977), pp. 7, 8.

For Eugene Goodheart, however, belief in the redemptive power of art is dead; *The Cult of the Ego: The Self in Modern Literature* (1968) offers a somber assessment of the rise and inevitable fall of the Romantic self, precluding any optimistic return of the sort Morris and Langbaum envision to the vital, restorative powers of a Wordsworth or a Yeats. Wylie Sypher's *Loss of the Self in Modern Literature and Art* (1962), which charts the progress of the modern self through its Romantic, Existentialist, and "anonymous" phases, beholds in the present the final deromanticizing of man's anthropomorphic view of the world: "we are walking in a universe where there is no echo of the 'I.' "[56] Although much of the text would support a view of Sypher as the most tough-minded of these historians of the Romantic self, he manages to find even in the desolation of Beckett a possible basis for what he terms, tentatively (and somewhat paradoxically?), "a defensive humanism" not to be confused with "any romantic notion of selfhood": "Defeated as he is, Beckett implies in his anti-novels that we cannot, in spite of everything, annihilate selfhood—there is a self that wishes to die quietly."[57]

What these literary and cultural historians share, and this is my point, is a conviction that there is—or was—such a thing as "the Romantic self," the product of a given moment in the historical unfolding of human culture. The moral vision that motivates their inquiries testifies to a belief that the models of the self in a culture—in its art and literature and philosophy—exert a decisive influence on the form and content of

[56] *Loss of the Self in Modern Literature and Art* (New York: Random, 1962), p. 79. For a similar development of this theme, see Alain Robbe-Grillet, *For a New Novel: Essays on Fiction*, trans. Richard Howard (New York: Grove, 1965). These books by Sypher and Robbe-Grillet are but two prominent examples of an extensive literature on the condition of the self in modern culture. See also, e.g., Lionel Trilling, *Sincerity and Authenticity* (Cambridge: Harvard Univ. Press, 1972).

[57] *Ibid.*, pp. 14, 156. Sypher uses the phrase "a defensive humanism" as the subtitle for the final chapter, "The Anonymous Self." This phrase is adapted from Jean Grenier's *Essais sur la peinture contemporaine* (Paris: Gallimard, 1959).

206

the self in any individual. As to this latter point, we have seen it confirmed in the autobiographies studied in previous chapters, whether it be the model of the popular girl in *Memories of a Catholic Girlhood*, the young American male as war hero in *Notes of a Son and Brother*, or the great writer as child in *The Words*. The literature of autobiography is replete, moreover, with texts explicitly proposing the self and life of the writer as a model for the reader: conversion narratives, from St. Augustine to Malcolm X, and success stories, from Benjamin Franklin to Booker T. Washington to Norman Podhoretz, amply illustrate the didactic paradigm.

To conclude this section on the origins of the self, I want to look briefly at F. Scott Fitzgerald's "Crack-Up" essays, for not only do they dramatize the general process of the determination of the self by dominant models in the surrounding culture, they document as well the specific influence of the concept of the Romantic self, which I have considered in Morris, Langbaum, Goodheart, and Sypher. When Glenway Westcott observed that Fitzgerald "always suffered from an extreme environmental sense,"[58] he identified that aspect of Fitzgerald's personality which has made him a figure of perennial fascination for social and cultural historians. He was afflicted, as it were, by an acute case of culture, taking on chameleonlike the subtlest colorations of its unspoken ideas and assumptions and giving them utterance in his work. So intimate is the symbiotic relation involved between self and society that it would be pointless to attempt to determine whether Fitzgerald was spokesman *of* his culture or *for* it—he was both, modeled and model. This interdependency, this intense identification between his own life and the life of his time, was the basis for Fitzgerald's belief in himself as a representative individual. Thus he could write as follows of the affective shape of his career: ". . . I think that my happiness, or talent for self-delusion or what you will, was an exception.

---

[58] "The Moral of Scott Fitzgerald," in F. Scott Fitzgerald, *The Crack-Up*, ed. Edmund Wilson (New York: New Directions, 1945), p. 327.

It was not the natural thing but the unnatural—unnatural as the Boom; and my recent experience parallels the wave of despair that swept the nation when the Boom was over."[59]

Precisely because others were willing to grant him the representative status that he claims in this passage, the self-revelation of the three "Crack-Up" essays, which concluded with this unwelcome assessment of the state of his own and the nation's soul, acquired the power to shock and dismay. In these pieces, published in *Esquire* in 1936, a "posthumous" Fitzgerald performs his own autopsy, an autobiographical *tour de force* in which the demise of the first person is recorded by a self who claims no longer to exist: "so there was not an 'I' any more . . . ." " 'I felt—therefore I was' "—this is the "Cartesian" premise of the model of Romantic selfhood that Fitzgerald had embraced in his youth. Now, with the definitive collapse of the moral structure of his personality in the aftermath of a nervous breakdown, Fitzgerald repudiates "the old dream of being an entire man in the Goethe-Byron-Shaw tradition." This consciousness of models is a characteristic and pervasive feature of these essays. As he proceeds, painfully, to reconstruct the past, Fitzgerald realizes the extent to which the apparent wholeness and independence of his inner life was in effect derivative, its content borrowed from others whose influence he now itemizes in a list (Edmund Wilson functioned as his "intellectual conscience," and so forth). In the final essay we see Fitzgerald in the process of inventing a new self: "I would get me a smile," "I am working with a teacher on the voice." This new model for the self is to be relentlessly dehumanized, no longer a person but "a writer only," a thing, a "cracked plate" "to hold crackers late at night or to go into the ice box under left-overs," "a correct animal" who "may even lick your hand."[60]

The death of the Romantic self, which Fitzgerald delivers in a disturbing mix of the clinician's chill detachment and the

[59] Fitzgerald, p. 84.
[60] *Ibid.*, pp. 79, 80, 84, 79, 82, 83, 75, 84.

dog's raw bite (*Cave Canem* is the chosen motto for his new identity), is of course an old story, and dates from the very beginnings of Romanticism. Wordsworth, Coleridge, and Whitman, for example, all experienced what Hawthorne termed the death of the heart. From " 'I felt—therefore I was' " to "I see, not feel, how beautiful they are!" the spiritual trajectory is the same for both Coleridge and Fitzgerald. What distinguishes the "Crack-Up" essays from "Dejection: An Ode" is the explicitness with which what we recognize as a characteristic utterance of the Romantic self is perceived by Fitzgerald in terms of the model as such. It is perhaps precisely when the exhaustion of the model in the individual coincides with its exhaustion in the culture as well that its status *as a model* achieves a paradigmatic clarity and is most easily recognized. Fitzgerald's self-consciousness in this regard would be hard to overstate: "I wanted to put a lament into my record, without even the background of the Euganean Hills to give it color. There weren't any Euganean hills that I could see."[61] Fitzgerald's allusion to Shelley here, like his formulation of the Romantic self as "the old dream of being an entire man in the Goethe-Byron-Shaw tradition," may serve to remind us that, time and again in this section, pursuit of the origins of the self, both as entity and idea, has led us not inward, as one might expect, into some cul-de-sac of solipsism but always outward into a social dimension, to others, to culture, to language and literature. Now we need to look, to the extent that texts permit it, at the moment of language in which the self first finds its being.

## III. The Moment of Language

Helen Keller's writings offer a rare, possibly unique, account in the literature of autobiography of the emergence of selfhood that occurs, according to the theories of human development that we have considered, at the moment when lan-

[61] *Ibid.*, p. 75.

guage is acquired. Under normal circumstances this moment unfolds gradually over an extended period of time, thought to begin around eighteen months; in Keller's case it took place with the concentrated impact of a great discovery on April 5, 1887, when she was six and a half years old. Previously the unreflecting child had mastered a small vocabulary of finger-words spelled into her hand by her teacher, Anne Sullivan, which served her merely as a convenient mechanism to obtain more easily what she wanted.[62] Of the celebrated experience of the well-house, however, when Miss Sullivan placed one of Helen's hands under the spout and spelled into the other the word *water*, Keller wrote in *The Story of My Life* (1902):

> Suddenly I felt a misty consciousness as of something forgotten—a thrill of returning thought; and somehow the mystery of language was revealed to me. I knew then that "w-a-t-e-r" meant the wonderful cool something that was flowing over my hand. That living word awakened my soul, gave it light, hope, joy, set it free! There were barriers still, it is true, but barriers that could in time be swept away.
>
> I left the well-house eager to learn. Everything had a name, and each name gave birth to a new thought. As we returned to the house every object which I touched seemed to quiver with life. That was because I saw everything with the strange, new sight that had come to me. On entering the door I remembered the doll I had broken. I felt my way to the hearth and picked up the pieces. I tried vainly to put them together. Then my eyes filled with tears; for I realized what I had done, and for the first time I felt repentance and sorrow.
>
> I learned a great many new words that day. I do not remember what they all were; but I do know that *mother*, *father*, *sister*, *teacher* were among them—words that were to make the world blossom for me, "like Aaron's rod, with flowers." It would have been difficult to find a hap-

[62] Keller, *The World I Live In* (New York: Century, 1908), p. 116.

pier child than I was as I lay in my crib at the close of
that eventful day and lived over the joys it had brought
me, and for the first time longed for a new day to come.[63]

The burst of generative energy set in motion by the flow of
water from the spout colors the language of the entire passage
with an imagery of birth and beginnings. In this first version
of the decisive change in her life, Keller's emphasis quite naturally falls on her newly achieved, explicit understanding of
the concept of language ("everything had a name"), while her
related and equally momentous acquisition of the concept of
self remains implicit if prominent in the passage ("that living
word awakened my soul," "I realized what I had done, and
for the first time I felt repentance and sorrow"). It is worth
noting, moreover, that the list she gives of the new words she
learned that day is exclusively devoted to persons.[64]

In later versions of the well-house episode Keller stresses
its radical consequences for her sense of identity, and her recognition of the self as a concept is made explicit. Thus, in *The
World I Live In* (1908), she struggles to render in language a
mode of being preceding language and any sense of self:

> Before my teacher came to me, I did not know that I am.
> I lived in a world that was a no-world. I cannot hope to
> describe adequately that unconscious, yet conscious time
> of nothingness. I did not know that I knew aught, or that
> I lived or acted or desired. I had neither will nor intel-
> lect. I was carried along to objects and acts by a certain
> blind natural impetus. I had a mind which caused me to

[63] Keller, *The Story of My life* (1905; rpt. New York: Doubleday, 1954), pp.
36-37.

[64] Anne Sullivan's account of the well-house events in a letter written the
same day confirms the pairing of the linked concepts of language and person:
"She spelled 'water' several times. Then she dropped on the ground and
asked for its name and pointed to the pump and the trellis, and suddenly
turning round she asked for my name. I spelled 'Teacher.' " *Story*, p. 257.
See Bleich's analysis of the place of the doll in the context of the well episode
as a whole, in Bleich, pp. 58-61. His treatment of Keller created my interest
in her autobiographies.

feel anger, satisfaction, desire. These two facts led those about me to suppose that I willed and thought. I can remember all this, not because I knew that it was so, but because I have tactual memory.

Only after the event of the well-house did she achieve a conceptual grasp of self and of language, each inseparably linked to the other: "When I learned the meaning of 'I' and 'me' and found that I was something, I began to think. Then consciousness first existed for me." And again, "Idea—that which gives identity and continuity to experience—came into my sleeping and waking existence at the same moment with the awakening of self-consciousness. Before that moment my mind was in a state of anarchy in which meaningless sensations rioted, and if thought existed, it was so vague and inconsequent, it cannot be made a part of discourse."[65]

Many years later, in her biography of Anne Sullivan, *Teacher* (1955), Keller tried once more to illuminate the double darkness of her early years, "an unconscious yet conscious interval of non-personality," but she had to settle for referring to her nameless self in the third person as "Phantom." It is only after the watershed experience of April 5, 1887, that she begins, and her teacher with her, as an individual with a name: "From the well-house there walked two enraptured beings calling each other 'Helen' and 'Teacher.' " If we accept Keller's testimony, the episode of the well-house confirms the ontogenetic speculations reviewed in the previous seciton: the self ("my soul") emerges in the presence of language ("w-a-t-e-r") and the other ("Teacher"). As Keller put it in *Teacher*, "With the acquisition of speech I moved from the baby phase of my mental growth to my identity as a separate, conscious, and, to a degree, self-determining ego."[66]

Keller's performance in the well-house episode is comparable to the autobiographical act in three respects, which the

[65] Keller, *World*, pp. 113-14, 117, 159-60.

[66] Keller, *Teacher: Anne Sullivan Macy; A Tribute by the Fosterchild of Her Mind* (Garden City, NY: Doubleday, 1955), pp. 121, 37 ff., 40, 63.

climactic moment of the original passage places in suggestive configuration: it is an act of memory ("suddenly I felt . . . a thrill of returning thought"); it is an act of language in which experience is transformed into symbol ("she spelled into the other [hand] the word *water*. . . . my whole attention fixed upon the motions of her fingers"); and it is a constitution of self ("that living word awakened my soul"). The juxtaposition of self and language in the passage illuminates the nature of the link between them, that the self has a name or, as Keller later phrased it, "I learned . . . that I was something." In order to develop the parallel between the acquisition of language and the writing of autobiography that I want to explore here, we might say that it is the burden of autobiography to state "what we have learned we are." There are those who argue against the possibility of autobiography because they believe that the self is by definition transcendent and ineffable and hence resistant to any attempt to render its nature in language. Inquiry into the ontology of the self, however, both as entity and as idea, suggests the intimate interdependency of the capacities for language and for reflexive consciousness, as we have seen. (The famous dictum of Lacan, "The unconscious is structured like a language,"[67] would close the gap between language and personality altogether.) If the self in its origins is so deeply implicated in the emergence of language, then we should be prepared to entertain the *versimilitude* of the re-creation of self in the language of autobiographical discourse. If the self is itself a kind of metaphor, then we should be willing to accept metaphors of self in autobiography as consubstantial to a significant degree with the reality they presume to incarnate, a reality deeply linguistic, if not in the very texture of its being, at least in the quality of any knowledge of it that we may hope to attain.

In this perspective the writing of autobiography emerges as a symbolic analogue of the initial coming together of the individual and language that marks the origin of self-awareness;

[67] Quoted in Sturrock, *Structuralism and Since*, p. 125.

both are attempts, as it were, to pronounce the name of the self—this is the idea I want to develop in the rest of this chapter. Naming was the key to Keller's self-discovery in the well-house, as Anne Sullivan understood when she wrote of this event: "She [Helen] has learned that *everything has a name*."[68] In this moment of her own beginning in language Keller re-enacted the discovery that Susanne Langer identifies as the turning-point in the phylogenetic development of man's ca-pacity for symbol formation, "for the notion of giving some-thing a *name* is the vastest generative idea that ever was con-ceived."[69] The consequences of this step for the emergence of self experienced by Keller are stated by David Bleich as fol-lows: "We do not think of a thing without a name or a name without a thing; that is the nature of human self-awareness."[70] If Langer and Bleich are drawn to Keller's remarkable expe-rience in the well-house because it seems to throw into relief man's most distinctive, species-specific attribute, his capacity to form symbols, I am attracted to it more specifically as a dramatic instance of the genesis of the self, as a prefiguration in this respect of the symbolic dynamics of the autobiograph-ical act.[71]

Two qualifications are in order here with regard to my use of the Keller case as an analogue of this kind. First, in giving so much importance to the moment of the acquisition of lan-guage as the moment of the origin of the self, I do not mean to suggest that the individual's pre-linguistic experience is lacking in autobiographical significance, nor is it quite as in-accessible as we might think. Keller herself, for example, draws on the evidence of what she terms "tactual memory," distin-guishing it from conscious, remembered knowledge, when she reports her recollections of her life before Anne Sullivan and the well-house. Psychoanalysis at its boldest has demon-

---

[68] Keller, *Story*, p. 256.

[69] Langer, *Philosophy in a New Key*, 2nd ed. (1951; rpt. New York: New American Library, [c. 1951]), p. 126.

[70] Bleich, p. 61.

[71] Cf. Langer, pp. 34, 62-63; and Bleich, pp. 53-63.

strated procedures for the reconstruction of decisive moments of infantile experience, as in Freud's recovery of the *"primal scene"* from "the chaos of the dreamer's unconscious memory-traces"[72] in the remarkable case of the "Wolf Man." As a consequence, post-Freudian autobiographers (Conrad Aiken, Michel Leiris) and critics (John Sturrock and Philippe Lejeune), as we have seen in Chapter Three, have looked to psychoanalysis to provide the materials and techniques required for a more comprehensive account of life history than the conventional resources afforded by memory and narrative structure. The limitations of conscious memory, of course, are decisive here. Langer, for one, is prepared to accept "the period of learning language" as "the span which none of us recollect," while she asserts that "the conception of 'self' . . . is usually thought to mark the beginning of actual memory."[73] The life history of the individual in his or her earliest phase of development, pre-language, pre-"self," presents the autobiographer with problems analogous to the challenge of human pre-history. It remains to be demonstrated whether psychoanalysis will serve the autobiographer as the basis for a new archeology of the self, whether dreams and free association can provide the foundation for a carbon-dating of the earliest events of infantile experience.[74] Second, with regard to the normative calendar of child development, we must remember that Keller's acquisition of language occurs out of phase to a significantly older child. The conscious, *conceptual* recognition of one's self as a self, the recognition that the self has a name and that the name is one's own, does not necessarily or even usually coincide with the acquisition of language as it seems to have done in her case. (Language creates the potential for this pivotal event of consciousness; it enables it to take place, but it would be hard to demonstrate that it

[72] "From the History of an Infantile Neurosis" (1918), rpt. in *Three Case Histories*, ed. Philip Rieff (New York: Macmillan, 1963), p. 221.

[73] Langer, p. 111.

[74] See my discussion of the relation between psychoanalysis and autobiography in Chapter Three.

functions as its cause.) To the contrary, the literature of autobiography suggests that this experience insofar as it is remembered occurs at a considerably later date.

Notoriously outspoken in his scorn for the Freudian construction of the earliest phase of life history ("bitter little embryos spying . . . upon the love life of their parents"), Vladimir Nabokov dates the true beginning of his—or anyone's—autobiography from the moment the child consciously recognizes the reflexive nature of his consciousness, his existence as a self. The value of this moment—and of the autobiographical act that commemorates it—derives from Nabokov's view of human identity as a bulwark designed to ward off the child's elemental fear of nonexistence (in this Nabokov is closer to Erikson and to Freudian tradition than he would willingly acknowledge). Nabokov's autobiography, *Speak, Memory* (1951, 1966), opens precisely with an evocation of this fear, the "panic" he experienced as "a young chronophobiac" when, looking at "homemade movies that had been taken a few weeks before his birth," he witnessed a world in which "he did not exist." In the light of such a fear, which Nabokov (like Erikson) believes is common in childhood, it would be possible to view the characteristic blank of our earliest years as a beneficent repression, a salutary check against the impetus of retrospect which, left unrestrained, might push its quest for the origins of being over the threshold into nothingness. In Nabokov's case, this threat of nonexistence made visible on the screen transforms the "brand-new baby carriage," which will soon be his, into "a coffin"; it is "as if, in the reverse course of events, his very bones had disintegrated." The autobiographical act, which celebrates the world in which he does exist, thus becomes the sovereign remedy to stay the death-centered drive of "the reverse course of events," generating words to clothe the vulnerability of bones with the flesh of consciousness, and so, against the darkness of "the prenatal abyss," Nabokov juxtaposes the remembered light of his "first gleam of complete consciousness" on a summer day in August, 1903, when he was four years old:

I had learned numbers and speech more or less simultaneously at a very early date, but the inner knowledge that I was I and that my parents were my parents seems to have been established only later, when it was directly associated with my discovering their age in relation to mine. Judging by the strong sunlight that, when I think of that revelation, immediately invades my memory with lobed sun flecks through overlapping patterns of greenery, the occasion may have been my mother's birthday, in late summer, in the country, and I had asked questions and had assessed the answers I received. All this is as it should be according to the theory of recapitulation; the beginning of reflexive consciousness in the brain of our remotest ancestor must surely have coincided with the dawning of the sense of time.

The self, and autobiography, then, begin not with birth nor even with the learning of "numbers and speech" but with "the inner knowledge that I was I"; in this sense the experience constitutes "a second baptism."[75]

Nabokov's belief in the representative nature of this original experience of consciousness—its illustration of "the theory of recapitulation"—is shared by Jean-Paul Sartre, who asserts in his study *Baudelaire* (1947) that "everyone in his childhood has been able to observe the accidental and shattering [*fortuite et bouleversante*] apparition of the consciousness of self."[76] Citing the examples of such experiences supplied by Sartre (the cases of André Gide, Maria le Hardouin, and Richard Hughes), Herbert Spiegelberg argues that these "I-am-me experiences" are neither idiosyncratic nor infrequent, and he attempts to provide an empirical basis for what he regards as a widespread and normative category of experience, "particularly acute in

[75] Nabokov, *Speak, Memory: An Autobiography Revisited* (New York: Putnam's, 1966), pp. 20, 19, 22, 21.

[76] Quoted in Herbert Spiegelberg, "On the 'I-am-me' Experience in Childhood and Adolescence," *Psychologia: An International Journal of Psychology in the Orient*, 4 (1961), 136.

childhood but by no means restricted to it." Readers of autobiography can easily supply additional evidence to support Spiegelberg's view (we could argue that James's nightmare of the Galerie d'Apollon represents a variation of the basic paradigm), but it would be hard to match the intensity and clarity of Spiegelberg's initial example, an autobiographical fragment by Jean Paul Richter:

> I shall never forget what I have never revealed to anyone, the phenomenon which accompanied the birth of my consciousness of self [*Selbstbewusstsein*] and of which I can specify both the place and the time. One morning, as a very young child, I was standing in our front door and was looking over to the wood pile on the left, when suddenly the inner vision "I am a me" [*ich bin ein Ich*] shot down before me like a flash of lightning from the sky, and ever since it has remained with me luminously: at that moment my ego [*Ich*] had seen itself for the first time, and for ever. One can hardly conceive of deceptions of memory in this case, since no one else's reporting could mix additions with such an occurrence, which happened merely in the curtained holy of holies of man and whose novelty alone had lent permanence to such everyday concomitants.

Spiegelberg's preliminary findings, based on questionnaires he submitted to college students, lead him to believe that the "I-am-me experience" is "—at least to some degree—one of the fundamental facts of human existence." Spiegelberg distinguishes this experience from "the ordinary outward turn of our 'I'-consciousness,"[77] and it is, it seems to me, a second-level order of experience, a self-conscious experience of self-consciousness, explicit (*ich bin ein Ich*) whereas the reflexive nature of consciousness emerging with and enabled by the acquisition of language is characteristically implicit.

In the developmental picture I have been sketching out,

[77] Spiegelberg, 135, 146, 135.

following the acquisition of language and the "I-am-me" experience, the autobiographical act (if it comes at all) would figure as a third and culminating moment in the history of self-definition. Like the first moment, it is a coming together of self and language; like the second, it is characterized by a double reflexiveness, a self-conscious self-consciousness. The text of an autobiography is likely to recapitulate the second moment as a content, while the making of the text re-enacts the first moment as a structure. All three moments yield a constitution of self, and language, if I am correct, is not merely a conduit for such self-knowledge but a determination and constituent of it.

No one has explored the relation between self and language in autobiography with greater insight than Elizabeth Bruss, who identifies the self and autobiography as homologous linguistic structures:

> . . . the structure of autobiography, a story that is at once by and about the same individual, echoes and reinforces a structure already implicit in our language, a structure that is also (not accidentally) very like what we usually take to be the structure of self-consciousness itself: the capacity to know and simultaneously be that which one knows. . . . Indeed to be a "self" at all seems to demand that one display the ability to embrace, take in, one's own attributes and activities—which is just the sort of display that language makes possible.[78]

The logical extension of this view is explored in *Autobiographical Acts* (1976), where, as I discussed in Chapter One, Bruss advocates an approach to autobiography on the model of the speech act. If, following John R. Searle, Bruss can conceptualize autobiography as a form of illocutionary action, then she can—and does—propose that it is the task of the critic of autobiography, working from linguistic clues or markers embedded in the text, to reconstruct the context of the origi-

---

[78] Bruss, "Eye for I," in *Autobiography*, p. 301.

nal "utterance" and, in so doing, to gain a key to the private world of the autobiographer. Inherent in the speech-act theory from which this critical program is derived is a fundamental optimism about the possibilities of language as a medium of communication, an optimism clearly expressed in this analysis of the act of speech from Searle:

> In speaking I attempt to communicate certain things to my hearer by getting him to recognize my intention to communicate just those things. I achieve the intended effect on the hearer by getting him to recognize my intention to achieve that effect, and as soon as the hearer recognizes what it is my intention to achieve, it is in general achieved. He understands what I am saying as soon as he recognizes my intention in uttering what I utter as an intention to say that thing.[79]

If we accept the writing of autobiography as a kind of speech, and if we posit that it is the "intention" of such a text to communicate the nature of the author's self (the "effect"), then we may entertain the possibility that autobiography, like speech, could afford a medium in which for both the autobiographer and his or her reader the self might be apprehended in its living presence.

This, of course, would be to assign to autobiography an ideal capacity for self-expression, and there is little likelihood of its realization in any particular instance. As T. S. Eliot reminds us in his own spiritual autobiography, *The Four Quartets*, "Words strain,/Crack and sometimes break, under the burden. . . ."[80] For an illustration of what the moment of living presence in autobiography might be like, we may turn to the well-known climax of the early part of Walt Whitman's "Song of Myself," to the moment when the "I" invites the "you my soul" to "loafe with me on the grass." In the preced-

---

[79] *Speech Acts: An Essay in the Philosophy of Language* (Cambridge: Cambridge Univ. Press, 1969), p. 43.

[80] *The Complete Poems and Plays: 1909-1950* (New York: Harcourt, 1952), p. 121.

ing lines the poet seeks to distinguish the separate identity of "the Me myself" from the welter of experience and sensation: "Apart from the pulling and hauling stands what I am." Then the invitation to the soul initiates an attempt to penetrate to the fundamental reality of selfhood, beginning with an invocation of speech but reaching to some immanent reality of being at the heart of language:

> loose the stop from your throat,
> Not words, not music or rhyme I want, not custom or
>    lecture, not even the best,
> Only the lull I like, the hum of your valvèd voice.

The referential dimension of language is rejected here; the words do not represent anything; they are simply sound, the "hum" of "voice," of life as living process.[81] As this moment of the apprehension of being unfolds and deepens, the act of speech becomes a daring metaphor for an experience of self-communion which takes the form of a physical, sexual union of the self with itself:

> I mind how once we lay such a transparent summer
>    morning,
> How you settled your head athwart my hips and gently
>    turn'd over upon me,
> And parted the shirt from my bosom-bone, and plunged
>    your tongue to my bare-stript heart,
> And reach'd till you felt my beard, and reach'd till
>    you held my feet.

In this epiphany language and flesh partake of the transparency of the hour, and the self is revealed in its totality, from the "bare-stript heart" at its center to the "beard" and "feet" at its circumference. This extraordinary meditation on the self concludes with lines affirming the transcendent knowledge of

---

[81] For another example of the moment of presence in autobiography, see my discussion in Chapter Two of Henry James's experiences of "taking in" the "hum" of reality.

being that has been attained: "Swiftly arose and spread around me the peace and knowledge that pass all the argument of the earth."[82]

The sacrament of presence that Whitman celebrates here, presence of the self to itself, is the fundamental project of all his poetry, a project sustained by his belief in the power of language to effect a transubstantiation of reality. In this passage of incarnation the "hum" of the "voice" becomes the plunging "tongue"; reciprocally, strong in his belief in the agency of an organic art, Whitman could assert that the flesh could become word as well. Thus, in the preface to the first edition of *Leaves of Grass* (1855), he could counsel the reader, who is always for Whitman a metaphor of self, to "read these leaves in the open air every season of every year of your life" to the end that "your very flesh shall be a great poem." And in "So Long!" Whitman offers his most radical version of his organic philosophy of presence in which the poet and his reader, the self and the other, transcend even the immediacy of language to achieve a more perfect union:

> Camerado, this is no book,
> Who touches this touches a man.
> (Is it night? are we here together alone?)
> It is I you hold and who holds you,
> I spring from the pages into your arms—
> decease calls me forth.[83]

---

[82] Whitman, *Leaves of Grass*, ed. Sculley Bradley and Harold W. Blodgett (1965; rpt. New York: Norton, 1973), pp. 32-33.

[83] *Ibid.*, pp. 717, 505. Whitman's faith in language as an instrument for self-expression, however, was severely challenged by his personal experience of loss, and the buoyant mood of "Song of Myself" was followed four years later by the black despair of "As I Ebb'd with the Ocean of Life" (1859). Here the "barbaric yawp" of the omnipotent self has become "all that blab whose echoes recoil upon me." Of "Song of Myself," "Crossing Brooklyn Ferry," and the other autobiographical poems written in the flood-tide of self-confidence, the speaker of "As I Ebb'd" observes: ". . . before all my arrogant

Walt Whitman's invocation of the "hum" of the "voice" as the avenue to total self-communion, Elizabeth Bruss's conception of the autobiographical act as a form of speech act—in these instances the practice and theory of autobiography reflect what Jacques Derrida has identified as an inveterate tendency in Western epistemology to privilege speech as the foundation of our knowledge of reality. Derrida's analysis of this phenomenon in *Of Grammatology* formulates the dynamics of the encounter between the self and language as follows:

> It is not by chance that the thought of being, as the thought of this transcendental signified, is manifested above all in the voice: in a language of words [*mots*]. . . . It is the unique experience of the signified producing itself spontaneously, from within the self, and nevertheless, as signified concept, in the element of ideality or universality. . . . Within the closure of this experience, the word [*mot*] is lived as the elementary and undecomposable unity of the signified and the voice, of the concept and a transparent substance of expression. This experience is considered in its greatest purity—and at the same time in the condition of its possibility—as the experience of "being."[84]

This is not the place to rehearse the knotty metaphysical problems posed by the Cartesian *cogito* and by the transcendental reduction of Husserl, Heidegger, and the phenomenologists, key moments in the Western philosophy of presence that it is Derrida's ongoing project to deconstruct. Jonathan Culler's capsule version of Derrida's elaborate argument about the place of speech in our metaphysics will suffice to suggest the extent to which the theory and practice of autobiography

poems the real Me stands yet untouch'd, untold, altogether unreach'd" (p. 254).

[84] *Of Grammatology*, trans. Gayatri Chakravorty Spivak (Baltimore: Johns Hopkins Univ. Press, 1976), p. 20.

(also, as we have seen, a phenomenon peculiar to Western culture) have been colored by a similar style of thought:

> The moment of speech can play this kind of role because it seems to be the one point or instant in which form and meaning are simultaneously present. Written words may be physical marks which a reader must interpret and animate, supplying meanings which he deems appropriate but which do not seem to be given in the words themselves. But when I speak, my words are not external material objects which I first hear and then interpret. At the moment of utterance my words seem to be transparent signifiers coextensive with my thought; at the moment of speech consciousness seems present to itself; concepts present themselves directly, as signifieds which my words will express for others. Voice seems to be the direct manifestation of thought and thus the meeting point of the physical and the intelligible, body and soul, empirical and transcendental, outside and inside, etc. This is what Derrida calls the system of *s'entendre parler*, of hearing and simultaneously understanding oneself speak: my words give me direct and immediate access to my thoughts, and this form of self-presence, this circuit of self-understanding, is taken as the model for communication in general—what true communication consists of when there are no external difficulties or forms of interference.[85]

The desire for presence that the moment of speech promises to fulfill (and by extension the desire for the experience of self-presence to which autobiography aspires)—this is for Derrida impossible to realize, for speech (really a form of writing) and the writing that records it are "always already" at one remove from the reality of being. This is the sobering lesson of his deconstruction, and the light of such knowledge seems to have contributed to Bruss's second thoughts about

---

[85] "Jacques Derrida," in Sturrock, *Structuralism and Since*, pp. 169-70.

autobiography as a form of illocutionary action which could provide access to the original speech of the self. In her essay on film, from which I quoted earlier, she speaks in a kind of nostalgic retrospect of "the old self-knowledge" and "the old self-deceptions" of "classical autobiography." Quoting Derrida, she emphasizes her chastened sense of the fundamental limitation of any autobiographical text which her study of the failure of autobiography in film has taught her: "one potential effect of film is to 'deconstruct' the autobiographical preoccupation with capturing the self on paper, demonstrating the delusion of a subjectivity trying to be 'through and through present to itself' in the very writing that is the mark of its own absence."[86]

Even if we accept Derrida's analysis of the mistaken premise of the metaphysics of presence, as Bruss seems to here, it is nonetheless the case (as Derrida himself suggests when he posits the system of *s'entendre parler* as the basis of self-presence) that, psychologically speaking, reflexive consciousness—the self's sense of itself as a self—is liveliest and most immediate in the moment of speech. To this extent there is, then, an experiential plausibility to the speech act model of the autobiographical act, and it is also true that the circumstances of composition of some autobiographies—I am thinking of the dictated (e.g., Henry James) or "as told to" (e.g., Malcolm X) varieties—promote a conception of autobiography as a mode of utterance. Moreover, as we have seen, it is possible to view the autobiographical act as the culminating phase in a history of self-consciousness which originates in the acquisition of language. It is, however, by no means true that every autobiographer conceives of the autobiographical act in this way, even though alternative formulations often prove to be the metaphoric equivalent of speech, as we shall see in the cases of Frank Conroy and Alfred Kazin. Furthermore, when they do situate the autobiographical act in an ontogenetic history of self-development, they tend to link it,

[86] Bruss, "Eye for I," in *Autobiography*, pp. 318, 317.

as Nabokov does, not to the period of language acquisition (which often eludes memory altogether), but rather to key experiences of the "I-am-me" variety in childhood and adolescence.

Accordingly, without abandoning the genuine insight of the speech act model, I would like to propose a more comprehensive conception of the autobiographical act as both a re-enactment and an extension of earlier phases of identity formation. As the research of Spiegelberg and the testimony of many autobiographers suggest, there is frequently a special order of experience in the life itself that for the autobiographer is inseparably linked to the discovery and invention of identity. Further, these self-defining acts may be re-enacted as the autobiographical narrative is being written. That is to say that during the process of autobiographical composition the qualities of these prototypical autobiographical acts may be re-expressed by the qualities of the act of *remembering* as distinguished from or in addition to the substantive content of the *remembered* experience. The autobiographer may even be drawn to suggest in the completed narrative that such a re-enactment has taken place. Thus the act of composition may be conceived as a mediating term in the autobiographical enterprise, reaching back into the past not merely to recapture but to repeat the psychological rhythms of identity formation, and reaching forward into the future to fix the structure of this identity in a permanent self-made existence as literary text. This is to understand the writing of autobiography not merely as the passive, transparent record of an already completed self but rather as an integral and often decisive phase of the drama of self-definition.[87]

For obvious reasons it would be hard to prove the truth of this thesis about the autobiographical act, since supporting

---

[87] For further discussion of the concept of the completed self, see Ross Miller, "Autobiography as Fact and Fiction: Franklin, Adams, Malcolm X," *Centennial Review*, 16 (1972), 221-32, and Paul John Eakin, "Malcolm X and the Limits of Autobiography," *Criticism*, 18 (1976), 230-42, rpt. in *Autobiography*, pp. 181-93.

biographical evidence for such a reading of the place of an autobiography in its author's life is likely to come chiefly from the autobiography itself. Any behavioral patterns suggested by the text that link the present act of composition to past events that it reconstructs would be open to the charge that they are merely self-validating connections, retroactively imposed on the record of life history in the interest of producing an orderly, unified account of consciousness to serve aesthetic, psychological, or other designs. In earlier chapters I have myself supplied considerable evidence to support this charge. One of the chief lessons of Mary McCarthy's autobiography is that autobiographical truth is not a fixed but an evolving content, and my reading of James's autobiography demonstrates the extent to which the materials of life history are freely shaped by memory and imagination to serve the needs of present consciousness. It is nonetheless true that autobiographers themselves, when they do choose to dramatize and comment on the act of composition, frequently propose the creative process itself as in some fundamental way a mimesis of the rhythms of the life they are recreating. In this way, extending James Olney's view, we might speak of the autobiographical enterprise as doubly metaphoric: the autobiographical act, like the text it produces, would be a metaphor of self.[88] The autobiographies of Alfred Kazin and Frank Conroy illustrate this view of the autobiographical act as a re-enactment of earlier modes of identity formation. This construction of the autobiographical act does not, of course, preclude the possibility of other kinds of motivation at work; it should be recognized nevertheless as a prominent and perhaps the principal form of motivation.

In the first volume of his autobiography, *A Walker in the City* (1951), Kazin dramatizes the cultural conflict that structures his childhood, the struggle between "us" and "them,"

[88] See Olney, *Metaphors*, pp. 38-45, for Olney's concept of "the autobiographer duplex," for whom "the autobiographic process is not after the fact but a part and a manifestation of the living, and not only a part but, in its symbolic recall and completeness, the whole of the living" (p. 40).

Brownsville and Manhattan, the Jewish heritage of the Old World *shtetl* or village, personified in his immigrant parents, and the secular, urban values of the American community beyond his ghetto home. Kazin was by temperament a loner who found himself at odds with both the ghetto and the world beyond it, and he traces the origins of the act of accommodation required to complete the transcultural journey from Brooklyn to Manhattan, from the Old World to the New, to his solitary practice of walking. Kazin made his most explicit statement about the significance of walking in *The Open Street* (1948), a brief preliminary study for *Walker*. Walking, he writes here, is not merely his preferred means of self-expression but the supreme act of self-definition: "Walking became my way of personal meditation, and even now I feel most wholly myself only when I walk. . . . I go back and forth over streets that ring under my feet like the sound of my own name."[89] For Kazin, to walk is to pronounce the name of the self, to perform an originary speech, and, as we might expect, the "I-am-me" experience that he records in *Walker* is also associated with walking. It occurs on a "particular great day" during the summer heat of his sixteenth year as he walks along the city blocks of Brooklyn in a blazing afternoon:

> And then it came. All the way down that street, there seemed to be nothing but myself with a bag, the blazingly hot and empty afternoon, and silence through which I pressed my way. But the large shadow on the pavement was me, the music in my head was me, the indescribable joy I felt was me. I was so happy, I could not tell what I felt apart from the evenness of the heat in which I walked. The sweat poured out of my body in relief. I was me, me, me, and it was summer.[90]

In *The Open Street* Kazin asserts that he is "another in that long line of solitary American walkers" (21), and he forges a

---

[89] Kazin, *The Open Street* (New York: Reynal and Hitchcock, 1948), pp. 21-22.
[90] Kazin, *A Walker in the City* (New York: Harcourt, 1951), pp. 157, 158.

link to American culture by identifying Thoreau, and especially Whitman, as his predecessors. Whitman becomes the prototype of the American identity Kazin sought for himself, and there is in Kazin's elaboration of walking as a metaphor of self and knowledge, as a quest for an epiphany of self-presence, something of the flavor of Whitman's union in the grass with his "you my soul" in "Song of Myself": "How often have I had this longing for an infinite walk—of going on and on, forever unimpeded, until the movement of my body as I walked fell into the flight of streets under my feet—until I in my body and the world in its skin of earth were blended into a single act of knowing!"[91] *The Open Street* argues that the rhythms of Kazin's walks supplied him not only with an identity but with a principle of aesthetic form, and *Walker* relates that his discovery of his vocation as a writer unfolded during walks around the lake in Highland Park during which he read his first efforts at writing to a highschool teacher and mentor. Kazin believes that his art grew organically out of his walking, and in this sense *A Walker in the City* not only derives its title, theme, and structure from walking but the writing of the text emerges as Kazin's culminating act of self-definition, the "infinite walk" of which he dreamed. Kazin's parents embarked on a journey to America before he was born, and Kazin completes its final leg metaphorically in the performance of the autobiographical act.[92]

In Frank Conroy's case, no less than in Kazin's, the autobiography not only recapitulates the history of identity formation as a content but extends it as well by performing its basic structures during the process of composition. Such a comparison requires some justification, for although Conroy is a loner like Kazin, we need only juxtapose his pleasure in the experience of non-identity against Kazin's joyous affirmation of self in his walks to recognize that Conroy's sense of self is radically unlike anything we find in Kazin's account:

[91] Kazin, *Street*, p. 22.

[92] See Paul John Eakin, "Alfred Kazin's Bridge to America," *South Atlantic Quarterly*, 77 (1978), 39-53.

. . . I rediscover the exact, spatial center of my life, the one still point. . . . Waking in a white room filled with sunshine. The breeze pushes a curtain gently and I can hear the voices of children outside, far away. There's no one in the room. I don't know where I am or how long I've been there. It seems to be afternoon but it could be morning. I don't know who I am, but it doesn't bother me.[93]

Moreover, Conroy goes out of his way to emphasize his sense of the discontinuity between his past and his present. Thus the significance of the principal episode of the opening chapter of *Stop-time* (1967), Conroy's participation in the savage beating of a schoolmate, remains elusive for the autobiographer: "Although Ligget's beating is part of my life (past, present, and future coexist in the unconscious, says Freud), and although I've worried about it off and on for years, all I can say about it is that brutality happens easily. I learned almost nothing from beating up Ligget" (14). Again, in the last chapter, when he enters college, Conroy portrays himself as making a clean break with "a past I didn't understand, a past I feared, and a past with which I had expected to be forever encumbered" (295). Biographical materials like these—and they are characteristic—promise little as a legacy of identity formation, and we need to ask in what sense the writing of the autobiography is of a piece with the life it relates. That the autobiographical act established Conroy's public identity is not in question, for the earliest entry on Conroy in *Who's Who* reports that he is the author of his autobiography.

Before we consider what Conroy has to say about his life in the present, about the composition of his autobiography and his adult career as a writer, I want to suggest briefly the qualities of his past as reconstructed retrospectively in *Stop-time*. The shape of the life is in its basic outline a simple one, a story of decline and dispersion from a treasured moment of

[93] *Stop-time* (New York: Viking, 1967), p. 16. Subsequent references are to this edition and will appear in the text.

equilibrium in childhood. For a brief time in Florida, Frank enjoys a sense of security and stability, a freedom and happiness, which he associates with the only close and unshadowed relationship in the entire narrative, his friendship with a boy named Tobey: "The first year in Florida was my last good year until I became a man. The woods, Tobey, bikes, running, nakedness, freedom—these were the important things. It was the end of childhood." When his family leaves Florida, it is mostly downhill going for Frank, "until the fact of being alive became synonymous with the fact of being in trouble" (31). What follows is the story of a troubled youth who found little support in an unstable family of flawed personalities and frequent uprootings for his groping attempts to establish his own identity.

Accordingly, Frank develops two strategies that secure a protective withdrawal from his unsustaining surroundings, "spacing-out" and reading books. The most frequently described state of mind in *Stop-time* is a kind of trance on the verge of sleep, of loss of consciousness. Sometimes pleasurable and self-promoted, sometimes passive and frightening, this loss of identity becomes part of a recurring pattern of behavior, a potentially self-destructive drive that begins as a response to his constant boredom and disaffection with the conditions of his unstructured existence. "The *clarity of the world* in books" provides another avenue of escape from the demoralizing absence of pattern in his own life, "a vague, dreamy affair, amorphous and dimly perceived, without beginning or end" (149).

Standing out in bold relief in a life history of disintegration and drift is the boy's mastery of the yo-yo, his "first organized attempt to control the outside world." Frank's eventual achievement of the ultimate trick, "the Universe," only serves to underline the autobiographer's retrospective understanding of his childhood infatuation with the yo-yo as a desire to create a perfect, autonomous world of his own design. Yo-yoing was an experience of structure, of world building, that rectified the deficiencies of his daily life, supplying an ideal sur-

SELF-INVENTION

rogate for the missing warmth of interpersonal relations and
a developmental shape for an otherwise formless existence:

> [The yo-yo] fascinated me because I could see my prog-
> ress in clearly defined stages, and because the intimacy
> of it, the almost spooky closeness I began to feel with the
> instrument in my hand, seemed to ensure that nothing
> irrelevant would interfere. I was, in the language of jazz,
> "up tight" with my yo-yo, and finally free, in one small
> area at least, of the paralyzing sloppiness of life in gen-
> eral. (115)

Freedom, power, control—the boy performs here as the author, author of his world and of himself. He now knows who
he is: "I was without question the best yo-yo player around"
(134). Yo-yoing was for Conroy what walking was for Kazin,
a constitution of self and by extension the prototype of the
autobiographical act.[94]

Conroy has given important clues on two different occasions to the relation between the writing of the autobiography
and the biographical history it relates. In the first of these, a
"Foreword" to *The Autobiography of a Schizophrenic Girl* which
he published in 1968, he suggests that Renée's (a pseudonym)
account of her loss of identity and her eventual recovery sustained him in his struggle to write his own story: "it proved
that a writer could successfully re-create states of consciousness despite his failure to understand those states when they
had originally occurred." When he praises the courage of her
imaginative re-entry into the world of her illness so "soon
after her cure," he emphasizes the extent to which he understood his own performance of the autobiographical act as a
painful re-enactment of the past: the "four-and-a-half years of
work on *Stop-Time*" were "years in which there were many
violent and unexplained emotional storms battering me about,

[94] Tony Tanner reads in the boy of the yo-yo episode "the outlines of the
future writer" he would become. See *City of Words: American Fiction, 1950-
1970* (New York: Harper, 1971), p. 321.

232

arising presumably from the solo (I was not in analysis) redis-
covery of my childhood." The example of Renée's narrative
"reinforced" Conroy's "faith in the act of writing": "She had
faith in words, believing in their ability to carry inexpressible
messages, trusting that what cannot be said can somehow be
borne aloft by what can be said. She was right."[95]

Two years later, in an interview published in *Esquire* (1970),
Conroy characterizes his practice of writing as a feat of skill,
a balancing act necessary to his survival:

> Conroy: I have to write. I would write even if I were
> strung up by my toes.
>
> Myself: I don't think you would be able to write under
> those circumstances.
>
> Conroy: But I would, you know, I know I would. In
> fact, I wrote the last part of *Stop-time* when I was at
> the brink of being institutionalized.
>
> Myself: This is not the same as being strung up by the
> toes.
>
> Conroy: But it is! . . . When I'm writing, I'm not con-
> cerned with the consequences of publication.
>
> Myself: I don't believe you. To divide your mind in half
> like that you would have to be a schizophrenic.
>
> Conroy: Well, a writer is a sort of schizophrenic.
>
> Myself: A schizophrenic and a sort of schizophrenic are
> not the same thing.
>
> Conroy: Listen. When a man is writing—and I'm talking
> about a serious writer—when a man is writing, he is
> living in a different world. He is free. That is what
> writing is all about. It is a way to freedom. Money,
> publication, the names of people, none of these things
> concern me when I'm writing. And I'm not just talking
> off the top of my head. Believe me, I know about this.

[95] "Foreword," to *Autobiography of a Schizophrenic Girl*, ed. Marguerite
Sechehaye (1968; rpt. New York: New American Library, 1970), pp. ix, xi,
xii.

> I've dedicated my whole life to books. I've been work-
> ing six hours a day, five days a week, for ten years![96]

It is worth noting that Conroy's association of his own story
with Renée's story of the loss and recovery of identity apparently surfaces again in this exchange with the interviewer. In
any case, his assertion that writing provides him an entry into
a world of freedom of his own design suggests that, like the
yo-yo, like reading, it functions for him as a symbolic analogue to the childhood experience of identity and security in
Florida.

*Stop-time*, then, not only dramatizes young Conroy's search
for a viable stance toward experience, but the writing of the
autobiography is itself a further, more sustained testing-out
of what will work when performed by the adult Conroy. Conroy himself encourages this interpretation of the autobiographical act when he speaks of yo-yoing and writing in reciprocal terms. If he likens writing to an exhibitionistic
demonstration of physical skill, he speaks of his performance
on the yo-yo as an utterance, a linguistic materialization of
reality, in effect a work of art: "The Trick! There it is, brief
and magic, right before your eyes! My hands are frozen in
the middle of a deaf-and-dumb sentence, holding the whole
airy, tenuous statement aloft for everyone to see" (119). Similarly, Conroy characterizes the world of books and the world
of the yo-yo in the same way; both forms of imaginative activity offer the clarity and form that he contrasts to the otherwise dispiriting formlessness of his living. All the various accounts of the experience of reading in *Stop-time* suggest that
reading is deeply implicated in the working-out of the boy's
identity problems. Reading is invariably understood as a
withdrawal or escape *from* an unpleasant, boring, or frightening reality, and reading is always sought because it provides
the boy with an entry *into* an alternative world where he is
safe and free. That is to say that reading is at once passive,
escapist, oriented toward nonidentity, and also active, crea-

[96] From Barton Midwood, "Short Visits with Five Writers and One Friend,"
*Esquire*, 74 (Nov. 1970), pp. 152-53.

tive, and identity-affirming. We may conjecture that it is not a surprising step in the psychological economy of Conroy's development for the reader of these alternative worlds in books to become the writer or maker of them.

To link Conroy's activity as a writer to formative childhood experiences with the yo-yo and with reading is not necessarily to suggest that these earlier experiences are to be understood as causes of his present identity. It is not so much that these earlier moments determine the autobiographical act but rather that they prefigure its motivation. Finally, we should note that writing is quite possibly only a provisional solution and not the ultimate trick in Conroy's troubled quest for identity. As far as Conroy is concerned, his need to test out what will work with life, "to experiment with those balanced elements, . . . trying, in the least dangerous way, to find out what they were" (153), is not settled previous to the writing of the autobiography. The narrative of *Stop-time* is framed by a prologue and an epilogue designed to remind the reader that Conroy's vocation as a writer offers no resting-place in his search for—himself? Seeking "something invisible, something I never found," Conroy goes to London "once or twice a week" (3) only in order to drive home at breakneck speed through the darkness of the English countryside. The young man's compulsion to "streak through the dark world" (4), "my brain finally clean and white" (3-4), becomes a stunning metaphor for a self in conflict. "The drive home was the point of it all" (3), he writes, and the same might be said of the making of *Stop-time*. What remains unclear both to Conroy and to us is whether the reckless driving, the latest in the unfolding series of feats of skill, represents a creative liberation of a self repressed or a desperate exercise in self-destruction. "My brain finally clean and white"—you can read it either way.

IV. SAUL FRIEDLÄNDER AND THE CHILDREN OF
TULSA "WHO WANTED TO SPEAK AND COULD NOT"

There are, of course, all sorts of reasons for writing an autobiography, and I readily acknowledge that my own inquiry into autobiographical motivation has focused exclusively on cases of felt need, on individuals who seem to be writing as much to work through something for themselves as to present some finished thing—self or life—for others. Proceeding in this way, I have left unexamined the more obvious kinds of motives, profit and publicity, politics and power, that inevitably govern a large (if not the largest) share of the autobiographies written today. My principle of selection, my attraction to autobiographers like Mary McCarthy and Henry James, Jean-Paul Sartre and Frank Conroy, has been largely instinctive, as though I were strangely sensitized to respond most deeply to texts that seem to be the product of some imperative authorial necessity. "I have to write," Conroy confides, "I would write even if I were strung up by my toes."

For Kazin, as for Conroy, autobiographical discourse seems to be integral to the personality, not merely an epiphenomenon or some ancillary means of communication, but a primary manifestation of self, an incarnation of its mode of being. Kazin recalls himself as a hopeless stutterer in school, and his quest for an unimpeded mode of self-expression became the search for a voice: "I could speak in the fullness of my own voice only when I was alone on the streets, walking about," he remembers, and his impassioned response to the street singers of Brownsville prefigures the peripetetic identity he would choose for himself, a solitary singer in the Whitman tradition with a voice (and a self) that could resist the tremendous pressure of environment and so come into his own:

> But it was not for their music I listened—it was to the voice itself rebounding against brick; the voice that crept up each window to the roof, insinuated itself into every back bedroom and down the hollows in a woman's back as standing against the window, she raised her hands to pull a dress over her head—a voice struggling to be heard against the pandemonium that filled the yard, that was sometimes entirely lost in the swish of the sheets and the clatter of the pulleys as the clotheslines were brought in,

but always bounding up again hard and clear in the great narrow shaft, forced me to look through the tangled web of clotheslines to the figure standing alone in the middle of the yard.

This is the pattern of emergent selfhood that Kazin re-enacts at the climax of *Walker*, in the charmed moments of his discovery of his vocation, when he reads his work aloud as he walks around the lake in Highland Park, knowing "the harsh exultant pain of hearing my own voice ring out on that quiet path."[97] I have been arguing that the autobiographical act in instances like these not only recapitulates but performs anew the psychological rhythms of identity formation that pattern the autobiographical text, and I would like to consider now two recent autobiographies, Saul Friedländer's *When Memory Comes* (1978) and Maxine Hong Kingston's *The Woman Warrior* (1976), which foreground the encounter between self and language that is always the basis but only occasionally the theme of any autobiographical project. In these narratives the achievement of speech becomes the controlling metaphor for the constitution of self, suggesting that the autobiographical act functions symbolically as a second acquisition of language. These texts offer, accordingly, an especially instructive opportunity to pursue yet again the relation between narrative and the fundamental structures of consciousness that I have explored in earlier chapters.

The epigraph to Saul Friedländer's autobiography is from Gustav Meyrink's *The Golem*, and it reads as follows: "When knowledge comes, memory comes too, little by little. Knowledge and memory are one and the same thing."[98] Friedländer's inversion of the relation between memory and knowledge in the title of his narrative, *When Memory Comes*, suggests that to

[97] Kazin, *Walker*, pp. 24, 111-12, 155.

[98] *When Memory Comes*, trans. Helen R. Lane (1979; rpt. New York: Avon, 1980). Subsequent references are to this edition and will appear in the text. Originally published in French under the title *Quand vient le souvenir* (Paris: Seuil, 1978).

engage in autobiographical retrospect is to move toward united consciousness. The title contains other meanings as well, however, meanings which qualify this idea of a process of gradual restoration, making it stand in relation to the narrative more as a kind of wish than as any reference to an achieved experience of identity, of wholeness, of being "one and the same thing." As Friedländer unpacks the significance of the epigraph in the narrative, he uncovers a network of conflicting associations that organizes his memories of his childhood in Prague, associations with the legend of the Golem, with his father, and with his own early fears of abandonment and death.

Friedländer recalls three different versions of the legend of the Golem, the robot of clay fashioned by the grand rabbi Loew to serve the Jewish community of Prague. In the first of these, the robot goes berserk, rampaging through the ghetto, and is destroyed when his creator reverses the process of his creation: "To breathe life into him, the Hebrew word *emeth*, 'truth,' written on a scrap of parchment, had been stuck to his forehead. To destroy the robot, it was necessary to efface the first letter, which left *meth*, 'dead' " (18). In this rendering of the legend the author of the Golem is himself destroyed, for language if all-powerful is also dangerous: in the life sign, the symbolic name, of this monstrous identity, "dead" dwells at the heart of "truth."[99] In the second version, Friedländer's favorite, language, inversion, de-creation, and loss of identity are again the central features of the story of the creature's destruction. Given the link that Friedländer supplies in the epigraph between *When Memory Comes* and these legends, the story of the Golem begins to look more and more like a disturbing parody, a nightmarish inversion and undoing, of the work of the autobiographical act: "At the time of the creation of the robot, the rabbi and his aides had placed themselves at the feet of the clay statue stretched out on the ground and recited the magic formulas of the Sefer Yetzirah, the Kabbalist Book of Creation; this time they posted themselves behind

---

[99] See my discussion of death as the source of meaning in Chapter Three.

the Golem's head and the phrases of the Sefer Yetzirah were read backward" (19). The epigraph from Meyrink, whose phrasing Friedländer *inverts* significantly in his title, may lead us to wonder about the nature of the spell that his re-creation of the past is designed to perform. The words of the epigraph seem to promise the advent of wholeness and identity, while language in these versions of the legend acts instead as the exorcism of a threat, deconstituting a created being into a mass of clay.

Friedländer's associations with the third version of the legend, the "strange retelling" (20) from Meyrink, are equally ambiguous; they center on the figure of his father, who owned a handsome, illustrated copy of Meyrink's *The Golem*, with a picture of the robot on the cover, " 'hairless face, with prominent cheekbones and slanted eyes' " (56). Friedländer does not supply a plot for this version of the story, focusing instead on his memory of the many childhood daydreams that he links to the reading of "this haunting, spellbinding book" (20) with his father. He mentions twice that this volume was one of the few books that his father managed to take with him when the family fled from Czechoslovakia to France in 1939, and he speculates that it may have come to form for him—with the other books—"a magic screen against an unbearable reality," opening up "an inner domain of calm and isolation" (56). Interestingly, the image of his father reading a book seems to have functioned in a similar way for Friedländer himself during a period of childhood anxiety in Prague. A prey to an unreasoning fear of being abandoned, the child would rise from bed and sneak to the library door, where, through the keyhole, he would derive a sense of reassurance and security from the knowledge that his father "was there, in his usual place" (14), reading a book. His father seems, in fact, to have been a rather unapproachable and inexpressive figure, unsuited for the role in which the child's need had cast him— the autobiographer remembers, for instance, the painful moment of loss when his father confiscated the pillow which, at age four, the boy "considered the most faithful and intimate of companions" (150). Friedländer speaks of his father's "reserve" and "extreme timidity," and he regrets that he himself lacked the spontaneity as a child to "leap up onto my father's lap, and throw my arms around his neck" (6). Ironically, the child, in his search for a bulwark for his identity, is fated by circumstance to depend on a man whom the autobiographer portrays as himself mortally stricken by an incurable malady of identity.

"Thinking back on my father sitting there, motionless in the dying light" (55), Friedländer interprets his father in the period preceding his deportation to Auschwitz as the victim of historical forces which hunted him down "for what he had refused to remain: a Jew." Like the fate of the Golem, "his desperate straits had become an impossibility of being" (56). The autobiographer reconstructs with dismay the paralysis of the will that seems to have prevented his father—indeed both his parents—from saving themselves from the Holocaust; their initiatives of flight seemed inevitably belated and doomed to failure. If the central image of the father reading a book was a symbol of security for the boy, the autobiographer suggests that it is also a " 'screen image' " (13), concealing the origins of the fear of abandonment and death that darkened his childhood. The memories associated with this image—a traumatic recollection of "a body cut in half by the wheels of a streetcar" (14) and (a proleptic anticipation of the horror of the death camps) a disturbing vision of the cremation of the director of his school—underline the recurrent theme of the lesion and loss of identity, a dark countercurrent to the sentiment of the epigraph from Meyrink.

Nevertheless, in retrospect, Friedländer's childhood in Prague speaks to him of an integrity of personality which was always missing later on. The autobiographer asserts that there is "an impassable line of cleavage somewhere in our memories" (33), dividing the world of childhood, where "the essential part of my self was shaped," from "the terrible upheavals that followed" (32). The aspiration of the narrative toward wholeness, expressed in the title and epigraph, is readily understood

when we consider the constant uprootings and radical shifts—
in place, in language, in religion—that structure Friedländer's
story in *When Memory Comes*. The child who was Pavel (Pa-
velicek, Gagl) in Czechoslovakia became in France first Paul
(who "could have been Czech and Jewish") and then Paul-
Henri (who "could be nothing but French and resolutely
Catholic"). Later, after the war, when he leaves France at age
sixteen to begin a new life in Israel, Paul-Henri becomes Shaul
and then Saul ("a compromise between the Saül that French
requires and the Paul that I had been"). Meditating on the
long, transpersonal, transcultural itinerary reflected in these
many changes in his name, Friedländer observes, "it is impossible to know which name I am, and that in the final analysis seems to me sufficient expression of a real and profound
confusion" (94).

Friedländer seems to have been predestined to the experience of dissociation; in every situation, early and late, he is
always the isolated individual. During the brief period of his
stay in a "home" for Jewish children outside Paris, for example, the lack of orthodox piety in his own formation marks
him as "a non-Jew, a *goy*" (44). Again, later on, the teenager
who had abandoned his studies at the Lycée Henri IV in
Paris to join the fight for Eretz Israel finds himself to be "a
person divided" (62) in the land of Zion; he steals away to
read Fromentin's *Dominique* alone on the beach, a symbolic
gesture of affiliation with "the permanence of a culture that
remained the only one that mattered in my eyes" (12)—a gesture, moreover, which recalls his father's refuge in France behind "the magic screen" of the books he had brought from
Czechoslovakia. The most drastic of these experiences occurs
when, prior to their own last, desperate, and unsuccessful
attempt to escape the net of the Holocaust, his parents prepare an alternative future and identity for their son by enroll-
ing him in a Catholic school under an assumed name.

This transformation of Pavel Friedländer into Paul-Henri
Ferland constitutes a total rupture of identity: "I became
someone else" (79). This is the essential rhythm of Friedlän-

der's experience, a relentless discontinuity, a repeated movement from the safety of the known self into the unknown world of the other. As a child he was separated from his parents; as an adult he feels himself separated from his earlier selves. The image for this fundamental experience of discontinuity which is inseparably joined to Friedländer's sense of identity is inevitably martial; in this book of many wars which, stretching from Hitler's war against the Jews to the wars of Israel in 1948, 1967, and 1973, constitute the primary matter of his vision of history, the self is defined by circumstance as a survivor, a veteran. Yet, behind and beneath the forces of change and separation that, from the vantage point of an Israeli present, reduce the world of his French Catholic past "to a fine dust . . . blown away, like a house slowly eaten away by termites," the autobiographer detects a possible principle of identity, of sameness in difference, uniting an otherwise divided consciousness: "perhaps I am the one who has become totally different, perhaps I am the one who now preserves, in the very depths of myself, certain disparate, incompatible fragments of existence, cut off from all reality, with no continuity whatsoever, like those shards of steel that survivors of great battles carry about inside their bodies" (110).

This striking metaphor of self is a metaphor of repression, antithetical to the autobiographical act which would assemble and integrate "disparate, incompatible fragments of existence" into a pattern of relation, and Friedländer comments extensively on the repressive resistance of his memory which his autobiographical project would have to reverse in order for the narrative to fulfill the promised wholeness of its title and epigraph. In *When Memory Comes* Friedländer argues that, for much of his life, his memory functioned recessively as a forgetting, especially during the period of his French Catholic identity as Paul-Henri Ferland. Thus he wonders at "the extraordinary mechanism of memory": "the unbearable is effaced or, rather, sinks below the surface. . . . The first ten years of my life, the memories of my childhood, were to disappear, for there was no possible synthesis between the person I had been and the one I was to become" (79-80).

Repression, moreover, by his own account, continues its agency right into the present moment in which the autobiography is being written. Following his account of his brief stay at a Jewish children's home in the summer of 1942, from which he narrowly escapes deportation by the Pétainist *gendarmes*, Friedländer reflects on the fact that he has never sought to learn the fate of the other children who remained behind, and he shrewdly observes that "even a story complete to the last detail sometimes turns into an exercise in hiding things from ourselves" (75). He identifies this habit of repression as characteristic of the Jewish response to "harrowing memories," and to illustrate the defensive strategies of memory he adduces an analogue to his own performance of the autobiographical act in his recollection of a radio program commemorating the twenty-fifth anniversary of the uprising in the Warsaw ghetto.

As Friedländer and his wife Hagith listen, a survivor recalls that one night, hearing a child crying in the street for a piece of bread ("*a shtikl broit*" [75]), he throws his last piece of bread out the window to the child below, but the child, now lying on the pavement, fails to respond to his promptings ("Look, lift up your head, there's bread right next to you!"), and suddenly he understands that the child is dead. When Friedländer and his wife discuss this story with a number of people the next day, she is shocked at the inadequacy of the response—the paralysis—not only of the narrator of the story but of all those who heard it twenty-five years later as well. To Friedländer, who later in the narrative identifies himself in his role of autobiographer as a survivor carrying the shrapnel of recollection buried deep in his flesh, she explains: "Don't you see, either? Instead of throwing the bread down and calling out directions through his window, the narrator should have gone downstairs, opened the door, and taken the child in his arms . . ." (76). The narrator's story of the stricken child is indeed, as Hagith Friedländer reads it, "an exercise in hiding things from ourselves," and in dedicating *When Memory Comes* to his children and to "Hagith, who has always understood," Friedländer seems to invoke the freedom and directness of her response as an ideal against which his own quest for autobiographical truth is to be measured.

Elsewhere in the narrative Friedländer supplies clues that help to explain his choice of this particular episode, and the breaking of the archetypal bond between parent and child which it symbolizes for Hagith, as an emblem of the repression his autobiography seeks to lift. If the distance between the narrator in the safety of his room and the dying child in the street exemplifies the distance between the autobiographer and his past, it is also true that Friedländer portrays this quality in himself as a child, as we have seen, lacking in the spontaneity and naturalness that might have enabled him to break through his father's timidity and reserve to express his love, to "leap up onto my father's lap, and throw my arms around his neck." The narrative suggests a more obvious bond of identification, however, between Friedländer and the stricken child who dies alone in the streets of the Warsaw ghetto: his persistent and increasingly well-founded fear of abandonment by his parents. In making provision for his safety, his parents did conclude that his separation both from them and from his Jewish past was the only avenue to survival. When they entrust him to a Catholic school and a new name, Paul-Henri Ferland, the boy runs away and rejoins them in a tearful reunion which brings the first section of the narrative to its climax and conclusion. The boy finds his parents on the eve of their final attempt at flight, and he instinctively guesses "the real meaning of our separation" when his father, always timid and reserved, "hugged me to him and kissed me" (87).

Following this initial resistance to his new identity, Friedländer surrenders to it in despair; isolated, friendless, a stricken Paul-Henri attempts to drown himself. The ironies here are overwhelming, for the salvation chosen by his parents for their son nearly destroys him, just as it may have destroyed them as well; Friedländer later learns that refugees with children were accepted at the Swiss border point where his parents, leaving him behind at the Catholic school, tried to cross and were turned back. It is as though, like the Golem, the boy were killed by the letter of his new name, as though his parents had inscribed the word *meth* on his forehead. During his long convalescence, he re-enacts in his delirium yet another painful memory of separation, which dramatizes in all its rawness the intensity of his inveterate and incapacitating anxiety; afterward, he does indeed emerge as "someone else," a Paul-Henri Ferland in identity as well as in name, a French Catholic of an ardent Pétainist stamp who "felt at ease within a community of those who had nothing but scorn for Jews" (121). This phase of anti-identity,[100] sustained during the war years by the repression of his feelings about the disappearance of his parents, swiftly collapses when he eventually faces the fact of their death in the year after the war. Paul-Henri has been confirmed, made his first solemn communion, and is already contemplating the priesthood, Friedländer writes, when a wise priest at St. Etienne, Father L., "helping me to renew the contact with my past" (138), asks him point-blank: "Didn't your parents die at Auschwitz?" (137).

Saul Friedländer's story in *When Memory Comes* falls into two distinct and complementary phases, a disintegration and repression of his original identity and his Jewish past, followed by a lifting of repression, return to the past, and reconstitution of self through the writing of history and autobiography. His meeting with Father L. marks the beginning of the shift from the first phase to the second, initiating a movement which Friedländer is still completing thirty years later in the creation of *When Memory Comes*. The priest not only reveals to the ignorant youth the facts of the Holocaust ("Auschwitz, the trains, the gas chambers, the crematory ovens, the millions of dead"), but he provides as well a model of their importance for the Jewish individual by reading to the boy "a few pages of an autobiographical text in which a historian

---

[100] See Erikson on the concept of "negative identity," p. 102.

who was a French Jew describes how, when still a child, he discovered anti-Semitism for the first time" (138). It would be hard to overstate the impact of these revelations at St. Etienne, for Friedländer would eventually become a historian of the Holocaust and of himself. The new knowledge has the force of a conversion, an "astonishing discovery," accomplishing a "secret work," awakening a "buried" instinct, precipitating an "obscure rupture" (139) in his sense of identity. "For the first time, I felt myself to be Jewish" (138), he writes, and he decides to abandon his "borrowed name" and to reassume "the name that was mine" (139). Paul-Henri Ferland becomes Paul Friedländer once more.

To the autobiographer, however, looking back, his transformation from a French Catholic candidate for the priesthood in 1946 into a Zionist freedom fighter in Israel two years later remained in certain important respects an incomplete if radical change. Discontinuity and repression continued to govern his life in Israel as they had at the Catholic school in France, with this difference, that he seems to have accepted repression consciously as a strategy for psychic survival:

> It took me a long, long time to find the way back to my own past. I could not banish the memory of events themselves, but if I tried to speak of them or pick up a pen to describe them, I immediately found myself in the grip of a strange paralysis. When I finished my military service, since I could not forget the facts, I made up my mind to view everything with indifference; every sort of resonance within me was stifled. (102)

In this larger perspective the meeting with Father L. at St. Etienne in 1946 was only the beginning of a process of reintegration of identity of which the autobiography itself is a final fruit.

The critical phase of this process occurs ten years later during a visit in Sweden to his Uncle Hans, who was the director of an institution for emotionally disturbed children. The autobiographer places his account of this visit of 1956 just beyond the midpoint of the narrative; it is the structural and psychological heart of his story. Despite the fact that he and his uncle almost never speak of the past they share—their memories of Prague—Friedländer finds that the presence of the past is inescapable and insistent in "this year outside of time" at Tulsa. Reading in his uncle's library, he discovers three volumes by Martin Buber, which open up a new dimension of his Jewish heritage, awakening a deeper feeling of Jewishness than his comparatively "superficial" identification with Israel. Another, more immediately personal and painful encounter with the past takes place when he experiences an instinctive and visceral revulsion to a German friend, also working at the institution, when Wolf reveals that he had served in the Waffen SS. The impact on Friedländer is that of a "violent blow." If repression had served him as "a *modus vivendi* workable for the time," as Henry James would have said, it could do so no longer, for he could not but read the evening with Wolf as "an urgent summons to turn toward this chapter of history, for nothing could be forgotten yet, and in fact nothing was over" (104).

The year in Sweden had yet another lesson about the past to teach, more profound than either the revelation of the reading in Buber or the shock of the evening with Wolf. Both of these taught the necessity and value of taking the road back to the past; contact with the disturbed children at the institution, on the other hand, suggested the impossibility of doing so. These are children "who wanted to speak and could not, . . . who desperately sought to establish human contact and would merely repeat a name, for hours" (103), and the apparently permanent inaccessibility of their lives in a closed world of fantasy and delirium becomes for Friedländer "an obsessive symbol" of "powerlessness" (105). The basis for his identification with their autistic condition is not far to seek, for they embody an extreme nightmare version of the isolation that Friedländer had always feared for himself. The institution and its setting in Sweden remind him of the Catholic school he attended in France, and it was at this school that he had suf-

247

fered the collapse of his own identity and had attempted suicide, events which occur in the narrative immediately preceding the pages devoted to the year at Tulsa. Musing at his sense of dissociation from himself in this darkest phase of his own story, Friedländer asks: "Was this sick child really me?" (100). This "sick child" joins the autistic children of Tulsa, the dying child of the Warsaw ghetto, and even the Golem as links in a lengthening chain of imagery associated with the themes of isolation and abandonment, repression and disintegration, that bind together so many of the episodes of this life of discontinuity.

Friedländer's encounter with the children of Tulsa occurs, we should recall, at a time in his own life when "a strange paralysis" frustrated any attempt to speak or write of the past. In this context the two episodes involving these children emerge as symbols of both the need for autobiographical discourse and the frustration of this need. The first of these concerns a fifteen-year-old boy named Arne, who "would pour out an incomprehensible flood of words and gesticulate endlessly as he told himself stories whose meaning only he could understand" (105). During a winter walk Friedländer and the boy become separated, and, when Friedländer overtakes him, he finds him surrounded by a gang of teasing schoolchildren who have driven him to screams and convulsions. In the last extremity of desperation, tantalizingly poised at the edge of his silence, driven almost to communication, to the language of the self—this is the instant in which Friedländer fixes Arne forever:

> At that point Arne suddenly sat down, gripped one of my hands, and raised his face to me. Everything that was locked inside Arne's head, everything that he was never to express, all his howling, dumb suffering was there on the contorted face covered with tears, mucus, slaver, and melted snow. Arne blinked his eyes, trying to tell me

everything, but how could he do it? "Herr Friedländer,"
he burst out, "Herr Friedländer!"—and could say no more.
(106)

It is a truly haunting moment; to pronounce the name of the
self and its story lies beyond his powers.

The second episode, which deals with a slightly younger
boy named Bert, is equally harrowing, and Friedländer's involvement, if anything, is more intense, for this time he functions not merely as the helpless spectator of helplessness but
as someone determined somehow to rescue the boy from his
isolation. The only time when Bert would interrupt his ceaseless repetition of "one meaningless phrase, '*Svalla ble*' " (106),
was when he read, and Friedländer tries accordingly to reach
him through reading:

> We began to read, and as usual I tried to kindle for a
> moment a fleeting spark of communication. All of a sud-
> den, I raise my hand, my fingers leave the page; Bert
> stops reading and looks at me. I wait for the "*Svalla ble*,"
> but Bert says nothing. He is still looking, his lips move,
> he is about to say something, a vague smile hovers on his
> lips. Still nothing. The smile persists. Is it possible that
> . . . ? No. His eyes grow dull again, his face assumes its
> fixed expression, its total vacuity once more, his lips open,
> and hesitantly though distinctly the "*Svalla ble*" pours out.
> (107)

The urgency of Friedländer's identification with the boy is
suggested by the shift to the immediacy of present tense, and
by the expansion of language to slow the lapse of time to a
second-by-second pulse. As with Arne, however, the hope for
a breakthrough into a truly human exchange is aborted; the
possibility of personality recedes and the boy reverts to his
"unbearable" (106) parody of human speech, the anti-language
of "*Svalla ble*."

The burden of frustration, of an isolation forever unredeemed by language, in the cases of Arne and Bert seems to have shocked Friedländer to adopt a new posture toward the private world of his own past. If these cases vividly represent the failure of the autobiographical act, their muteness also speaks of its necessity in human terms, and it is in this sense that Friedländer can interpret his encounter with "the powerlessness" of Arne and Bert as not only "an obsessive symbol" but "on a personal level . . . an actual provocation" (105). When he leaves Tulsa, he leaves behind him not only Arne and Bert but the isolate, closed condition of his own personality as well, the "sick child" he had been and the "paralyzed" adult he had become: "When the *Gripsholm* slowly pulled away from the Göteborg docks, I knew that this strange stay in Sweden had opened doors for me that would never close again" (107).

The pages on Sweden in 1956 interrupt Friedländer's account of his life at the French Catholic school in 1942, separating the moment of Paul-Henri's suicide and collapse from the period of his convalescence and recovery. In this context the "strange paralysis" of the pre-Tulsa self emerges as a kind of illness, and the sense of "opened doors" signals for the post-Tulsa self the beginning of a cure, the return to a wholly integrated personality. The progress of this return, as the title and epigraph suggest, was to be measured in the gradual emancipation ("little by little") of his memory from the bondage of repression. It is especially significant in this regard that Friedländer should characterize his buried memories of his Catholic identity a few pages after the events in Sweden in language that supports the parallel between his own condition and that of Arne and Bert. Like them, he carried within "the very depths" of his personality "certain disparate, incompatible fragments of existence, cut off from all reality"; like them, he was afflicted with an incapacity of speech.

The earliest of his attempts to articulate his sense of the past that Friedländer records takes place after the end of the war, and before his departure for Israel in 1948. This first effort to write about the Holocaust, about Belzec and Maidenek, is completely abortive—"nothing happened"—and in a passage of commentary for which the epigraph provides a gloss, the autobiographer interprets the cause of this failure as a function of his isolation from history and of a deep-seated dissociation and lack of wholeness, which had left him "incapable of feeling an identification without any reticence, incapable of seeing, understanding, and belonging in a single, immediate, total movement." When he goes on to add, "Hence— need I say?—my enormous difficulty in writing this book" (155-56), the autobiographical project takes its place as the climax of a psychological recovery spanning more than thirty years. Friedländer's historical works are the milestones of the earlier stages of this process.

*When Memory Comes* offers only the briefest glimpse of Friedländer's career as a historian of the Holocaust, a career which began in earnest in 1961, four years after the decisive year in Sweden that turned him irrevocably toward the past. Within the text we are shown Friedländer performing the work of the historian only once, in an interview in Germany in 1962 with Admiral Doenitz, the man who had commanded Hitler's navy. There is no little irony in his account of this scene, for, having exchanged his private repression of the past for a profession devoted to its total recall, the young historian is confronted with willful repression once more in Doenitz's solemn oaths that he "knew nothing about the extermination of the Jews" (146). In Friedländer's own work, however, the Holocaust moves steadily to become the central focus of his inquiry into the past. While there is no important mention of it in his first book, *Prelude to Downfall: Hitler and the United States, 1939-1941* (1963), it dominates the second and third, *Pius XII and the Third Reich, a Documentation* (1964), dedicated "To the memory of my parents killed at Auschwitz," and *Kurt Gerstein: The Ambiguity of Good* (1967). In these inquiries and in later books, including *L'anti-sémitisme nazi: histoire d'une psychose collective* (1971) and *History and Psychoanalysis* (1975), Friedländer developed a psychohistorical approach to the past, becoming one of the most distinguished contemporary students of collective psychoses and repressions.

For Friedländer, to write history and finally autobiography is not merely to recover the lost content of the past; it is to perform metaphorically a work of personal restoration. This is the connection the autobiographer makes between his own history and the history of his people in a meditation on his "first Seder" in 1946, just after he had shed his French Catholic identity to become a Jew once more. The feast of the Passover becomes for him doubly symbolic, a celebration not merely of the exodus from bondage in Egypt but of his own emancipation from a false identity as well. Unlike the inexpressive private rites of the children of Tulsa, Arne's "incomprehensible flood of words" and the "unbearable" meaninglessness of Bert's "*Svalla ble*," the language of traditional Jewish ritual functions as the instrument of liberation, of identity, of belonging:

> . . . it is the holy words, repeated over the centuries, that give the general symbol its particular force, that mark the sinking of roots in a group, the sinking of roots in history and in time. Because they have never been entirely clear, and always open to exegesis and explanation, it is the holy words that open the doors of imagination and allow the humblest of participants to understand, in his own way, the story and the feeling of liberation, knowing that these traditional words are his anchor and foundation within the community. (152)

The communal experience of language here is the antithesis of the repression symbolized by the fate of the Tulsa children and the stricken child of the Warsaw ghetto. The words of the Haggadah become a metaphor for the end of isolation, teaching the lesson Friedländer was to learn again in his own private passover in Sweden: the necessity and the possibility of the opening of doors to the past.

Friedländer specifically suggests that his ability to write about the past of his people and, still later on, his own life history signals the gradual lifting of an inveterate habit of repression: "It took me a long, long time to find the way back to my own past." We could make a similar observation about Henry James's decision at seventy to investigate in public the most private passage of his personal history, the "obscure hurt" that determined the shape of his life at age eighteen, and Mary McCarthy proposes precisely such an interpretation of her own belated return to the episode of the hated nickname, "C.Y.E.," and, still later on, to the loss of her parents which had cut her life in half. In order to test this view of the psychological significance of the autobiographical act, we are entitled to ask, in what respects can the writing of autobiography be said to minister to the experience of wholeness? Friedländer himself is decidedly ambivalent on this score. On the one hand, he analyzes his motivation as an involuntary return to the repressed, "an imperious resurgence of the past that has contributed, at least in part, to the writing of this book, the . . . surfacing of the obscure questions of my adolescence, now returned and influencing my day-to-day outlook." This "need for synthesis, for a thoroughgoing coherence that no longer excludes anything" (114), which drives him to write of the past is counterbalanced by deep misgivings about the power of language to perform the work of restoration: "When I leaf through these pages I often feel deeply discouraged: I will never be able to express what I want to say; these lines, often clumsy, are very far removed, I know, from my memories, and even my memories retrieve only sparse fragments of my parents' existence, of their world, of the time when I was a child" (134). If he perseveres in the work of commemoration, then, it is because language offers the only possible avenue to the lost experience of presence upon which alone a wholeness of identity can be founded: "I must write, then. Writing retraces the contours of the past with a possibly less ephemeral stroke than the others [surviving letters and "two or three yellowed photographs" (134)], it does at least preserve a presence, and it enables one to tell about a child who saw one world founder and another reborn" (135).

The narrative in *When Memory Comes* is given a distinctive coloration by this tension between the possibilities and the limitations of autobiographical discourse, and I would venture to add that this tension is invariably a central feature of those autobiographies which we variously identify as the truly great ones, the texts that compel belief. One of the things that writing the autobiography does succeed in doing is to return Friedländer in imagination to the "earliest setting of my life" where "the essential part of my self was shaped" (32), and he speaks of his reluctance to terminate his evocation of this period of relative security and to move forward in the narrative. Once past this moment of stasis in Prague, however, the narrative re-enacts his separation from his parents repeatedly; each of the three sections of his story concludes by reverting in fact or symbol to this central experience of loss. Again, through the constant juxtaposition of time frames and the presence in the text of dated entries dramatizing the successive stages of its composition, the narrative posits in its structure an interconnectedness among the various phases of his life. The constant alternation between pasts and the present blends at the last into a single moment, his arrival on the shores of Israel in 1948. The promise of the ending, of this moment of symbolic reunification of the boy with his people and with himself, however, is undercut by Friedländer's insistence early on and throughout the text of his recurrent sense of dissociation from Israel and its nationalistic culture: "Should I confess that since the beginning I had nonetheless had vague, confused, intermittent feelings that something was missing?" (12).[101]

Friedländer suggests that the writing of the autobiography has itself been a kind of metaphor or analogue to the boy's search for a homeland, a motive stilling once for all his manifold doubts about the autobiographical act:

> This story is drawing to a close and once more the question arises: have I succeeded in setting down even so much as a tiny part of what I wanted to express? As a matter of fact, this quest, this incessant confrontation with the past during these months, has become sufficient reason

[101] See also pp. 22-23 and 124 for similar passages.

in itself, and a necessary undertaking. And the words of
Gustav Meyrink leap to mind once more: "When knowledge comes, memory comes too, little by little . . ."—a
sequence, however, that has been inverted here: when
memory comes, knowledge comes too, little by little. . . .
"Knowledge and memory are one and the same thing."
(182)

"A sequence that has been inverted here"—to write autobiography is in its way to perform a kind of spell, a deliberate
reversal of process of the sort displayed in the legends of the
Golem. The inversion in the title, I think, points to the fundamental wish motivating the narrative: to reverse process here
is to return to the lost parents, to the vanished integrity of
the childhood self; to reverse process is to cure the sick child
whose presence pervades these pages. The power of the narrative resides in its unflinching recognition of this wish as a
wish, in its chastened knowledge that the experience of
wholeness resides, not in any recoverable period of history,
but rather—if at all—in a work of words, in a fiction of the
self.

## V. MAXINE HONG KINGSTON: "I HAD TO TELL MY MOTHER SO THAT SHE WOULD KNOW THE TRUE THINGS ABOUT ME AND TO STOP THE PAIN IN MY THROAT"

"It took me a long, long time to find the way back to my own
past," Friedländer writes, and he traces the decisive shift from
repression of his early life to representation of it in autobiographical narrative to his experience with the autistic children
in Sweden, as we have seen. His encounters with Arne and
Bert, frozen in the isolation of the inarticulate, function as the
symbolic heart of his narrative, for they shocked him into
awareness of the living death of silence, the indispensable contribution of language to the constitution of the wholly integrated self. If, in the perspective of Tulsa, Friedländer's creation of his autobiography is revealed as an act of speech, it

is nonetheless true that he always characterizes his lifelong attempts to deal with his own history and that of his people as attempts to write. For Maxine Hong Kingston, on the other hand, who shares Friedländer's belief that the exercise of language is necessary to the realization of self, the autobiographical act and the text it produces are always conceptualized as spoken rather than written performance. The reasons for her view are cultural, for Kingston was nurtured in an oral tradition, and she specifically models herself as an autobiographer on her mother, who was a teller of "talk-stories." Like Sartre, like Friedländer, Kingston understands that the art of self-invention is governed by a dialectical interplay between the individual and his or her culture. *The Woman Warrior: Memoirs of a Girlhood Among Ghosts* confirms both as theme and gesture that in our life in culture the self and language exist in an irreducible relation of mutually constituting interdependency.

Kingston inaugurates her memoirs by speaking her mother's injunction to silence:

> "You must not tell anyone," my mother said, "what I am about to tell you. In China your father had a sister who killed herself. She jumped into the family well. We say that your father has all brothers because it is as if she had never been born."[102]

The mother presents her story of the "no name woman," the aunt whose adultery shamed her family and the entire village, as a cautionary tale designed to communicate to the listening Maxine at her entrance into womanhood the lesson that a woman is defined exclusively in terms of her relation to her community. When the aunt violates the strict code governing the conduct of women in the village culture of China, breaking with the discourse of tradition, her behavior becomes "un-

---

[102] *The Woman Warrior: Memoirs of a Girlhood Among Ghosts* (1976; rpt. New York: Random, 1977), p. 3. Subsequent references are to this edition and will appear in the text.

speakable" (6), as Maxine's mother insists ("No one said any-thing. We did not discuss it" [3-4]). The villagers visit on her family in the most literal fashion the destruction and violence of her transgression of the laws of the community, and the aunt drowns herself and her infant child in the family well. Her punishment is complete when, following the rigorous logic of an ancient ancestral culture in which language is the foun-dation of identity, the family expunges her name from the annals of the honored dead. The imposition of silence, the denial of name, is tantamount to the extinction of personality: "it is as if she had never been born." It becomes, accordingly, the task of the Chinese-American girl, "always trying to get things straight" as she makes a place and an identity for her-self in her transcultural journey from China to America, to try to understand her mother's cryptic telling of what she claims must never be told, an effort that will lead Kingston in her turn "to name the unspeakable" (6) in *The Woman War-rior*.

Rejecting the conventional wisdom of her mother's "talk-story," Kingston explores an alternative reading, remaking the figure of the rebellious aunt into a "forerunner" (9) of her own aspiration toward self-determination; only in this way, she writes, can "I see her life branching into mine" (10). The aunt is punished by the villagers, not so much because she com-mitted adultery, as Kingston's mother would have it, but be-cause she acted "as if she could have a private life, secret and apart from them." There is no place for the self—especially that of a woman—apart from community in the narrowly cir-cumscribed moral universe of the village patriarchy; to violate the perfect closure, the " 'roundness,' " of the village world is to end in the void: "one human being flaring up into violence could open up a black hole, a maelstrom that pulled in the sky" (14). The attempt to lead the life of the single, separate person is against the law of nature. The violent consequences of the aunt's assertion of her individuality balance in searing intensity the depth of the villagers' commitment to cultural determinism and conformity. The quest for selfhood, so familiar in the literature of the West, unleashes a rush toward annihilation in this stark and somber tale from the East. Following the ritual enactment of the death penalty upon her family and herself in the villagers' raid ("You've killed us. . . . You've never been born" [16]), unable to bear the limitless space into which the expression of her individuality has propelled her, the "no name woman" seeks the sheltering confinement first of a pigsty, where she gives birth to her illegitimate child, then of the family well, where she drowns both herself and the baby. Order in this traditional universe can be restored only when the "black hole" ripped open in the firmament of convention by the assertion of autonomous selfhood is plugged by the death of self, the surrender of the bodies in the well.

When Kingston breaks her mother's injunction to silence, ending twenty years of complicity in her family's unrelenting punishment of the wayward aunt, her telling of the story "No Name Woman" becomes unmistakably an act of defiance both of her mother and of the communal values the mother seeks to transmit. At the same time, her narrative is not only a mimesis of her mother's traditional "talk-story" but an observance of Chinese custom as well. Haunted by the ghost of her aunt, who wanders unappeased by any of the paper gifts that ancestor worship prescribes for the well-being of the honored dead, Kingston makes of her narrative a surrogate offering of respect: "I alone devote pages of paper to her." To honor tradition, however, is as dangerous as it is to defy it, and the "no name woman" becomes at the last an unsettling model of self and self-expression: "I do not think she always means me well. I am telling on her, and she was a spite suicide, drowning herself in the drinking water. The Chinese are always very frightened of the drowned one, whose weeping ghost, wet hair hanging and skin bloated, waits silently by the water to pull down a substitute" (19).

Kingston's telling of "No Name Woman" suggests the ambiguity of the autobiographical act that created *The Woman Warrior*: her narrative becomes a symbolic analogue not only of the aunt's initial defiance of tradition in her search for a private space in which individuality could dwell "secret and apart," but also of the aunt's subsequent plea for the observance of tradition in the endless search of her ghost for the place and the recognition of a name that only community has the power to confer. We begin to see what Kingston means when she writes, somewhat later in the narrative, "Even now China wraps double binds around my feet" (57). Like the aunt's story, Kingston's performance as an autobiographer is a complex mixture of deference and defiance: to write the story of "no name woman" is to speak "the unspeakable," yet we do well to note that *The Woman Warrior* is dedicated "To Mother and Father."

Flanking the portrait of "no name woman," who is condemned forever to the silence of the nameless, the limbo of the incomplete, is Kingston's portrait of Fa Mu Lan, the woman warrior, the embodiment of speech in action, whose superlative achievement of identity is confirmed by the passage of her name into legend. As before and throughout *The Woman Warrior*, Kingston is concerned with the fate of the woman who dares to be different; only this time the failure of the nonconforming individual is transposed into a success of mythic dimensions. "No Name Woman" is structured by the contrast between Maxine's mother's "talk-story" version of the aunt, reported as direct discourse, and Maxine's own imaginative reconstruction of her portrait; in either case, however, the reading is the same: the possibility for difference, for wholeness of the private self, is definitively foreclosed in the village culture. Kingston wisely keeps her distance from this disturbing figure of the defeated rebel in her family past: "I do not think she always means me well." In "White Tigers," on the other hand, although Kingston traces her intimate familiarity with her legendary subject to its source in her mother's "talk-stories," she presents the events of the life of the woman warrior as unfolding in an extended reverie or daydream, a girl's wish-fulfilling fantasy of the acquisition of the power requisite to the formation of an autonomous identity. Here the identification between Kingston and the woman rebel is on a different footing: so great is the attraction of the girl to her heroine that distance between them gives way to a merged identity in Kingston's discourse, an "I" who is Maxine-as-Fa Mu Lan.

"White Tigers" affirms that there really is a separate, secret place for self-development, and the story opens when this fantasy-Maxine is summoned to it by a magical bird. Here an old man and woman take charge of her education, training her for seven years to become a warrior, skilled in the arts of survival, war, and storytelling, since the art of narration is just as much a part of heroic conduct in Kingston's Chinese legend as ever it was in *The Odyssey*. Her mentors instruct her that she is destined to lead the Han people in rebellion against the oppression of a cruel baron who has conscripted her brother and her father to serve in the wars of the empire. Determined to take her father's place, the woman warrior returns to her village, where she is welcomed by her parents with all of the honor traditionally prescribed for a son. Her parents complete her consecration as the female avenger by carving revenge on her back, "words in red and black files, like an army, like my army" (42). In this astonishing rite of passage, in which birth, menstruation, and sacrificial death mingle in "the iron smell of blood," the flesh of the woman warrior becomes a living text, an act of war, a work of art, a deadly weapon: "The list of grievances went on and on. If an enemy should flay me, the light would shine through my skin like lace" (41). In Maxine's fantasy version of the life of Fa Mu Lan, then, the figure of the rebel is literally the spokesman incarnate of the family and the village community, reversing in this regard the nightmare of alienation that is the fate of her counterpart, the "no name woman" who was destroyed by her difference from her culture.

Like the adulterous aunt, the woman warrior is by definition a forbidden identity for women in the patriarchal culture ("Chinese executed women who disguised themselves as soldiers or students, no matter how bravely they fought or how high they scored on the examinations" [46]), but the contrast between them is total: where the consequences of the life of difference, of individuality, were dishonor, death, and exclusion from history, they are now fulfillment and an honored place in legend. Significantly, moreover, although the woman warrior disguises her identity as a woman, she is not required to sacrifice it—this, I would wager, is doubtless a principal attraction of the story of Fa Mu Lan for Maxine Hong Kingston. If the woman warrior goes forth into battle dressed as a man, she is nonetheless no virginal Chinese Joan; visited in secret by her husband, she becomes pregnant, "a strange human being indeed—words carved on my back and the baby large in front" (47). It is both as a warrior and as a woman that Fa Mu Lan-Maxine performs the climactic action of her tale. In this final exploit, identifying herself as "a female avenger," she confronts the wicked baron and calls him to account for his crimes against the villagers, against her brother, against defenseless women, against her own childhood. The war between the sexes shows here as a war of words. The baron defends his alleged wrongdoing by quoting "the sayings [she] hated": " 'Girls are maggots in the rice.' 'It is more profitable to raise geese than daughters' " (51). To the repressive sexist text of the patriarchal culture the woman warrior displays her own power, her countertext, her body of words, her sword:

> "You've done this," I said, and ripped off my shirt to
> show him my back. "You are responsible for this." When
> I saw his startled eyes at my breasts, I slashed him across
> the face and on the second stroke cut off his head. (52)

Language and sex are inseparably linked here as the constituent parts of the power of the self.

What the events of the story of Fa Mu Lan display is the prodigy of a versatile, all-purpose, composite identity, in which each of her various roles as son and daughter, surrogate father, wife, military leader, and mother complements all of the others. Language and culture are in perfect harmony: the identity of the woman warrior is consubstantial with her story:

"From the words on my back, and how they were fulfilled, the villagers would make a legend about my perfect filiality" (54). The redemptive paradox of the world of legend is that the achievement of identity in difference, as rebel, as female avenger, is the result, not of defiance but of obedience to family, not of a break with the culture but of a fundamental allegiance to it.

By contrast, Kingston writes, "My American life has been such a disappointment" (54), teaching her at every turn the disparity between the reality she lives and the legend she dreams. For the would-be woman warrior, there is no bird to call her, no magical horse to ride, no old people to be her "gurus"; still worse, her parents and even language itself are in league with the enemy. Like the sexist baron of the legend, her parents quote to her "the sayings [she] hated" (" 'Better to raise geese than girls' " [54]); "I watched such words come out of my own mother's and father's mouths . . . and I had to get out of hating range" (62). The hatred, moreover, includes self-hatred, for Fa Mu Lan's legendary weapon of words proves to be a double-edged sword for a Chinese-American girl like Maxine: "There is a Chinese word for the female *I*—which is 'slave.' Break the women with their own tongues!" (56). How can language be made the instrument of identity when it is instrumental in the denial of identity? One more double bind.

It is to language, nevertheless, however compromised and contingent, that Kingston turns now in her autobiography in her search for reconciliation with family and culture and with herself, just as she turned to it instinctively as a child. Even then her war was a war of words. Maxine's response to the hated sayings of her parents was to scream in reply, "I'm not a bad girl," as her mother recalls, "talking-story about my childhood." Kingston adds, "I might as well have said, 'I'm not a girl' " (55).[103] The impressionable child, seeking to emulate the triumphant self of Fa Mu Lan, recognized that "it

[103] See Erikson's discussion of Luther's fit in the choir, which he interprets as a repudiation of a negative identity, pp. 23-40.

was important that I do something big and fine" (54). Looking back, the older woman concedes her failure to locate a theater of action in which to enact the legendary paradigm of self-hood: "I went away to college—Berkeley in the sixties—and I studied, and I marched to change the world, but I did not turn into a boy. I would have liked to bring myself back as a boy for my parents to welcome with chickens and pigs" (56).

Deeper than this difference between Maxine Hong Kings-ton and Fa Mu Lan, however, lies a redemptive principle of identity binding the autobiographer to her chosen eponym:

> The swordswoman and I are not so dissimilar. May my people understand the resemblance soon so that I can return to them. What we have in common are the words at our backs. The ideographs for *revenge* are "report a crime" and "report to five families." The reporting is the vengeance—not the beheading, not the gutting, but the words. And I have so many words—"chink" words and "gook" words too—that they do not fit on my skin. (62-63)

In making her autobiographical discourse a re-enactment of Fa Mu Lan's execution of the wicked baron, Kingston pro-poses for herself the resolution that awaits the woman war-rior, reunion with her parents and her culture, completion of the circle of selfhood. The irreducible reflexiveness of the im-age captures perfectly the essence of Kingston's dilemma: if "the words" are the equivalent of heroic action, are "the be-heading" and "the gutting" of "the sayings I hated" that refuse identity to women, they also refuse native identity to the for-eigner, "chink" or "gook." What Kingston as woman warrior does is done to her; in this logomachy what she writes is writ-ten in her flesh. In uttering the text that is her body the au-tobiographer has had to "flay" herself, paying in pain so that "the light would shine through [her] skin like lace." This is the dynamic of Kingston's art of self-invention, the making for herself in language a second skin—this text—of legendary proportions, in order to contain all the words that would not fit on the original body of the self.

Kingston comes to this special view of language, this conception of the autobiographical act as heroic and violent conduct, by way of her mother, "champion talker" (235); the person and the performance of Brave Orchid link the swordswoman Maxine dreams of being as a child and the wordswoman she becomes in writing her childhood in *The Woman Warrior*. When the autobiographer reconstructs her mother's own story as "Shaman," the longest and central section of the narrative, Brave Orchid emerges as a real-life Fa Mu Lan who re-enacts the paradigm of the legend, for she "had gone away [from her village] ordinary and come back miraculous, like the ancient magicians who came down from the mountains" (90). Like the woman warrior, Brave Orchid is a woman who manages to reconcile her choice of an unconventional identity for a woman with a profound allegiance to the traditions of her culture. Thus, if she seems to live out a Chinese version of women's liberation when she attends medical school, free from "servitude" to her "father's tyrant mother with the bound feet" (73), she emerges in Kingston's account of this period not so much as a student of medicine but rather as a master of ancient ghost lore; when a huge "sitting" ghost named Boulder terrorizes the other women students in her dormitory, Brave Orchid is the "capable exorcist" (108) who defeats him with the power of her speech. Similarly, although Brave Orchid is constantly associated with the traditional uses of language in her culture, with spells, with "talk-stories," with endless formulas of ritual, the import of her linguistic performance is unmistakably radicalizing to the listening Maxine: "She said I would grow up a wife and a slave, but she taught me the song of the warrior woman, Fa Mu Lan. I would have to grow up a warrior woman" (24).

Where did Brave Orchid finally stand, what did she really believe, what model of womanhood did she want her daughter to embrace? Given the conflicting signals her mother sends her, it is not surprising that these are questions of endless speculation for Kingston early and late, and they become especially urgent at moments when she suspects that her mother has joined forces with the patriarchal enemies of female identity in Chinese culture. When Brave Orchid tells Maxine a harrowing tale of her attendance as midwife at the birth of a child without an anus, who was abandoned in an outhouse "so that the family would not have to hear it cry," Kingston's comment underlines what was for her always the essential ambiguity that clouds her relationship with her mother and her power of words:

> I hope this holeless baby proves that my mother did not prepare a box of clean ashes beside the birth bed in case of a girl. "The midwife or a relative would take the back of a girl baby's head in her hand and turn her face into the ashes," said my mother. "It was very easy." She never said she herself killed babies, but perhaps the holeless baby was a boy.

Small wonder, then, that Maxine should have punctuated her early years with tantrums, screaming at her mother, "I'm not a bad girl" ("I'm not a girl"). The "holeless baby" functions here not only as a nightmare surrogate for a Maxine destroyed by the sayings she hated, slain by her mother for the irremediable insufficiency of her female identity, but also as a symbolic analogue for Kingston's anguished view of discourse as necessary to the survival of the self. The child instinctively transposes this stuff of nightmare to the circumstances of her own experience, "a naked child sitting on a modern toilet desperately trying to perform until it died of congestion" (101), and the "congestion" she suffers from in her overstimulated imagination is precisely the threatening id-like content of this and many another of her mother's tales. Again and again Kingston uses the imagery surrounding Brave Orchid's endless performance of "talk-story" to stress the pressure, the violent physical assault, of Chinese lore upon the unprotected consciousness of the impressionable Maxine: "My mother funneled China into our ears" (89), or again, "[my mother] pries open my head and my fists and crams into them responsibility for time, responsibility for intervening oceans" (126). In the instance of "the holeless baby" the child's only recourse is repression: "To make my waking life American-normal, I turn on the lights before anything untoward makes an appearance. I push the deformed into my dreams, which are in Chinese, the language of impossible stories." What is repressed is communicated nonetheless, Kingston is marked for life, and so she concludes, "Before we can leave our parents, they stuff our heads like the suitcases which they jam-pack with home-made underwear" (102). It is these strange wonders of her crowded consciousness that Kingston unpacks with the violence of an explosion in *The Woman Warrior*.

If identity is determined by sex in the culture of Brave Orchid, as Maxine's wish to be both not-a-girl and "American-normal" makes clear, it is also profoundly linguistic. For mother and daughter language is not merely a means of self-expression; it is itself a mode of being, the primary act of the self. The listening Maxine recognizes that she is "in the presence of great power, my mother talking-story" (24). "Funnel," "pry," "cram," "jam-pack"—in the unrelenting aggression of the mother's speech, language is something done to the daughter. Gradually, as Maxine grows toward the adult self that will crystallize in her own performance of "talk-story" in her autobiography, language becomes something she does, too, and Kingston tells this story of her emergence in language, this shift from made to maker, in "A Song for a Barbarian Reed Pipe."

In this final section of the narrative she traces her ultimate identity as the woman warrior to a founding, originary event that is fully as remarkable as anything in the legendary formation of her alter ego, Fa Mu Lan: the cutting of her tongue by Brave Orchid:

She pushed my tongue up and sliced the frenum. Or maybe she snipped it with a pair of nail scissors. I don't remember her doing it, only her telling me about it, but

all during childhood I felt sorry for the baby whose mother
waited with scissors or knife in hand for it to cry—and
then, when its mouth was wide open like a baby bird's,
cut. . . .
"Why did you do that to me, Mother?". . .
"I cut it so that you would not be tonguetied. Your tongue
would be able to move in any language."

In Kingston's ontogenetic account of her self, to begin is to
begin in language, and the acquisition of language, quite literally of mother tongue, is, accordingly, the great primal moment of her life history, virtually coextensive with her birth,
for it is "the first thing my mother did when she saw me"
(190). The mother's posture here as the woman with the knife
identifies her as an avatar of the woman warrior, presiding
over the birth of the woman warrior-to-be. The historicity of
this alleged event remains as problematical for Maxine as a
girl as that of "the *primal scene*" witnessed by the "Wolf Man"
in Freud's celebrated reconstruction, and perhaps the cutting
of the tongue is a similarly fictive piece of aetiology, a myth
of origin disguised as history. In any case no reader of *The
Woman Warrior* will dispute Kingston's invocation of her mother
as the woman "who marked [her] growing with stories" (6).

What is not clear to Kingston, however, is how to construe
this marking, the double-edged sword of language wielded by
her mother: "Sometimes I felt very proud that my mother
committed such a powerful act upon me. At other times I
was terrified" (190). As in Friedländer's legends of the Golem,
the ambiguity here is fundamental, for creation and mutila-
tion are inextricably intertwined, recalling Kingston's anxiety
about her mother's part in the birth of "the holeless baby." In
theory, Brave Orchid performs with the knife a kind of consecration, a laying on of tongues, for if she is the author of
Maxine's "congestion," she is also midwife to its release in
language, providing in the paradox of this symbolic action the
"hole" that is necessary to make Kingston whole.

The immediate consequence of Brave Orchid's "powerful

act," however, fully justifies Kingston's sense of its ambiguity, for the first fruit of the mother's gift of speech is the daughter's silence. Even now, she writes, "I have a terrible time talking" (191), while in her early years at an American school it was a misery to speak up in class. Part of the inhibition was cultural, for self-reference in English seemed to lack the protective intricacy of the Chinese "I" with its seven strokes. Yet even at the Chinese school speaking was an ordeal: Maxine managed to be loud but her voice was cut and painful, the utterance of the mutilated self, full of "splinters," of "bones rubbing jagged against one another," "a crippled animal running on broken legs" (196).

Maxine's smoldering anxiety about speech as the *sine qua non* of identity explodes in the sixth grade in an astonishing outburst of violence and hatred against another "quiet" Chinese girl whose weakness and silence perfectly mirror her own fears of failed selfhood. The reflexiveness of the psychological situation is unmistakable, the hatred self-hatred, the murderous aggression suicidal. Cornering her alter-ego in the bathroom after school, Maxine pours out a torrent of verbal and physical abuse that recalls the double motivation she attributes to her mother in the episode of the cutting of her tongue; in fact, the encounter in the bathroom, in which Maxine determines to force the quiet girl into speech ("I am going to make you talk, you sissy girl" [204]), is in essence a re-play of the earlier episode, with Maxine performing her mother's role, the warrior woman midwife of speech. The impulse to mutilate is painfully insisted on as Kingston relives moment by moment her sadistic pinching and squeezing of the quiet girl's face, her yanking on her hair: "If she had had little bound feet, the toes twisted under the balls, I would have jumped up and landed on them—crunch!—stomped on them with my iron shoes" (208).

The counter-impulse to create wholeness of self through language is the burden of the hysterical tirade Maxine voices while she beats her victim: "If you don't talk, you can't have a personality. You'll have no personality and no hair" (210).

In a very real sense the encounter represents the making of self, and if Maxine fails to bring her adversary into the life of speech ("quarts of tears but no words" [209]), she succeeds in speaking herself in a voice of sustained and awesome power. The episode is, then, both a warning against the muteness of the isolate individual, that living death of self in which the quiet girl resembles the autistic children of Tulsa, and a prototype of the autobiographical act in which Kingston's quest for self through language finds its culmination.

Following her attack on the quiet girl, Maxine succumbs for eighteen months to a "mysterious illness" ("there was no pain and no symptoms" [211]) in which she lapses with undisguised pleasure into the regressive passivity of her hated alter-ego. When her mother terminates the retreat into the womblike security of a life seemingly outside history where "nothing happened," Maxine is faced once more with that acquisition of language which she seems destined to re-enact continuously in her living and writing: "at school I had to figure out again how to talk" (212). What Kingston learns, however, is that the freedom and selfhood that speech enacts is not absolute and autonomous but bound and determined by culture, for the Chinese "want to capture your voice for their own use" (196).

The isolation of the Chinese-American girl is deepened by her growing sense of entrapment in a perplexing network of linguistic prohibitions. Thus the apparent inclusion in community fostered by the parental injunction to "lie to Americans" (214) is subverted by the programmatic refusal of the parents to initiate the children into the mysteries of the language of the tribe. Constantly witnessing the performance of rituals for which all explanation is declined, Maxine is hard put to account for the survival of an unspoken culture: "If we had to depend on being told, we'd have no religion, no babies, no menstruation (sex, of course, unspeakable), no death" (216). Thus "talk-story," the traditionally sanctioned instrument for the transmission of cultural discourse, becomes a source of confusion, as we have seen, devoted as it is to speaking the "unspeakable": "You must not tell anyone . . . what I am about to tell you"; or again, "she said I would grow up a wife and a slave, but she taught me the song of the warrior woman." Even the simplest exchange like the following between Kingston and her mother becomes problematical, paradoxical, contradictory, self-cancelling:

> [Brave Orchid] "I didn't say you were ugly."
> [Maxine] "You say that all the time."
> [Brave Orchid] "That's what we're supposed to say. That's what Chinese say. We like to say the opposite." (237)

Moreover, in addition to the inherent confusion of discourse within culture, Maxine discovers that there is neither life nor language for the self outside culture. Only if her speech is understood by others can she break free of the isolation imposed by silence and solitude: "I thought talking and not talking made the difference between sanity and insanity. Insane people were the ones who couldn't explain themselves. There were many crazy girls and women" (216). Sex, sanity, and identity are inseparably linked to language here as Kingston delineates yet another version of the Chinese double bind for women. If the culture sanctions no self for women ("maggots"), and women cannot locate a self beyond the matrix of culture, it is hardly surprising that Maxine is surrounded by models of failed, female identity, especially crazy women like the woman next door, like Crazy Mary, like Pee-A-Nah the wild woman, and she comes to think of insanity as a familiar and even inevitable occurrence in her world, a likely future for herself, for any woman: "I thought every house had to have its crazy woman or crazy girl, every village its idiot. Who would be It at our house? Probably me" (220).

Despite her anxiety about her sanity, Maxine assumes for a time the difference of a crazy persona complete with limp, ugly quacking voice, and general clumsiness as a defense against her parents' attempt to make of her the traditional wife and slave by marrying her off to a young Chinese immigrant. Maxine is soon forced to abandon this model of difference, however, when her crazy act threatens to pair her for life with a hulking, mentally retarded Chinese boy who divides his time between infatuation for Maxine and the pleasures of his pornographic magazines. For all the legendary triumph of Fa Mu Lan (who was obliged to become a man in order to be the woman of her choice), difference is dangerous, essentially "unspeakable," as Maxine's "no name" aunt learned to her cost. When Brave Orchid tells Maxine about a harmless crazy lady who was stoned to death by her village, she makes it clear that the penalty for the failure to be understood is death.

At the heart of Maxine's fears for her sanity are her misgivings about the normality of her prodigiously active imagination, for "there were adventurous people inside my head to whom I talked" (220). When she attempts to naturalize the difference of this private speech, however, asking her sister ("the person most like me in all the world"), "do you talk to people that aren't real inside your mind?" her appeal for reassurance, for the likeness of shared experience, is met with an uncomprehending "*what?*" (221). There is, nevertheless, one woman in Maxine's world who succeeds first in China and then in California in achieving through the medium of "talk-story" the difference of selfhood without at the same time sacrificing her place in the community of the sane and same. Brave Orchid is in this fundamental respect the antithesis of all of the silent, incomprehensible, and unspeakable women destroyed by the failure of language, and she becomes accordingly the focus of Maxine's attempt to utter her self: "Maybe because I was the one with the tongue cut loose, I had grown inside me a list of over two hundred things that I had to tell my mother so that she would know the true things about me and to stop the pain in my throat" (229). In this latest version, the cutting of the tongue, initially associated with birth, is extended backward to include the moment of conception as well; Brave Orchid becomes the generative principle of Maxine's reflexive consciousness, author of the author.

Kingston's fascinating account of her list and of the pain in her throat suggests, to be sure, that this phase of her development anticipates the content and motivation of the autobiographical act that created *The Woman Warrior*. It is much more to the point, however, to reverse this formulation of the relation between life and art, or better still to abandon such a pairing of terms altogether, for the autobiographical act is revealed here as a mode of self-invention that is always practiced first in living and only eventually, sometimes, formalized in writing. The child instinctively recognizes the paradoxical desire for sameness that is the price of the achieved difference of selfhood, for to be someone, to be the "me" constituted by the "true things" on the list, is to be separate and alone: "If only I could let my mother know the list, she—and the world—would become more like me, and I would never be alone again" (230). Not to be alone, not to have a list, not to have a pain in the throat to speak—this is in essence a wish to retreat to the sheltering silence before self and language, to a prenatal existence within the mother prior to the cutting of the tongue and the ensuing role of mother to her nascent self.

If we accept Maxine's list as the analogue and prototype of Kingston's autobiography, then we can recognize that a profound resistance to self-invention is central to her performance of the autobiographical act, for the point of Maxine's telling of her list is to shorten it, to reduce the number of items to zero. The list is by definition untold, all of the things she has not said to her mother, the secret, the forbidden, the repressed, her guilts and misgivings, her unasked questions about the mysterious practices of Chinese culture. Maxine's narrative program, which calls for confessing one item to her mother each day, is potentially as death-centered as Poulou's, for she not only proposes to herself a telling that will lead her to the end of her list, but an event-free living that will end her need for list and telling in the first place. Thus, having told the first item (how she killed a spider), she thinks:

Just two hundred and six more items to go. I moved carefully all the next day so as not to do anything or have anything happen to me that would make me go back to two hundred and seven again. (231)

The list proves, however, to be coextensive with consciousness, for, even as Maxine tells it, it continues to grow, and, still worse, Brave Orchid, fed up with "senseless gabbings," soon repudiates her daughter's autobiographical initiative as "madness." The difference of selfhood generates a pain in Maxine's throat ("vocal cords taut to snapping"), and the pain motivates a speech that would bridge her separation from her mother; her mother stops her speech and returns her to the isolation and loneliness of difference once more; then the pain in her throat re-doubles and the cycle of the list resumes: "I shut my mouth, but I felt something alive tearing at my throat, bite by bite, from the inside. Soon there would be three hundred things, and too late to get them out before my mother grew old and died" (233). Maxine seems condemned to join the line of crazy women, "the ones who couldn't explain themselves," for the list-teller never seems to find in her mother the "higher listener" she seeks, and she can only conclude, "No listener but myself" (237).

*The Woman Warrior* ends, however, with a fable of reconciliation, the discovery of a viable, that is to say speakable, mode of difference. "Recently, when I told her I also talk-story"—Kingston's announcement to her mother of this principle of likeness between them is the occasion for the final "talk-story" in the narrative, and Kingston presents this story as a work of collaboration between them ("the beginning is hers, the ending, mine" [240]). Brave Orchid's story is an anecdote about Maxine's grandmother's love of the theater and an encounter with bandits, in which the grandmother draws the whimsical moral that her family "was immune to harm as

273

long as they went to plays" (241). To this tale Kingston adds
a narrative of her own about the life of the poetess Ts'ai Yen,
and it is altogether fitting that this last utterance of the war-
rior-woman autobiographer should echo in capsule form some
of the themes of the legend of Fa Mu Lan: the life of soldier-
ing and childbirth, the absence from home and the eventual
return, and especially the power of language to create a perfect filiality, a bridge between the separateness of the isolate
self and the circle of communal belonging. Carried off as a
young woman by an invading tribe, Ts'ai Yen spends twelve
lonely years of captivity among the barbarians as a chieftain's
bride, giving birth to two children who defeat her attempts
to speak to them in Chinese. No listener but herself, Kingston
might have added. For Ts'ai Yen, the principal language of
the primitive Hsiung-nu, "their only music," is the "death
sounds" (242) made by their whistling arrows in battle, until
she hears hundreds of her barbarian captors playing one night
on flutes. Then, in the generative moment of language that
follows, in which Ts'ai Yen achieves her spiritual freedom,
Kingston captures the drama of her own discovery of a voice
and a circle of higher listeners:

> Then, out of Ts'ai Yen's tent, which was apart from the
> others, the barbarians heard a woman's voice singing, as
> if to her babies, a song so high and clear, it matched the
> flutes. Ts'ai Yen sang about China and her family there.
> Her words seemed to be Chinese, but the barbarians
> understood their sadness and anger. Sometimes they
> thought they could catch barbarian phrases about forever
> wandering. Her children did not laugh, but eventually
> sang along when she left her tent to sit by the winter
> campfires, ringed by barbarians. (243)

The language that enables the self to move here from its
place apart to join in the ring of others who understand is an
art of discourse in which difference and sameness peacefully
coexist ("her words seemed to be Chinese, but the barbarians
understood their sadness and anger"). The ending of the story

274

of Ts'ai Yen prefigures the resolution of Kingston's own story in the performance of the autobiographical act, the re-integration of the self in culture through the medium of art: "She brought her songs back from the savage lands, and one of the three that has been passed down to us is 'Eighteen Stanzas for a Barbarian Reed Pipe,' a song that Chinese sing to their own instruments" (243). Kingston's "talk-stories," all of them, are about women who cross the boundaries of traditional culture, as Chinese women must if they are to escape the double binds that would limit them to the maggot nonidentities of wife and slave. Only some of them, however, survive the transcultural quest for selfhood, and these are the ones who can explain themselves, can tell their lists. "If you don't talk, you can't have a personality," Maxine admonishes the quiet girl; this is the law of self-invention. We can say of Kingston's speech in *The Woman Warrior*, as she observed of the songs of Ts'ai Yen, "it translated well" (243).[104]

## VI. The Autobiographical Imperative:
## "I have to write . . ."

The present climate for autobiography is curious and contradictory, both unusually hospitable and extremely forbidding. There is a distinct gap between certain recent kinds of theorizing about autobiography, on the one hand, which understand it as a discourse of muteness, privation, and death, and, on the other hand, the immense popularity of autobiography itself, which is clearly a response to the felt need of writers and their readers for a literature of the self. The teachings of Structuralism have made the death of the subject as commonplace a concept in contemporary criticism as its predecessors, the death of God and the death of the novel. Fredric Jameson, for one, is prepared to attribute to this phenomenon the

---

[104] Kingston invites this comparison by adopting the title of one of Ts'ai Yen's songs, "Eighteen Stanzas for a Barbarian Reed Pipe," as the title for the final section of *The Woman Warrior*, "A Song for a Barbarian Reed Pipe."

broadest cultural significance. He identifies this "refusal of the older categories of human nature and of the notion that man (or human consciousness) is an intelligible entity or field of study in himself" as a form of "militant anti-humanism," and he reads it as a sign of "the intellectual, cultural, and psychic decay of post-industrial monopoly capitalism."[105]

To complicate matters, autobiographers themselves constitute a principal source of doubt about the validity of the art they practice. Although the motive to invent the self in language—or re-invent, I should say, in the light of the ontogenetic schema of self-realization I presented earlier—is as vigorous now as it has been at any time in the history of autobiography, response to this motive seems fated to lead many an autobiographer willy-nilly to the discovery of the limits or even the theoretical impossibility of his art. As a privileged theater of difference, the autobiographical act may seem to be as various as life itself, as protean as desire, but it seems to promote with a predictable sameness an overwhelming sense of the elusiveness of self-knowledge. Georges Gusdorf has documented this tendency extensively in his study of Amiel and the other major French students of the self, showing how time and again the self as an object of inquiry seems to dissolve in direct proportion to the intensity with which it is pursued.[106] From this perspective, then, the Deconstructionists emerge as only the most recent to remind us of the perennial gulf between life and language, person and text, which has always been one of the principal truths taught by the practice of autobiography. Yet the enduring autobiographers—Henry James is one, Jean-Paul Sartre is another—help us to cross this gulf, introducing us into the illusion of presence even as they make us know it for the illusion it is. These are the writers—and I could mention others, Kingston,

---

[105] *The Prison-House of Language: A Critical Account of Structuralism and Russian Formalism* (Princeton: Princeton Univ. Press, 1972), pp. 139, 141. See also "Autobiography and the Problem of the Subject," special issue of *MLN*, 93 (May 1978), 573-749.

[106] Gusdorf, *La découverte*, pp. 57-64.

for example, or Nabokov—who savor the generative principle at work in the writing of autobiography. This is what James meant, I think, when he spoke to Henry Adams of the autobiographical act as "an act of life," and even Sartre, despite the pervasive consciousness of death that colors his autobiographical meditations early and late, is fascinated by the possibility of rebirth in narrative: "I keep creating myself; I am the giver and the gift."

Even though no one can ever confirm the existence of the self as an ultimate fact, autobiographies attest by their very existence to the reality of the autobiographical imperative, the pain in the throat of which Kingston spoke that can be assuaged only by the creation of narrative. Readers in their turn reciprocate, for it is hard to undo the art of self-invention once it has been ably performed, hard to unhear the voice of presence in the text. Thus James, contemplating "the small Boy" he had made, could speak of him as "locked fast in the golden cage of the *intraduisible*," and I would liken the reader's encounter with the "I" of autobiographical discourse to Nabokov's account at the end of *Speak, Memory* of the irreversible solution to a puzzle picture ("Find What the Sailor Has Hidden") "that the finder cannot unsee once it has been seen."[107]

In these studies of the art of self-invention, as performed by McCarthy, James, Sartre, Friedländer, and Kingston, I have emphasized the presence of fiction in autobiography, yet in speaking of self as an artifact I have not meant to confuse autobiography with other works of the imagination. I regard the self finally as a mysterious reality, mysterious in its nature and origins and not necessarily consubstantial with the fictions we use to express it, and I find it altogether fitting that it should be Nabokov, one of the great believers in the self in our time and one of our greatest artificers, who captures for me best this sense of mystery:

But even so, the individual mystery remains to tantalize the memoirist. Neither in environment nor in heredity

[107] Nabokov, p. 310.

277

can I find the exact instrument that fashioned me, the anonymous roller that pressed upon my life a certain intricate watermark whose unique design becomes visible when the lamp of art is made to shine through life's foolscap.[108]

In this striking image from the opening of *Speak, Memory*, Nabokov encapsulates many of the themes of my inquiry in these pages, the integrity, the uniqueness, the textuality of the self, the problematical agency of its origin (shrouded here in passives), the counterpoint of discovery and invention in its revelation by "the lamp of art." The ambiguity of "foolscap" here is decisive and profound, for it allows for the possibility of deception even as it affirms the principle of design in our inward experience. Whether the self, that "certain intricate watermark," is literally dis-covered, made "visible" in autobiography, or is only invented by it as a signature, a kind of writing, is beyond our knowing, for knowledge of the self is inseparable from the practice of language. "How can we know the dancer from the dance?"

[108] *Ibid.*, p. 25.

# INDEX

*a Cold Eye*, 32; "C'est Le Premier Pas Qui Coûte," 33, 37; "C.Y.E.," 27-33, 34, 35, 36, 37, 43, 54, 253; "The Figures in the Clock," 37, 42; *Memories of a Catholic Girlhood*, 10-17, 27-55, 207; "Names," 33-35, 36, 46; "Settling the Colonel's Hash," 18; "A Tin Butterfly," 12, 13-17, 35, 37, 40, 46; "To the Reader," 11, 15, 37, 39-40, 40, 43, 46, 54; "Yellowstone Park," 37, 42; "Yonder Peasant, Who Is He?", 12, 37, 40, 41, 46, 54
Malcolm X, 152, 159n, 207, 225
Man, Paul de. *See* de Man, Paul
Mandell, Barrett John, 176
Mansell Darrel, 17-19
Marcus, Stephen, 170
Maxwell, William, 6, 8
Mazlish, Bruce, 24n, 25, 169
Mehlman, Jeffrey, 127n, 158n
memory: nature of, 151. *See* autobiographical act; autobiography; Friedländer, Saul; James, Henry; McCarthy, Mary
Meyre, Norbert, 153
Meyrink, Gustav, 237, 239, 240, 255
Midwood, Barton, 234n
Mill, James, 25
Mill, John Stuart, 24, 25, 205
Miller, Ross, 226n
Mink, Louis O., 134, 134-35
Misch, Georg, 183, 201
Molière, Jean-Baptiste, 148
Monod, Auguste, 125n
Montaigne, Michel de, 202
Morot-Sir, Edouard, 162n
Morris, Colin, 202n
Morris, John N., 26n, 205, 206, 207
Mozart, Wolfgang Amadeus, 148
Musset, Alfred de, 177

Nabokov, Vladimir, 216-17, 277, 277-78
Nadali, Jean, 83
narrative: as cognition, 131, 134-35, 154, 171; and consciousness, 8, 9, 130-35; and death, 147, 272; and experience, 130, 162, 163, 178; and historical understanding, 134-35, 154; as perception, 131-34, 154; phenomenology of, 135, 172-74; in psychoanalysis, 170, 171; and teleology, 134, 154, 164-65; and temporal experience, 131n, 151, 172-74. *See* autobiography; Sartre, Jean-Paul; self
Niebuhr, Elisabeth, 32
Nietzsche, Friedrich Wilhelm, 183
Nizan, Paul Yves, 153
Norton, Charles Eliot, 94, 119

Olney, James, 22, 152n, 182, 183, 184, 187-91, 199, 200-201, 227
origins, as epistemological problem, 193

Pascal, Roy, 56, 201n, 202
Pell-Clarke, Henrietta, 120
Perry, Thomas Sergeant, 113n, 114, 120n
Piaget, Jean, 133
Pike, Burton, 19n, 22, 165, 167, 173
Pingaud, Bernard, 39n, 59n
Piriou, Jean-Pierre, 162n
Plato, 189-90
Podhoretz, Norman, 207
Poe, Edgar Allan, 4-5, 163
Popper Karl R., 193-94, 195, 196, 197
Propp, Vladimir, 133
psychoanalysis: narrative in, 170; and origins of self, 214-15. *See* autobiography

*Library of Congress Cataloging in Publication Data*

Eakin, Paul John.
Fictions in autobiography.

Includes index.
1. American prose literature—20th century—
History and criticism. 2. Autobiography. 3. Self
in literature. 4. Fiction—20th century—History
and criticism. 5. Sartre, Jean Paul, 1905—
Biography. 6. Authors, American—20th century—
Biography. 7. Authors, French—20th century—
Biography. I. Title.
PS366.A88E26 1985     818'.508'09     84-42941
ISBN 0-691-06640-X (alk. paper)